Weight of Modernity

Cathy Banwell • Dorothy Broom
Anna Davies • Jane Dixon

Weight of Modernity

An Intergenerational Study of the Rise of Obesity

Springer

Cathy Banwell
National Center for Epidemiology
& Population Health
Australian National University
Canberra, Australia

Dorothy Broom
National Center for Epidemiology
& Population Health
Australian National University
Canberra, Australia

Anna Davies
National Center for Epidemiology
& Population Health
Australian National University
Canberra, Australia

Jane Dixon
National Center for Epidemiology
& Population Health
Australian National University
Canberra, Australia

ISBN 978-90-481-8956-4 ISBN 978-90-481-8957-1 (eBook)
DOI 10.1007/978-90-481-8957-1
Springer Dordrecht Heidelberg New York London

Library of Congress Control Number: 2012956194

Printed on acid-free paper

Springer is part of Springer Science+Business Media (www.springer.com)

Acknowledgements

We are grateful for support and assistance from many friends, colleagues and organisations. In particular, Graham Giles and the Cancer Council of Victoria supplied welcome support in recruiting the oldest generation of our participants (enrolled in the Melbourne Collaborative Cohort Study) and accommodation for the interviews to take place, giving us access to a unique group of people and the time to invest in hearing their stories when we would otherwise have been absorbed in the tedious task of finding and recruiting appropriate participants.

We received able research assistance from Susan Butler, Megan Shipley and Christine Winter. Ben Freeman carried out the laborious task of assembling the references in one location and Maxine McArthur formatted the manuscript, undertook copy editing and prepared the index quickly and expertly. We appreciate all their contributions.

For Chap. 7, we invited our former student Dr. Sarah Hinde to assist us to interpret the material on changing patterns of car use and to contribute insights from her earlier study of the cultural economy of car reliance in twentieth century Melbourne. We are grateful for her input, and it was a pleasure to work with her again.

Shepherdson's work which introduces Chap. 10 appeared in an exhibition 'The Contested Landscapes of Western Sydney' mounted by the Australian National University School of Art, 2010. The artist explains the work as being about branching growth patterns in land use and the disappearance of productive agricultural lands under "the weight of development".

Funding for the research was supplied by an Australian Research Council Discovery Grant DP0559439, and by investigator salaries paid by the National Centre for Epidemiology and Population Health. Social science research often depends on the willingness of ordinary citizens to supply information, and doing so often entails giving of their time—sometimes a considerable amount of time. The three generations of participants were enormously generous with their time and life stories, and we are deeply grateful to them. Their words breathe life into the analysis and argument we present here.

We also express personal appreciation to Colin Sindall, Martin Banwell, Alistair Usher, and finally we thank Bernadette Deelen-Mans and Evelien Bakker at Springer who have been enormously patient with delivery of the manuscript.

Canberra 2012

Contents

Chapter 1
The Big Australian: Obesity in the Modern World

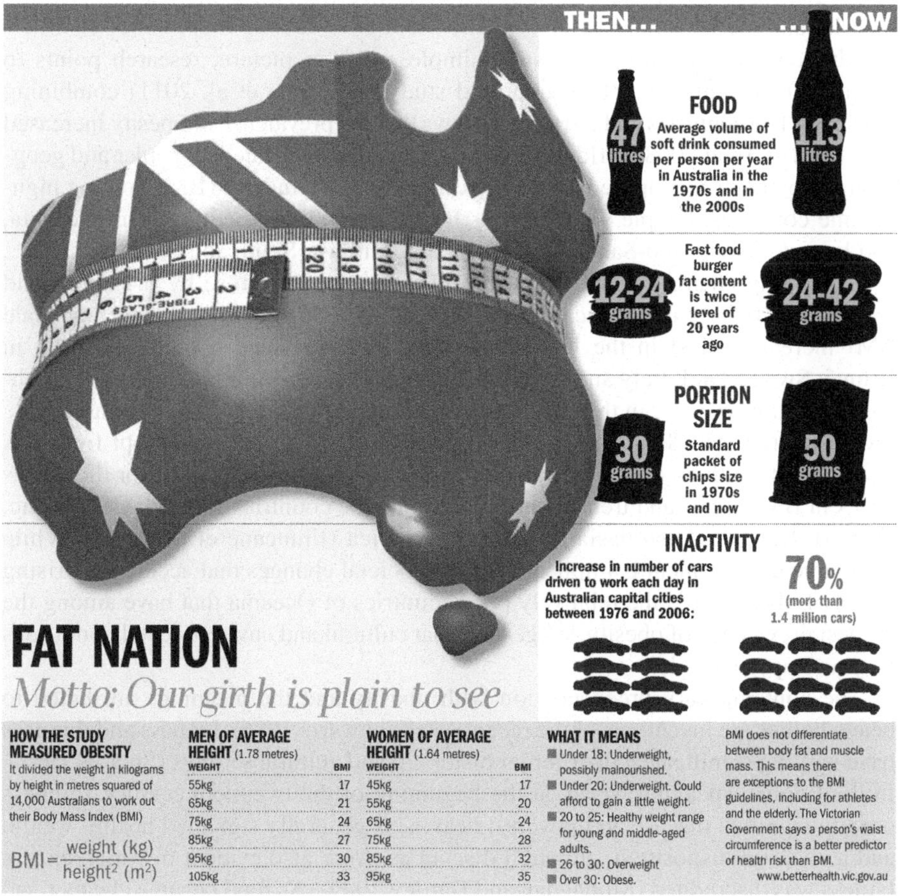

Image 1.1 The Fat Nation. Source: THE AGE 23 July 2008

C. Banwell et al., *Weight of Modernity: An Intergenerational Study of the Rise of Obesity*,
DOI 10.1007/978-90-481-8957-1_1, © Springer Science+Business Media Dordrecht 2012

1.1 Introduction

During the first decade of the twenty-first century, public health and popular publications were full of statistics about an 'epidemic of obesity', and predictions that this epidemic threatens to overwhelm health-care budgets and to generate premature mortality amongst ever-younger cohorts around the world. While we do not subscribe to the stigmatising and alarmist language that has characterised much obesity discourse, there is no doubt that the population prevalence of obesity has risen dramatically, with a doubling in numbers since 1980 (World Health Organization 2010). Given the close links between obesity and a range of serious illness conditions, such striking changes are significant for the health of people in Australia and in most other wealthy economies, and increasingly for people in developing countries as well. Because it has emerged so rapidly, so much heaviness cannot be understood as a product of genetics, but requires investigation using social scientific theories and methods.

Although the headline suggests a simple, uniform picture, research points to significant diversity. A WHO-supported study (Finucane et al. 2011) combining data from 199 countries and territories shows that the prevalence of obesity increased between 1980 and 2008 worldwide, but with differences related to gender and geography. Japan and Singapore had the lowest Body Mass Indices (BMI) among high-income countries. People were heaviest in Nauru and other countries in Oceania, and lowest in some sub-Saharan countries, and in East, South and Southeast Asia.

Examining changes in prevalence, men's average BMI rose by 0.4 kg/m^2 and women's by 0.5 kg/m^2 per decade. Among high-income countries, the average male BMI increased most in the US followed by Australia, and it increased least in Brunei, Switzerland, Italy and France. The largest increases in female BMI in high-income countries were in the US, New Zealand and Australia while increases were lowest in Italy and Singapore. Only a minority of countries are exempt from this trend. As the authors of this study note, explanations are now needed for the differences in BMI levels and trends among high-income countries such as Asia-Pacific, Western Europe, Australasia and North America (Finucane et al. 2011). While economic development is implicated in the societal changes that accompany rising levels of obesity, it is the relatively poor countries of Oceania that have among the highest prevalence of obesity, suggesting that cultural and environmental conditions play an important role.

The contemporary preoccupation with obesity and the meanings attributed to heavy bodies are inventions of the recent past (Schwartz 1986). Fatness and thinness have varying significance in different historical and cultural settings (Stearns 1997). In the English-speaking world, at the beginning of the twentieth century, thinness usually signified disease and poverty; heaviness generally signalled health, wealth and a cheerful disposition, although discourses were also evident in which excess fatness was discredited (Monaghan and Hardey 2009). As food became cheaper and more abundant, fatness was a less consistent marker of distinction, since *anyone* (not only the wealthy) could become heavy. Both the dominant signification and epidemiological distribution changed over the century, until now heaviness has become a symbol of personal failure and is correlated with low socio-economic status (SES). In epidemiological terms, the direct gradient (heavier people were generally better off economically) at the beginning of the century had, by the end of the century, reversed, and heavier people came to be concentrated among those who are less educated and poorer.[1] Such a negative gradient between SES and a health risk factor is typical of the relationship between class and most measures of health risk or outcome (Commission on Social Determinants of Health 2008).

Of course, international and historical comparison is challenging, because data are unavailable from some very poor nations, and incomplete or unreliable for many others. Nevertheless, broad trends are evident. Cross-sectional comparisons between poor, middle-income and economically developed nations tend to report positive (direct) associations between SES and weight in poor nations; mixed results in middle-income nations; and negative associations in developed nations (McLaren 2007). These patterns are not absolute: some societies have both under – and over-nutrition in the same population subgroups (Doak et al. 2005; Valera-Silva et al. 2009). However, the burden of obesity tends to shift toward lower SES as the country's gross national product increases (Monteiro et al. 2004).

In Australia, obesity prevalence is now distributed like most other chronic disease risks, and overall prevalence differs little between the sexes (Australian Institute of Health and Welfare 2003a, b). In addition, data reported previously (Friel and Broom 2007) show that when education is used as the indicator, the typical pattern of declining obesity prevalence with increasing levels of education is evident for both women and men. However, when income (rather than education) is the indicator, the patterns for men and women are no longer the same. The expected negative association is fairly consistent among women, but is less distinct or even absent for men. Indeed, there are suggestions of a positive relationship between obesity and income (men on higher incomes are more likely to be obese) in some surveys which is contrary to both the typically inverse association usually observed for health risk, and also to the pattern observed for women. Similar gender-differentiated patterns have been reported in several international studies (Ljungvall and Gerdtham 2010; Roskam et al. 2010; Zhang and Wang 2004), lending confidence to the conclusion that these apparently anomalous patterns for income are not errors or artefacts of particular surveys.

As with the variations in national patterns that do not necessarily follow the stage of economic development, explaining the variation in gender patterns requires greater attention to national and sub-population cultural trends and everyday practices. According to Glassner (1989), both structural and cultural explanations are needed to understand how and why social trends evolve in the way they do. In other words, a rise in population wealth can explain the population rise in obesity levels, but explaining different obesity patterns between and within countries requires cultural analysis.

[1] Similar shifts appeared in the distribution of cigarette smoking over the twentieth century. Adopted first by men and later by women, smoking was initially a habit for elites which was gradually democratised when mass production and rising demand lowered tobacco prices. As the health hazards became more widely documented, better educated people quit first, and the gradient—initially direct—reversed and now the majority of smokers, like people who are obese, are of lower SES.

1.2 Explaining Rising Obesity

A wide range of explanations has been proposed to account for rising obesity. Most relate to a specific aspect of modern daily life (the nutrition transition, the physical activity transition), but one unique explanation is the 'thrifty gene' theory which has been applied to formerly nomadic indigenous populations. It is hypothesised that during the millennia before European colonisation, such people experienced periodic food shortage, resulting in genetic selection for those members who were genetically predisposed to accumulate somatic fat stores during times of plenty, weight which was gradually depleted when food was short. The logic is that this predisposition was an adaptive advantage in times of alternating abundance and shortage, but that it has become a disadvantage with the end of the nomadic way of life, the advent of settlement and the industrial supply of energy-dense processed food. While the thrifty gene hypothesis is proposed as a partial explanation for higher obesity prevalence amongst indigenous people, most explanations are more generic than genetic.

Generally, rising obesity has provoked a search for single-cause explanations (such as consumption of fast food or the popularity of screen-based leisure), and readers interested in such accounts will have no difficulty finding them. Although we think it unlikely that there will ever be unanimous agreement on one 'main culprit', even if a specific factor is eventually shown to be especially important, its deleterious effects will not be reduced much by simple or singular interventions. A 2006 summary of the evidence on obesity prevention and intervention shows that very little works (Baker and Young 2006). More potentially fruitful in our view is an approach to both analysis and interventions that considers how socio-economic, physical and cultural environments have become 'obesogenic'(Egger and Swinburn 1997), that is, have come—subtly but relentlessly—to foster ways of life and individual behaviours that lead to excess weight, and to make it increasingly challenging to live in ways that promote healthy weight. We fill a research gap by characterising the obesogenic environment and its antecedents (Kirk et al. 2009).

Our previous volume (Dixon and Broom 2007) began to canvass a range of explanations for rising obesity. Since that time, some of the most strident 'moral panic' surrounding obesity may have abated slightly, and there are suggestions that the rate of increase in Australia has begun to level off, at least among some groups of children (Hardy 2010). Nevertheless, popular and public health interest remains intense, with a continuing proliferation of weight loss products, programs and services. Popular culture in the form of commercial television programs and human interest stories in the print media maintain the spotlight on excess weight and its management. Voices of resistance are raised by 'obesity sceptics' (Gard and Wright 2005) alongside a growing obesity rights discourse objecting to the stigmatising of heavy people (Broom and Dixon 2008; Julier 2008), and exposing the ineffectiveness of diets and most other interventions (Aphramor 2005; Kwan 2009). Rising above the cacophony (Lang and Rayner 2007), the overwhelming themes are however that excessive weight is harmful to health, and that the high rates of heaviness bode ill for personal wellbeing, family resources and the national health-care budget.

1.3 Our Emphasis

Obesity is often referred to as a 'lifestyle disease' because it is conceived to be a condition which individuals can consciously act upon through their dietary practices and physical activities. However, for social scientists like Weber, Mills, and Giddens, instead of lifestyles being the realm of unfettered agency, whim or choice, they are constrained or mediated by historically embedded life chances relating to structures such as gender, social and economic position, ethnicity and the physical environment. In contrast to the typical portrayal of obesity as the outcome of individual failure to manage diet and activities, we argue that obesity is a site of struggle for the majority of the population: a struggle between social structure and agency, or between chance and choice.

In order to understand the rising prevalence and changing pattern of obesity and provide input for strategies which take account of the social dynamics propelling the obesogenic environment, we use and build upon research approaches adopted in health sociology. Our basic building blocks involve deploying concepts of 'lifestyle' and social practice (Cockerham et al. 1997; Frohlick and Potvin 2002; Williams 2003, 1995) to explain changes and patterned variations in health behaviours. However, as Cockerham notes, public health research has too often focused on lifestyle choices (such as diet and activity) made by individuals, without regard for the significance of what he calls the 'structural conditions' influencing these choices (1997). Discussion of lifestyle tends to attribute health outcomes to personal choice and behaviour, as if people were solitary individuals rather than socially and culturally situated actors engaging in meaningful social practices. It can neglect how personal behaviours are structured, constrained or encouraged. Our interest is in how structures 'get under the skin' to affect human health.

We conceive of social structure and individual agency in ways generally accepted in sociology. Social structure is observed through the institutions and processes of the polity, economy and culture, which constitute the period or context in which particular populations (cohorts) live their lives. An important element of the social structure is to organise populations in terms of socio-economic status, sex, ethnicity and religion (attributes that may be referred to as social position). Another element is the generation of socio-cultural trends, or more sedimented meaning-action systems. Both aspects of social structure provide populations with differing life chances, or resources and capacities to use resources. Similarly, agency has several dimensions: it is a "temporally embedded process of social engagement, informed by the past (in its habitual aspect), but also oriented toward the future (as a capacity to imagine alternative possibilities) and toward the present (as a capacity to contextualise past habits and future projects) within the contingencies of the moment" (Emirbayer and Mische 1998, p. 963). Agency is exercised by individuals when they consider strategically the choices they have in a context of their life chances. Agency guides behaviours and lifestyles, which can be considered a routinised set of meaningful behaviours.

The research presented here responds to the call from Williams (2003) to investigate "… the complex intersection of structure and agency within the material world of everyday life", and to develop a "robust historical perspective on both agency and

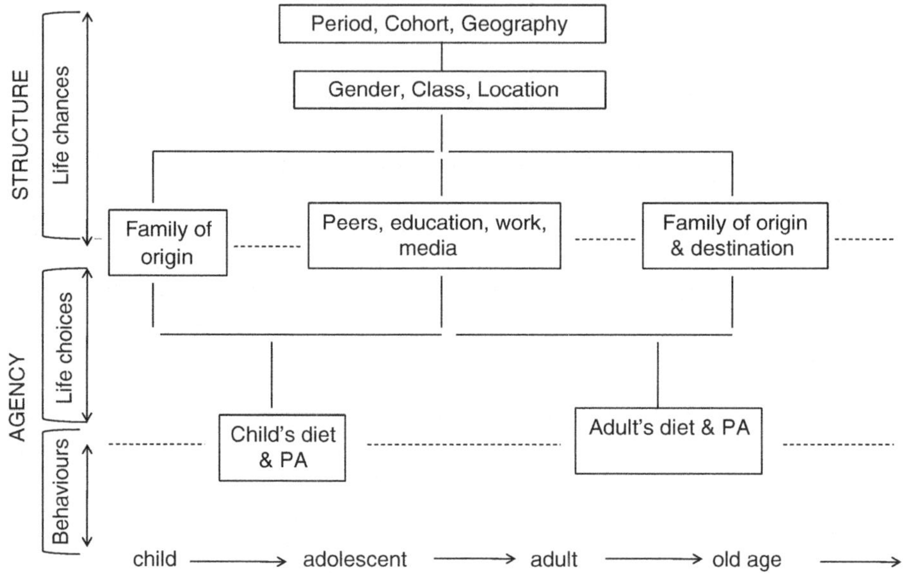

Fig. 1.1 Social structure, agency and weight related behaviours over time and the lifecourse

structure" (p. 139). Such a perspective requires more than cross-sectional snapshots of contextually embedded behaviours. Thus, we also present data on what Williams calls generative mechanisms: the social forces that imbue historically specific socio-cultural trends with currency and appeal. Cassell and Giddens say "the most deeply ingrained practices gain their identity and structuring potential only through their endurance in the *longue duree*, the 'long haul' of time" (1993, p. 17).

To provide social structure with an historical dimension we focus on socio-cultural trends. Agency will be 'given a history' by adopting a lifecourse perspective on people's action reflections towards the trends.

Figure 1.1 shows the relationships between the major foci of our research. That is, the interactions between social structure, individual agency and the two health behaviours we are most interested in. We will examine the behavioural responses to life chances over the lifecourse of individuals from three different generations.

Australia is close behind the US in having the greatest increase in BMI since 1980 among high-income countries. Thus, it is pertinent to explore what has happened in the lives of everyday Australians that has fostered such dramatic changes to Australian bodies.

Our research aims to yield a comprehensive description of the social and cultural environment as it is embodied and multiply determined. In particular this book addresses three questions: How have key socio-cultural trends generated what has come to be defined as an obesogenic environment in Australia over the last 50 years? How have generations of Australians embodied and experienced those trends? What are the social forces which provide the socio-cultural trends with their potency?

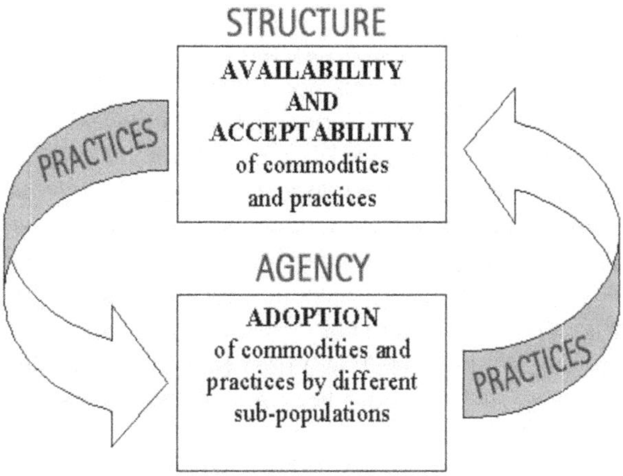

Fig. 1.2 Cultural economy framework

This research builds on findings from a Delphi study in which we consulted 50 Australian experts from a wide range of relevant backgrounds to obtain their views on which trends have driven the transformation of physical activity and food consumption practices in Australia over the last half century. The experts identified five key trends as the most important. Although all are intricately interconnected, three of the trends are linked particularly strongly with declining levels of physical activity: (a) car reliance (b) busyness and (c) changing forms of leisure; while two are more obviously related to food consumption: (d) aggressive marketing of food and (e) rising use of convenience foods, legitimated by busyness (Banwell et al. 2005). To systematise the study of the trends, we developed a framework drawing on the cultural economy literature and its methodology.

Cultural economy studies embrace the centrality of culture to the production, distribution and accumulation of resources (Amin and Thrift 2004; Dixon and Banwell 2004; du Gay and Pryke 2002). The approach calls into question dominant economic explanations of supply and demand by highlighting the processes that make commodities and practices 'good to think'. These processes are particularly pertinent to obesity, which as public health ecologists have noted can be partly attributed to transitions in culture (Lang and Rayner 2007). In examinations of changes to Australia's culinary culture and car culture since 1950, we previously (Dixon 2002; Hinde and Dixon 2007) concluded that a cultural economy perspective builds upon and improves both political economy and sociology of consumption approaches with their respective emphases on producer and consumer power.[2]

Figure 1.2 illustrates the approach which centres on two major processes that give order and structure to everyday life: the *availability* of goods and services and their *acceptability*. The third element in the framework concerns agency, or the *adoption* (and resistance to adoption) of goods, services and their associated routines and meanings.

[2] We have also successfully applied the approach to cigarette smoking (Dixon et al. 2009).

Using this framework, we developed the cultural economy audit method, which involves a synthesis of material related to availability, acceptability and adoption by actors. The key concepts pertinent to *availability* are used routinely in economics and include production, pricing, distribution and choice. The key concepts related to *acceptability* are deployed regularly in cultural studies: values and meanings, everyday practices, commodification and resistance. *Adoption* is captured in the interviews with people who reflect in detail on the trends.

For each trend we used existing documentary sources including historical, business, government and academic works, and relevant national surveys (e.g. Australian Bureau of Statistics Time Use Survey, Australian National Health Survey). The cultural economy approach pays particular attention to the cultural and economic processes that contribute to the social hierarchies, rules and resources that constitute structure.

The time period selected for the study is 50–80 years. While obesity prevalence has gathered momentum in the last 30 years, it is a cumulative process based on the *longue duree* (Australian Institute of Health and Welfare 2003a, b; Ferraro and Kelley-Moore 2003). We frame our material within a public health understanding of time. Hertzman et al. (1994) refer to a range of concepts of time used by epidemiologists, including:

biological time, referring to the point in the lifecycle when exposure takes place, otherwise known as an "age-related window of opportunity or expression";
cumulative time, referring to the time over which exposure takes place; and
historical time, referring to cohort effects or "the point in history of the society, as well as the organism". In this aspect of time, "the unfolding through time of the individual's response to particular circumstances can be influenced by when, in the course of evolution of the population, … events occurred" (Hertzman et al. 1994, p. 86).

In a quantitative analysis of how these three aspects of time—ageing (biological time), year of surveys (cumulative time), and birth cohort (historical time) relate to BMI and the prevalence of overweight and obesity in Australia, the NSW Centre for Overweight and Obesity (Allman-Farinelli et al. 2008) reported that:

1. weight increased for men and women with age in all birth cohorts except people born in 1925 or earlier;
2. men and women in each age group were heavier in 2000 than men and women in the same age group were in the previous two surveys (1990 and 1995); and
3. BMI is rising fastest among Generation X women and men (those born in the 1966–1970 period).

The researchers concluded that weight increases are not simply a result of growing older or ageing. Their main findings are that younger people are gaining weight faster than previous generations, and weight gain is accelerating as modern life influences weight patterns. The overall conclusions were that the times Australians live in are changing their weight, and that because people born most recently inhabit a more obesogenic environment than earlier cohorts, they are at greater risk of weight gain at younger ages. The findings highlight the interaction between biological, cumulative and historical time, including the circulation of socio-cultural and economic trends. We investigate these matters by interviewing three generations of Australians who are characterised as the Lucky Generation, born during the Depression; the Baby Boomers, who are children of the Lucky Generation; and the Baby Boomer children, Generation Y. The accounts from these three generations cover changes that have occurred in Australia over most of the twentieth century and the first decade of the 21st.

1.4 Structure of the Book

We provide more detail about our overall methodological approach in Chap. 2, as well as specifying the data collection and analysis techniques used. While we set out to explore the five socio-cultural trends mentioned above, we combined the aggressive marketing of food and the rise of convenience foods in conducting the interviews because their shared cultural economy histories made it difficult to disentangle them.

Changes in family dining are explored in Chap. 3, focusing in particular on the meal that Australians have most consistently eaten together: the evening meal. The plain and predictable food that older Australians remember consuming has given way to meals that are full of variety and the influences of European and Asian culinary cultures. While family meals are still held in high regard, modern Australian families struggle to maintain the family meal in the face of individualised food preferences and schedules that make it increasingly difficult to achieve commensality.

Chapter 4 deals more directly with a socio-cultural trend that is repeatedly implicated in rising levels of obesity, namely the rise of convenience foods and the production and marketing of industrial foods. It takes as a case study the dessert, once a fundamental part of the family meal, and examines the social, economic and technological changes that have contributed to its disappearance from the family menu. Now a plethora of mass-produced convenience foods is available and affordable, including after-meal confections. Increasingly frequently, Baby Boomer and Gen Y Australians eat commercially produced food products at home and in the form of takeaway, and at restaurants and cafés.

Chapter 5 weaves together cultural economy accounts of leisure (focusing specifically on non-obligatory physical exertion) and sporting activity (both organised and more spontaneous forms of play) across the twentieth century with how each of our three generations has interacted with their distinctive 'activity environments'. In addition to exerting themselves through play, sport and leisure pursuits, physical exertion is a by-product of other aspects of daily living including food provisioning, transportation and domestic and workplace technologies. Thus, this chapter needs to be read in conjunction with Chaps. 3, 7 and 8. The patterns reported there call attention to the way a wide variety of practices and environments both alter practical opportunities for physical activity and change how different forms of physical activity are culturally constructed and personally assessed.

Chapter 6 emerges from one of the key findings from Chap. 5, namely that leisure time physical activity has been far more structured and less social than in the past. We explore in greater depth two popular ways of achieving fitness: social dancing and gym-based exercise. Their appeal, positive and negative features and contradictions are described in terms of cultural and economic pressures bearing down on the three generations in the last quarter century: the pressure to ‘perform’ and excel even in leisure, and being efficient about getting and maintaining ‘fitness’ in a time pressured society. These perspectives have been largely ignored by previous researchers and commentators.

The gradual evolution of car reliance is the subject of Chap. 7. It builds on a detailed social history of transport and cars in Melbourne undertaken by our former doctoral student, Sarah Hinde. Her material describes how influential the automobile industry was in that city, and how a combination of urban planning and industry assistance decisions shaped the ready acceptance of the car. The effect of the car in relation to changes in popularity of active transport, of modes of food provisioning and leisure are canvassed through the experience of the three generations.

Chapter 8 takes up the complex and sometimes contradictory ways time pressure is represented and experienced, and the changes that are driven by its rise during the twentieth century. Unlike dietary practices and physical activity, time pressure is not implicated in weight in any direct way, but instead is a powerful socio-cultural element shaping and shaped by all the health behaviours discussed in the previous chapters. The imprint of time pressure is evident in people’s accounts of car use, dilemmas surrounding how to get or stay fit, problems scheduling family meals, and reliance on convenience food. In turn, these daily challenges feed back into the contemporary experience and understanding of time pressure.

Chapter 9 is divided into two parts. First, we summarise the findings from Chaps. 3 through 8, and then report on three additional socio-cultural trends which repeatedly appeared when the three generations were reflecting on their respective food and physical activity practices, namely: the rise of health consciousness; child-centred family practices; and the attenuation of habits and the embrace of cultural change. We illustrate these new trends by drawing on experiences from one of the three-generation families to have participated in our study. Throughout the chapters, we draw attention to the role of family socialisation and interrogate the structure-agency dynamic at work.

After summarising how the key socio-cultural trends have contributed to the obesogenic environment in Australia over the last 50 years and how three generations of Australians have embodied and experienced those trends, we turn to our second research aim: to identify the social forces that provide the socio-cultural trends with their potency. This part of the chapter uses material from three sources—our interviews, social policy, and social and economic histories—to ask whether there is evidence of fundamental social forces shaping the life chances, and hence life choices, of whole cohorts.

While the chapters rely on Australian data, that fact that Australia shares large increases in male and female BMI with other English-speaking advanced economies makes the overall findings pertinent to them at the very least. Chapter 10 begins by asking what pressure points for action exist in societies like Australia to reverse the rise in obesity. We focus on the realm of culture as an overlooked and contested sphere of both deliberate activity and incremental and unplanned change. If obesity is reframed as a sign of a deeply disturbed societal culture, then multiple pressure points are revealed. We draw inspiration from ecologists and resilience theorists to point to the broad types of government and civil society interventions that are required.

References

Allman-Farinelli, M. A., Chey, T., Bauman, A. E., Gill, T., & James, W. P. (2008). Age, period and birth cohort effects on prevalence of overweight and obesity in Australian adults from 1990 to 2000. *European Journal of Clinical Nutrition, 62*(7), 898–907.

Amin, A., & Thrift, N. (2004). *The Blackwell cultural economy reader*. Malden: Blackwell Publishing.

Aphramor, L. (2005). Is a weight-centred health framework salutogenic? Some thoughts on unhinging certain dietary ideologies. *Social Theory & Health, 3*(4), 315–350.

Australian Institute of Health and Welfare. (2003). Are all Australians gaining weight? Differentials in overweight and obesity among adults, 1989–2001. *AIHW Bulletin, December*, (11), 1–24.

Australian Institute of Health and Welfare. (2003). A growing problem: Trends and patterns in overweight and obesity among adults in Australia, 1980 to 2001. *AIHW Bulletin, September*, (8), 1–20.

Baker, P., & Young, M. (2006). *A summary of published Cochrane and non-Cochrane Systematics reviews – Systematic Reviews on Obesity*. http://www.health.qld.gov.au/ph/documents/caphs/32117.pdf

Banwell, C., Hinde, S., Dixon, J., & Sibthorpe, B. (2005). Reflections on an expert consensus: A case study of the social trends contributing to obesity. *European Journal of Public Health, 15*(6), 564–568.

Broom, D. H., & Dixon, J. (2008). The sex of slimming: Mobilising gender in weight-loss programs and fat acceptance. *Social Theory & Health, 8*(2), 148–166.

Cassel, P., & Giddens, A. (1993). *The Giddens reader*. London: Macmillan.

Cockerham, W. C. (2007). Health lifestyles and the absence of the Russian middle class. *Sociology of Health & Illness, 29*(3), 457–473.

Cockerham, W., Rutten, A., et al. (1997). Conceptualising contemporary health lifestyles: Moving beyond Weber. *The Sociological Quarterly, 38*(2), 321–342.

Commission on Social Determinants of Health. (2008). *Closing the gap in a generation: Health equity through action on the social determinants of health*. Geneva: WHO.

Dixon, J. (2002). *The changing chicken*. Sydney: UNSW Press.

Dixon, J., & Banwell, C. (2004). Heading the table: Parenting and the junior consumer. *British Food Journal, 106*(2/3), 181–193.

Dixon, J., & Broom, D. (Eds.). (2007). *The seven deadly sins of obesity: How the modern world is making us fat*. Sydney: University of New South Wales Press.

Dixon, J., & Banwell, C. (2009). Theoretically driven research for explaining health risk transitions: The case of smoking. *Social Science & Medicine, 68*(12), 2206–2214.

Doak, C. M., Aldair, L. S., Bentley, M., Monteiro, C., & Popkin, B. M. (2005). The dual burden household and the nutrition transition paradox. *International Journal of Obesity, 29*(1), 129–136.

du Gay, P., & Pryke, M. (2002). *Cultural economy: Cultural analysis and commercial life*. London: Sage.

Egger, G., & Swinburn, B. (1997). An "ecological" approach to the obesity pandemic. *British Medical Journal, 315*, 477–480.

Emirbayer, M., & Mische, A. (1998). What is agency? *The American Journal of Sociology, 103*(4), 962–1023.

Ferraro, K., & Kelley-Moore, J. (2003). Cumulative disadvantages and health: Long-term consequences of obesity? *American Sociological Review, 68*(5), 702–709.

Finucane, M. M., Stevens, G. A., Cowan, M. J., Danaei, G., Lin, J. K., Paciorek, C. J., et al. (2011). National, regional and global trends in body-mass index since 1980: Systematic analysis of health examination surveys and epidemiological studies with 960 country-years and 9.1 million participants. *The Lancet, 377*, 557–567.

Friel, S., & Broom, D. (2007). Unequal society, unhealthy weight: The social distribution of obesity. In J. Dixon & D. Broom (Eds.), *The 7 deadly sins of obesity*. Sydney: University of New South Wales Press.

Frohlick, K., & Potvin, L. (2002). A theoretical and empirical analysis of context: Neighbourhoods, smoking and youth. *Social Science & Medicine, 54*(9), 1401–1407.

Gard, M., & Wright, J. (2005). *The obesity epidemic: Science, morality and ideology*. London: Routledge.

Glassner, B. (1989). Fitness and the postmodern self. *Journal of Health and Social Behavior, 30*(2), 180–191.

Hardy, L. (2010). *SPANS 2010 NSW schools physical activity and nutrition survey executive summary*. Sydney: University of Sydney.

Hertzman, C., Frank, J., & Evans, R. G. (1994). Heterogeneities in health status and the determinants of population health. In R. G. Evans, M. L. Barer, & T. R. Marmor (Eds.), *Why are some people healthy and others not* (pp. 67–92). New York: Aldine De Gruyter.

Hinde, S., & Dixon, J. (2007). Reinstating Pierre Bourdieu's contribution to cultural economy theorising. *Journal of Sociology, 43*(4), 401–420.

Julier, A. (2008). The political economy of obesity: The fat pay all. In C. Counihan & P. V. Esterik (Eds.), *Food and culture: A reader* (2nd ed., pp. 482–499). New York: Routledge.

Kirk, S. F. L., Penney, T. L., & McHugh, T. L. F. (2009). Characterizing the obesogenic environment: The state of the evidence with directions for future research. *Obesity Reviews, 11*(2), 109–117.

Kwan, S. (2009). Framing the fat body: Contested meanings between government, activists, and industry. *Sociological Inquiry, 79*(1), 25–50.

Lang, T., & Rayner, G. (2007). Overcoming policy cacophony on obesity: An ecological public health framework for policymakers. *Obesity Reviews, 8*(Suppl 1), 165–181.

Ljungvall, Å., & Gerdtham, U.-G. (2010). More equal but heavier: A longitudinal analysis of income-related obesity inequalities in an adult Swedish cohort. *Social Science & Medicine, 70*(2), 221–231.

McLaren, L. (2007). Socioeconomic status and obesity. *Epidemiological Reviews, 29*, 29–48.

Monaghan, L. F., & Hardey, M. (2009). Bodily sensibility: Vocabularies of the discredited male body. *Critical Public Health, 19*(3), 341–362.

Monteiro, C. A., Conde, W. L., Lu, B., & Popkin, B. (2004). Obesity and inequities in health in the developing world. *International Journal of Obesity, 28*, 1181–1186.

Roskam, A.-J. R., Kunst, A. E., Van Oyen, H., Demarest, S., Klumbiene, J., Regidor, E., et al. (2010). Comparative appraisal of educational inequalities in overweight and obesity among adults in 19 European countries. *International Journal of Epidemiology, 39*(2), 392–404. doi:10.1093/ije/dyp329.

Schwartz, H. (1986). *Never satisfied: A cultural history of diets, fantasies and fat*. New York: The Free Press.

Stearns, P. N. (1997). *Fat history: Bodies and beauty in the modern west*. New York: New York University Press.

Valera-Silva, M. I., Azcorra, H., Dickinson, F., Bogin, B., & Frisancho, A. R. (2009). Influence of maternal stature, pregnancy age, and infant birthweight on growth during childhood in Yucatán, Mexico: A test of the intergenerational effects hypothesis. *American Journal of Human Biology, 21*, 657–663.

Williams, S. (1995). Theorising class, health and lifestyles: Can Bourdieu help us? *Sociology of Health & Illness, 17*(5), 577–604.

Williams, G. H. (2003). The determinants of health: Structure, context and agency. *Sociology of Health & Illness, 25*(3), 131–154.

World Health Organization. (2010). *Global database on body mass index*. Graphs. Retrieved January 14, 2010, from http://apps.who.int/bmi/index.jsp

Zhang, Q., & Wang, Y. (2004). Socioeconomic inequality of obesity in the United States: Do gender, age, and ethnicity matter? *Social Science & Medicine, 58*(6), 1171–1180.

Chapter 2
An Intergenerational Study Design

2.1 Generations and Cohorts

This study examines the experiences of older individuals who have lived through the unfolding of five selected socio-cultural trends as well as their children's and grandchildren's reflections on those same trends (more briefly). The trends already introduced are car reliance; busyness; changing forms of leisure; changing patterns of food consumption; and rising use of convenience foods. The study employs interviews conducted with people who could describe what it was like to grow up, work and raise a family amid transformations in basic aspects of daily life. Individuals' reflections on their lifecourse are contextualised through the use of a cultural economy approach in which historical and cultural texts illustrate broader economic and structural changes in the trends that acquire a personal voice in the stories from the people who have lived them. What this research does is to populate the cultural, social and economic trends that constitute the obesogenic environment with people's experiences and behavioural responses. Oft-used phrases like busyness, convenience foods, car reliance are contextualised in time, space and social structure. The interview material illustrates how the trends 'get under the skin' of people as they go about their daily lives, and provides insight into the very basic barriers to behaviour change.

The oldest generation of study participants match what Mackay (1997) calls the 'Lucky Generation', those who grew up in times of hardship and austerity in the Depression and World War II but later enjoyed the prosperity of the post-war boom at a time in their lives (as young adults) when they were best able to exploit it. Their children and our next generation of participants correspond to Mackay's Baby Boomers, characterised as the post-war generation who were in a sense the mirror image of their parents. They grew up in a period of "unprecedented prosperity" which was then followed by a life of "turbulence and hardship" (Mackay 1997, p. 59). We have diverged from Mackay's terminology to label their children (our third group of participants) Generation Y, a term widely used in Australia to describe those born in the last two decades of the twentieth century. The three generations and major historical events marking various stages of their lives are illustrated in Fig. 2.1.

C. Banwell et al., *Weight of Modernity: An Intergenerational Study of the Rise of Obesity*,
DOI 10.1007/978-90-481-8957-1_2, © Springer Science+Business Media Dordrecht 2012

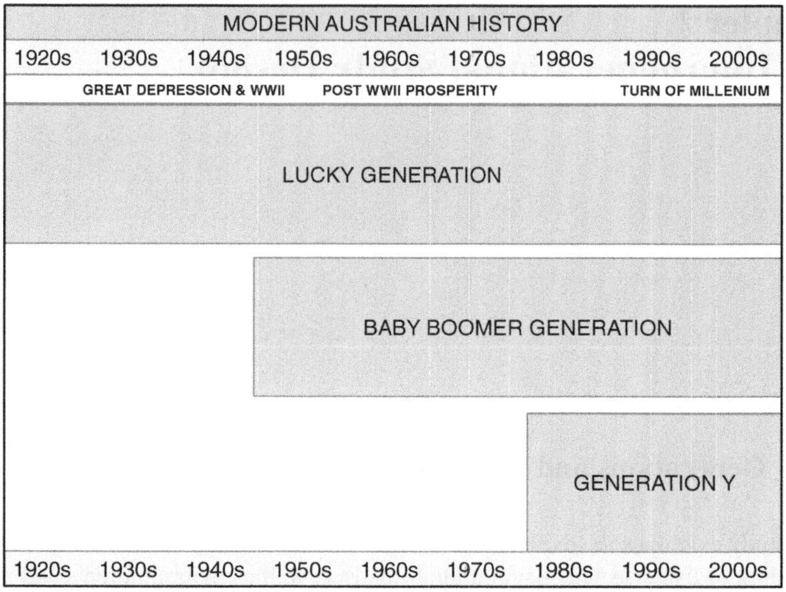

Fig. 2.1 The historical context and life-stage of each generation of participants

We consider how different generations of men and women experience the social trends that influence population weight levels at different life stages. This approach accords with what has been described as a "synthesis" between a cohort and generation approach (Mackay 1997). A cohort is typically defined as a group of people who experience the same event at the same historical time (Jackson and Heard 2000). Cohort members share the experience of major life events such as wars and socio-economic changes, while lesser ones such as leaving home, getting married and having children occurred in their lives at similar times. It is this nexus between their age and experience of lifecourse events that is understood to produce identifiable patterned cohort effects. Furthermore, the social, economic and cultural conditions that a cohort experiences shape "the outlook and life options and ultimately their life-time outcomes" (Jackson and Heard 2000). This understanding has most in common with the sociological concept of generations, which correspond to successive waves of new children who share a history and time period.

2.2 Generations of Memories

For the Lucky Generation in particular and to a lesser degree for the other two generations, the information they provided in qualitative interviews was based on their recollection of personal and historical events that sometimes occurred many years ago. The nexus between a generation and their memories of the socio-cultural trends discussed in this book is likely to reflect an identity and world view that is unique to each generation. A cohort or generation sharing outlooks and dispositions is predicated upon a concept of shared memories of similar experiences. Memory theorists (Connerton 1989; Golden 2005) argue that memory is primarily socially constructed and collective. For Connerton (1989, p. 3), "the memories of one generation [are] locked irretrievably, as it were, in the bodies of that generation". A generation's memories are intertwined with lived experiences of, for example, family meals, car use or choice of hobbies and may be visible in the body size and shape. People's reminiscences of how they have adopted, adapted and resisted change within their immediate family provide an insight into the broader social and economic forces that have motivated change over the last 50 years in Australia (Holtzman 2006).

Memories of the same event sometimes diverge, raising questions about their accuracy and reliability. However, it is not the 'truth' of remembered events that is important here but rather the "construction of knowledges and the process by which the enculturation of individuals into society is achieved" (Lupton 1994, p. 669). This book is based on participants' narratives which are not objective truths but, like all narratives, are creative accounts of their recent and distant past. Their accounts draw upon three kinds of linked autobiographical memory. The first is of "lifetime periods" and is often framed by developmental stages such as childhood, adolescence and adulthood; the second is of general events such as holidays, or years at university, and the third is event-specific, such as a special birthday or first day at school. Such autobiographical memories are likely to be based in part on shared family memories that reflect a collective family identity and culture (Shore 2009). When recalling family events such as meals, parties, holidays and hobbies, individuals will draw upon these shared family memories as well as their personal recollections. In summary, we have organised this study to tap into the collective memory of three generations to understand the interplay between individuals and their shared experience of historical periods, as well as personal and family memories of everyday events.

2.3 Cultural Economy Audit

Interwoven with the analysis of participants' narrative accounts of their experience of the social trends are references to documentary evidence gathered using a "cultural economy audit" method which involves a systematic, qualitative exploration of documentary sources of information related to the socio-cultural trends. As foreshadowed in Chap. 1, the choice of material to be included in the audit and ultimately in this book is driven by three key concepts regarding each trend. They are:

availability, which is used routinely in economics and includes production, pricing, distribution and choice;

acceptability, which is deployed regularly in cultural studies: values and meanings, everyday practices, and resistance to new trends;

adoption, or how a trend is taken up, is captured in the interviews with members of each generation.

For each trend we used existing documentary sources including historical, business, government and academic works, and relevant national surveys (e.g. ABS Time Use survey, National Health Survey). Textual material was collected before interviews began to inform the interview process and more was added during the fieldwork and writing stages.

2.4 Interviews

2.4.1 Recruitment

To access the Lucky or oldest generation, we worked with the longitudinal Melbourne Collaborative Cohort Study (MCCS). The cohort consists of over 40,000 Anglo, Italian and Greek men and women, recruited between 1990 and 1994, aged 40 to over 70 and resident in Melbourne, who had been surveyed in two waves (Giles and English 2002). We undertook a nested study of a selected group of participants, aged 65–70. The existing data on the cohort were used in an effort to select men and women with a range of body weights in the normal and above categories. Our aim was not for a representative sample, but a sample which would elucidate the qualitative themes relevant to body weight. (See Davis (2011) for a more detailed account of the methodological approach).

The MCCS runs periodic 'clinics' for the cohort during which weight is measured (height was recorded at baseline). When cohort members attended the clinics they were given information sheets on our research and an invitation to participate in our study. We recruited only those of Anglo-Celtic background as they are the largest and culturally dominant proportion of the Australian population, and have shown greater increases in obesity than the two other ethnic groups in the MCCS (Australian Institute of Health and Welfare 2003). As ours is the first study to broach the issues under discussion, we limited the ethnic, age and familial variation in the sample. (Future studies of other sub-populations would form valuable elaborations.)

Only MCCS participants who were parents were invited to participate. This enabled us to recruit two younger generations by asking interviewees for an opportunity to interview their adult offspring about the same trends over their lifetimes. The adult offspring were then asked to refer us to their adult children. We aimed to interview approximately 30 males and 30 females from the middle or Baby Boomer Generation, and as many of the youngest Generation Y members as possible (knowing that there would be comparatively fewer of them and that they would be the most difficult to recruit). This approach generated a sample that permits exploration of the intergenerational and familial patterns and responses to the trends and enables some exploration of age, lifestage and cohort effects. The basic recruitment strategy is illustrated in Fig. 2.2. While this type of qualitative research does not depend on representativeness for its authority, the project is strengthened by being a sub-sample from a large and representative sample.

The Lucky Generation were interviewed in the MCCS offices during June and July 2006 by Banwell Bloom and Dixon. The Baby Boomers were interviewed in

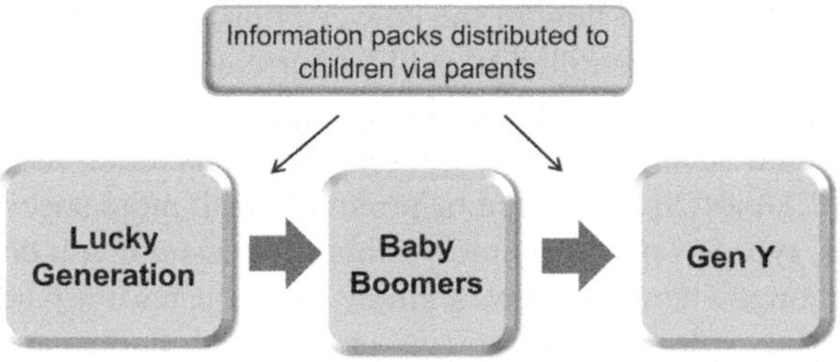

Fig. 2.2 Recruitment of baby boomers and generation Y participants

November 2006 and Generation Y in June 2007. Anna Davies conducted these interviews in participants' homes, workplaces and the ANU office in Melbourne.

Before beginning the more discursive part of the interview, we completed a brief questionnaire of background information including date of birth, schooling, whether they are employed, their main occupation during adulthood, their partner's occupation, and their father's and mother's level of education and occupation.

2.4.2 Interview Structure and Themes

All three generations of participants answered an open-ended semi-structured interview, including questions about everyday life and transition points. They were asked to reflect on their experiences of the trends in relation to their food consumption and physical activity practices throughout their lives, and the positive and negative impacts on body shape. Interviews started by asking participants to supply an overview of their life-span, beginning with their year of birth, the composition of the household into which they were born, and proceeding forward through major family events during childhood, schooling, adolescence, leaving home and establishing their own families, the arrival of children, transition to the 'empty nest' through to the current day. People were asked to indicate major personal and family landmarks in their life path which we marked on a sheet of paper as they spoke.

The sketch of their life-span was used as a reference point as the interview proceeded to questions on the socio-cultural trends. Where trends focused directly on food and physical activity, people were asked to describe their family's situation at three points over the life course: when the respondent her/himself was about age 10–12, when their own children were about age 10–12, and at the present. For example, to investigate patterns around eating and food, we asked participants to describe a typical evening meal when they were growing up: who was at the table, who had prepared the meal, what was served, whether they had a favourite food or were made to eat anything they hated. We also asked about school lunches and between-meal snacking. When they had given a detailed picture of how they ate when they were growing up, we asked similar questions about what happened when their children were in primary school. The questions on food concluded by asking them to describe what they had for their evening meal the night before our interview, how typical that meal was, and whether they usually ate anything between meals these days.

Depending on the natural flow of the conversation, most interviews were structured to explore the three identified broad lifecourse stages in succession (growing up, child-rearing and today) refracted through questions about each of the social trends. After a trend-specific framing question (e.g. 'As a kid, how did you spend your spare time?'), participants might be prompted with more specific probes (such as 'What games, types of play, pastimes, hobbies, sports did you do? Did you have any domestic chores when you were a child? Did you have a paid job when you were young?') The exploration of growing up included inquiry about whether any of the patterns described changed when the person became a teenager.

We were interested in the experience of all five trends through the lifecourse, but a different approach was required to explore the other three trends than the one used for eating and activity. The framing question about car use asked whether the family had a car when the respondent was a child. That was the basis on which to probe for more details about transport, how they got to school, how employed adults (parents, older siblings) commuted to work, and how transport for shopping and socialising were managed. If there was a car when they were growing up, we asked who drove it and what it was used for. If they recalled the event, interviewees were encouraged to describe the occasion when the family got its first car. They were then asked to tell us about when they got their own first car and why; how their children got to and from school and other activities while they were growing up; and finally to report on whether they still drive a car and for what purposes.

The examination of convenience goods and services consisted of completing a detailed checklist of devices and services, indicating both whether they *had* the technology in question, and whether they *used* it. We inquired about what they had found to be the most useful or favourite labour-saving device during their lifetime, how/why it was helpful, and whether it had any drawbacks. They were also asked to say what device or innovation they thought their mother had most welcomed, and the same for their father. Finally, they talked about what devices their children liked or found essential.

On the advice of the experts (Banwell et al. 2005), we had included time pressure or busyness in the theme list for our interviews. However, finding ways to investigate this theme, and subsequently interpreting interview responses generated as many questions as answers, problems we discuss in detail in Chap. 8.

Most interviews were structured to explore the three broad lifecourse stages in succession (growing up, child-rearing and today), although five of the Baby Boomer participants were not parents and hence did not have accounts of child-rearing, and only one Gen Y respondent had a child. We considered the use of convenience goods and services (including processed, prepared and catered food) in light of their potential relevance to time use. Time pressure *per se* was introduced by asking them when in their lives they were the busiest they had ever been, whether they felt rushed at that time and whether they needed to cut out doing anything or use short-cuts to cope with it. We also asked when they were the least busy, whether they felt the pace of life had been different for their parents than for themselves, and whether their children's lives were more or less busy than they themselves had been at the same age. In addition, the two younger generations were asked several specific questions with implications for time and time use, including what they would do with it if they had more time.

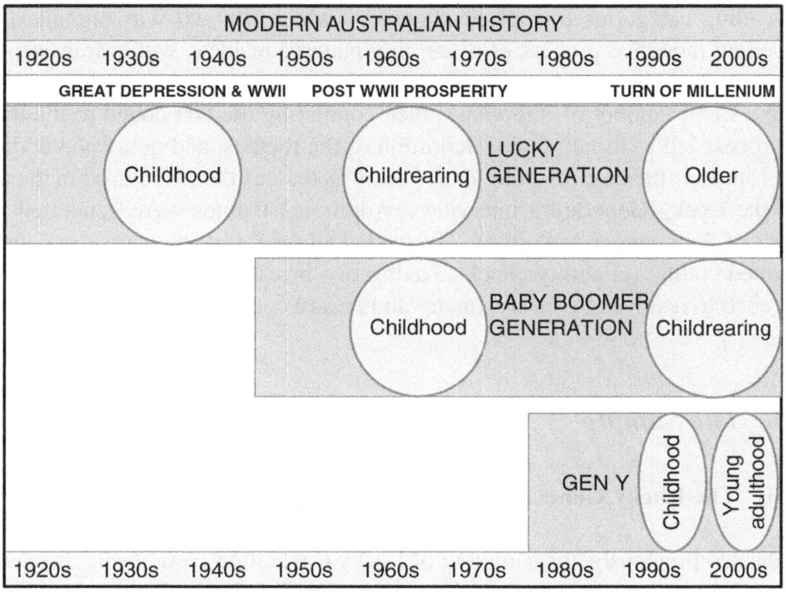

Fig. 2.3 The time periods about which each generation was questioned

The interviews concluded with some related (but not so trend-specific) questions asking people about whether their body size or shape had changed much over their adult life, how they felt about any changes, and what might have influenced them; whether there had been any other significant changes in their life (e.g. illness, injury, change in occupation) that might have affected their weight, and whether they ever weigh themselves. Finally, they were invited to propose advice to governments about what it could do to promote healthy weight.

The interview schedule for the Baby Boomers and their Generation Y children was based on the one described above. Additional themes were developed for the Baby Boomer and Generation Y interview schedules to gain a greater understanding of structural constraints and agency in participants' lives. These included sections on the media and social influences, health, wellbeing and what constitutes a healthy lifestyle and healthy weight. Because of the time-span covered and the participants' reflections on their parents and their children (as well as their own lives), our data shed light from multiple perspectives on everyday life in Australia over more than seven decades as shown in Figs. 2.1 and 2.3.

2.4.3 Interview Analysis

Interviews were audio-taped, transcribed, coded and sorted according to content, theme and narrative forms, using the computer programme ATLAS.ti for the management of qualitative textual data. The researchers jointly discussed and decided the main coding categories (or sub-headings) by which the text was organised. This involved an inductive process of discerning patterns of ideas within transcripts following repeated close readings of the data. This began with independent reading and coding a small number of interviews, then comparing the text coded to the themes. This process led to more precise definition of the themes, and generated additional themes and sub-themes, resulting in a total of 48 themes that were used in the analysis of the Lucky Generation interviews. Additional themes were generated in the analysis of the younger generations. We coded all the interviews ourselves, and also performed coding reliability checks, having two investigators cross-code five interviews each to resolve any discrepancies and ensure consistency in coding.

2.4.4 The Sample

2.4.4.1 The Lucky Generation

As indicated previously, the sampling of Lucky Generation participants dictated who was recruited in the other two generations and was therefore influential to the overall course of the study. We conducted interviews in 2006 with 111 Australian-born parents aged between 67 and 83. Although we had sought equal proportions of females and males, the actual sample contained 38 (34.2%) males and 73 (65.8%) females. Only the Lucky Generation had their weights and heights collected (through the Melbourne Collaborative Cohort Study). In our sample two thirds of participants (66.7%) fell within the healthy weight range and the remaining third (33.3%) were obese.

In part because most of the Lucky Generation had retired, they received relatively low incomes. More than half had an annual household income of $30,000 or below, that is, below the national average which would be expected in a sample with this age profile. Less than two thirds (proportionally more of the men than of the women) had any post-secondary education. There was a disinclination to identify as upper class in the whole sample, of which 60% labelled themselves as middle class while many more identified themselves as working class (20%) than upper-middle class (7%). The unequal distribution of Lucky generation participants by sex, BMI and class limited our ability to investigate the role and interaction of these variables in our analyses. Table 2.1 (at the end of this chapter) summarises the distribution of major demographic variables of the final sample.

As anticipated, there was some attrition in recruitment from the oldest to the youngest generations, since we relied on participants to recruit their children, a task they may have been more or less able and willing to undertake. We also limited the number of interviews conducted with Baby Boomers to a manageable number that also fulfilled the requirements of theoretical saturation. The Lucky Generation participants were already committed to taking part in population health research (as indicated by involvement in the MCCS), but the two younger generations did not necessarily share that commitment. Additionally, the younger cohorts were likely to be busier. This attenuation of numbers is evident in Table 2.1.

Table 2.1 Demographic characteristics of participants by generations

	Luckies N=111		Baby Boomers N=28		Gen Ys N=12	
	N	%	N	%	N	%
Gender						
Female	72	65	20	71	6	50
Male	39	35	8	28	6	50
Age range & mean	67–83 (75)		36–60 (49)		19–24 (24)	
Education						
To year 8	31	28	0	0	0	0
Years 9–10	32	29	1	4	0	0
Years 11–12	41	37	3	11	3	25
Post secondary education[a]	64	58	22	78	9	58
Net household income per annum						
Less than $30,000	49	44	0	0	0	8
$31,000–$70,000	29	26	8	25	4	25
$71,000 and over	14	13	20	75	8	66
Marital status						
Single	0	0	2	7	9	75
Married or defacto	75	67	21	75	3	25
Widowed	26	23	0	0	0	0
Separated or divorced	9	8	5	18	0	0
Work Force participation						
Full-time	1	1	19	68	4	33
Part-time	3	3	6	21	8	66
Casual	4	4	0	0	0	0
Pension	10	9	0	0	0	0
Retired/home duties	88	80	3	11	0	0
other	1	1	0	0	0	0

[a] The education columns do not add to 100%. Some people undertook post-secondary education in later life despite not completing high school. This does not include apprenticeships and trade certificates

2.4.4.2 Baby Boomers

Table 2.1 displays indicators of the different life stages of the three generations of participants as well as broad demographic changes that have occurred in the Australian population over the twentieth century. Reflecting demographic trends, the Baby Boomers had higher levels of education than their parents, higher incomes and higher divorce rates. As they were younger at the time of the research none were widowed and most were still in paid employment. We interviewed 28 people from this generation, 71% of whom were women. At the time of interview the Boomers in our sample were aged between 36 and 60 years, which is wider than the usual age range of Baby Boomers.

2.4.4.3 Gen Ys

The 12 participants from this generation have higher levels of education than their parents, with half of them studying at the time of the research as well as working either part – or full-time. They are evenly divided by gender. Given their comparative youth, a surprising proportion of them had household incomes over $70,000 but this is because in some cases they were living at home and this figure included their parents' incomes. However, in light of their age it is not surprising that 75% of them were unmarried. The age at marriage in Australia has increased from 25 years in 1986 to 30 years in 2005 for men and from 23 to 28 years for women over the same period (Australian Bureau of Statistics 2007).

2.4.5 Family Participation

The study is unique in that included 16 two-generation families (Lucky Generation grandparents and Baby Boomer parents) and seven three-generation families. The data from the three-generation families provided particularly vivid examples of the changes in social trends over time and enabled exploration of the role of family in reproducing patterned responses to social trends over time.

In the next six chapters, we present the combined findings from the interviews and cultural economy audits. Chapters 3 and 4 begin this process, concentrating specifically on aspects of food and eating.

References

Australian Bureau of Statistics. (2007). *Australian social trends—2007 4102.0*. Canberra: ABS.

Australian Institute of Health and Welfare. (2003). Are all Australians gaining weight? Differentials in overweight and obesity among adults, 1989–2001. *AIHW Bulletin, December*(11), 1–24.

Banwell, C., Hinde, S., Dixon, J., & Sibthorpe, B. (2005). Reflections on expert consensus: A case study of the social trends contributing to obesity. *European Journal of Public Health, 15*(6), 564–568.

Connerton, P. (1989). *How societies remember*. Cambridge: Cambridge University Press.

Davis, A. (2011). *Healthy citizenship in an obesogenic environment*. Canberra: Australian National University.

Giles, G., & English, D. (2002). The Melbourne collaborative cohort study. *International Agency for Research on Cancer Scientific Publications, 156*, 69–70.

Golden, C. (2005). Where does memory reside, and why isn't it history? *American Anthropologist, 107*(2), 270–274.

Holtzman, J. (2006). Food and memory. *Annual Review of Anthropology, 35*, 361–378.

Jackson, N., & Heard, G. (2000). *Population and globalisation: Australia in the 21st century*. Paper presented at the 10th biennial conference of the Australian Population Association, Melbourne.

Lupton, D. (1994). Food, memory and meaning: The symbolic and social nature of food. *The Sociological Review, 42*(4), 664–685.

Mackay, H. (1997). *Generations: Baby boomers, their parents and their children*. Sydney: Pan Macmillan.

Shore, B. (2009). Making time for family: Schemas for long-term family memory. *Social Indicators Research, 93*, 95–103.

Chapter 3
From Habit to Choice: Transformations in Family Dining Over Three Generations

Image 3.1 Dinner time (1940–1945) (Source: State Library of Victoria)

Over the lifetimes of the three generations of respondents widespread social and economic transformations have occurred which interact with, and ultimately reshape family dining patterns. For example, food sociologists have questioned whether the rules and structures around culinary systems in modern societies have diminished so far as to be replaced by a state of (gastro)anomie characterised by either a void or an over-abundance of conflicting rules (Fischler 1993). In similar vein, others have proposed that formal meals are being at least partially replaced by practices in which

C. Banwell et al., *Weight of Modernity: An Intergenerational Study of the Rise of Obesity*, DOI 10.1007/978-90-481-8957-1_3, © Springer Science+Business Media Dordrecht 2012

individuals eat what, where and when they choose (grazing) in the UK (Murcott 1997) or by vagabond eating in France (Poulain 2002). The trend is thought to be aided by the growth and accessibility of convenience and commercially prepared foods. The disappearance or significant modification of the family meal is proposed as one manifestation of post-modernity. This proposition has been contested, with some arguing that the family meal never really existed in its ideal form (Murcott 1997).

As well as practices, attitudes to food have also changed over this time. Elsewhere we have argued that the Lucky Generation of Australians growing up in economically restricted times was brought up to view food pragmatically, focusing on its cost and its ability to keep the family from feeling hungry. This practical attitude is also influenced by the dominant socio-cultural perspective on food, reflecting its Australian history as an English colony (Symons 1984; Walker and Roberts 1988) and the background of our respondents who were all of English-speaking descent. Later generations of Australians express enjoyment in food through their discussions of the taste, colour, smell and textures of dishes. There has been a corresponding growth in the promotion of pleasure in food via cook books, specialty food and wine magazines and television cooking shows.

Changes to family dining have been examined from socio-historical and gender perspectives (Charles and Kerr 1986; Luxton 1980; Murcott 1983), and recently attention has focused on the so-called 'obesity epidemic' particularly among younger generations. It appears that transformations in family dining have health (and weight) as well as social implications, although a plethora of theories are competing for attention. Some observers suggest that family dining may be protective if it excludes television viewing, (Veugelers and Fitzgerald 2005) as it may reduce the consumption of ready-made food (Gillman et al. 2000). In Australia, mothers' positive attitudes towards family dining were found to have greater impact on maintaining children's healthy weight than self-reports of the family eating together (Mamun et al. 2005). However, family dining has rarely been examined within and between specific generations or families. In this chapter we summarise the main trends in family dining over three generations and in the next chapter focuses on the growth of convenience food and the disappearance of home-made desserts as the final course in the everyday evening meal.

3.1 Growing Up During the Depression and War: The Lucky Generation's Childhood

Our oldest generation were children during the Depression when unemployment rates quickly rose to nearly 30% for male breadwinners, while wages dropped dramatically, forcing thousands of men to leave their families to tramp around the country looking for work (Kociumbas 1997), which was known as 'going on the wallaby'. In 1933, 33,000 men were of 'no fixed abode' (Fahey 1992). The effects of the Depression were compounded for country folk by a drought in the late 1920s

(Kociumbas 1997). In the cities the hardship of the Depression was quite class-specific, with the working class suffering greater economic hardship (Kociumbas 1997; Williams 1985). Associated with World War II, rationing lasted from 1942 until 1947. Butter, tea, sugar and meat were rationed and eggs were allocated to priority groups such as children under 5 years, while sausages, offal, canned meat, poultry, rabbits, fish, bacon and ham remained unrationed (Australian Bureau of Statistics 1945). Nevertheless, only the poorest few said they were hungry during their childhood. They developed a utilitarian view of food as a necessity to support life and activity but they expressed very little pleasure in the meals of their youth (Banwell et al. 2010). Furthermore, they were influenced like other Australians by the English, who valued plain food as wholesome and virtuous (Santich 1995), rather than pleasurable. A plain, 'no-frills' style of cooking was common, perhaps stemming from early colonial times when white Australians subsisted mainly on a monotonous and limited diet of meat and tea, and many suffered from vitamin deficiencies and scurvy due to lack of vegetables (Walker and Roberts 1988). The British roast dinner on Sundays was maintained, and as there were no refrigerators and few iceboxes, butchers remained open on Saturdays and some even on Sunday morning to allow the purchase of meat (Walker and Roberts 1988).

Our participants recalled that meals were based on low-cost cuts of meat, and usually three vegetables, sometimes home-grown. Joy's account reflects the dominant discourse about meals at this time and the need to eat cheaply.

> *We had very cheap food, [it] would have been a lot of potatoes and a lot of rice, boiled rice, rice puddings, the whole bit. I imagine we had meat, but I don't actually recall. I would say it would be the cheaper cuts because my father was earning a pittance, an absolute pittance.*

Maxine explained the enduring power of early childhood food habits that last even as they become unfashionable.

> *People can't understand why I like offal. And brains and lambs fry and all that. But we were brought up on that during the food rationing.*

As children, the Luckies, like Heather, most commonly dined on lamb or beef, often sausages or chops, which were cheaper, and steak less frequently, while chicken and other poultry were reserved for Christmas or very special occasions.

> *No, very seldom chicken. You know how in now days you can buy chicken all the time, well we had chicken perhaps we might have seen a chicken towards Christmas.*

At this time Australia was a large producer and exporter of sheep wool and meat, and some participants remembered their meat intake consisting almost entirely of lamb and mutton.

Many, like Eve, praised their mothers' abilities *to make a meal out of nothing* but the downside was that meals were humdrum, predictable, dictated by the limited availability and affordability. Joy's reference (above) to her father's earning capacity was accompanied by the memory that her mother would always serve *the husband and the four kids* first and herself last, reflecting the ideology of motherhood and the social and economic conditions of the time. Family meals expressed the hierarchies of the day with men often determining the timing of meals, the menu, the order of serving and sometimes the conversation. Women and particularly children wielded little influence. Participants remembered that family meals were dominated not only by some fathers' homecomings, but also by their food preferences and their emotional states. Joy recalled that her mother often ate her food cold because she always got up to serve her father first and then interrupted her meal to get him his dessert when he had finished his main course.

And I thought at the time, no way will I ever do that. But this was the role of the housewife back then, the man coming in from work was the most important person. And the wife always, you know, was very, very low down on the ladder, definitely...

As a consequence of dining as soon as her father arrived home, Joy's mother was required to prepare a light *supper* at about 10 pm at night because the children were hungry again by then.

Sixty-nine year-old Jenny recounted that her father insisted that the children were not allowed to talk at all. Children dined with the family and ate what they were given. *We weren't allowed to have dislikes, I don't think, with five kids. I think we ate most things.* They knew that food was scarce, particularly if rationed, and expensive. Lindsey said: *Times were hard and you didn't waste anything.* As children, they seemed to have absorbed this attitude with little resistance, even though they acknowledged it was a struggle to eat some foods. *I can remember sort of chewing it and chewing it and chewing it and having to sort of swallow it...*Lindsey continued. If they did not finish their meal they might be banished from the table, refused dessert or served their uneaten food for breakfast.

Informants gave accounts of structured evening meal patterns of main course and dessert, with the menu following a familiar pattern of meals over a weekly cycle, adding to the predictability but with a loss of spontaneity. Heather's account of the weekly meal cycle was typical. Nevertheless, her use of the phrase *just straight out of the oven* suggests that there was some enjoyment to be had in hot freshly cooked food.

We'd have a weekly roast with three vegetables and a sweet....And that would usually be Sunday lunch. Sunday night it would be cold meat and salads and homemade scones just straight out of the oven.

A somewhat looser seasonal cycle entailed lighter, cold meals such as salads and cold meat during summer, and heavier, hotter meals like lamb and beef stews, or sausages and chops during winter. These cuts of meat were supplemented by offal like lambs brains and tripe and by men's and kids' catch of fish and rabbits. During winter, potatoes, pumpkins, and *greens* such as brussel sprouts or cabbage were popular. The cycle was punctuated by special events such as Christmas and birthdays, which were not always celebrated with significantly richer meals because of the rationing that occurred during the war. The Luckies' accounts are confirmed by research at the time showing that the average adult worker between 1920 and 1925 consumed at the evening meal: meat, potato, pumpkin, rice pudding and two cups of tea (Teow et al. 1988). These patterns were a continuation of nineteenth century settler eating habits, which were heavily based on meat and tea

(Symons 2007). Sugar was comparatively cheap and large amounts were consumed in puddings or tea, which was the alternative drink to alcohol (Griggs 2006; Walker and Roberts 1988).

High unemployment in Australia in the inter-war years compelled men to find additional ways to provide for the family. Even city-dwelling men fished, hunted or scavenged so that rabbit pie or fresh fish occasionally appeared on family dinner tables. One woman described how her father would go to the nearby Sanitarium factory on his bicycle and buy a sackful of broken Vita Brits (cereal biscuits) which they would have for breakfast. Children often contributed to food provisioning by minding chickens, helping in the vegetable patch, or rabbit trapping.

During World War II the government launched a campaign to encourage men in particular to grow vegetables and raise fowls in suburban backyards. Fruit from trees in the garden supplemented the diet in many households. Participants consumed large amounts of fruit, both fresh and stewed—so much so that one woman refused to eat plums for the rest of her life. Neighbours shared or swapped their fruit, vegetables and eggs and extra food was often given to neighbouring families who were *battling*. Some suburban families had rural relatives who supplied them with meat and dairy produce. As rationing did not exist in outlying rural areas (Australian Bureau of Statistics 1945), farming families had access to larger amounts of red meat, fresh milk, fresh eggs from the domestic chook pen and a vegetable garden. In urban areas Chinese restaurants and fish and chips shops provided a different dining experience, although it was rare for cooked food to be taken home or for families to dine in restaurants, despite the fact that Cahn (1977) considers that many hotels sold food. These may have catered in particular to travellers and the very wealthy.

While a commercial food industry was developing and products such as biscuits and other commercial carbohydrates were readily available (Santich 1995) by the 1930s, the Lucky Generation remember that the food for family meals, including baked goods, was mainly produced in the family home by women who prepared, cooked and preserved food and provisioned the household.

> *Well it was all home-made so everything we had was home-made. My mother made all her jams, pickles, everything on the table and we'd have a weekly roast with three vegetables and a sweet.* (Marie)

Fahey's book on Australian food habits contains a Depression period recipe for jam using home-grown fruit dried in the sun and then boiled with sugar and stored in beer bottles that were cut down and covered with paper as they had no lids (Fahey 1992).

While women's labour and thriftiness created meals from basic materials, men were also vital to feeding the family. They were breadwinners and their ability to bring home an income was the main predictor of how much money a family had to spend on food. One woman remembered that the family meal was served exactly at 5 pm because that was when her father arrived home and he expected his meal to be ready.

> *He'd been out working and he used to walk five mile to work, five mile back. And when he got home, he'd be hungry, but 5 o'clock was dinner.*

Food was purchased from local shops or from merchants who travelled from door-to-door. Bread, milk, and other goods were often sold door-to-door, providing the housewife with a convenient supply of fresh food items. Mary recalled:

> *I can remember the man coming down the street, you know, and selling the rabbits and also the baker. We used to follow the baker's cart, the iceman. We used to go for bits of ice. When you think of it now...Yes, a wheelbarrow type thing. Yes and the iceman he had a car, a truck. The iceman did. And the baker had horse and cart. We used to follow him up with a shovel, a spade, a shovel and bucket from the garden.*

Becoming a teenager changed the Lucky Generation experience of food very little. Rarely did they eat at each others' houses; sometimes they knew that other families did not have food to share. Instead, young people continued to conform to the family dining pattern until they left home to establish their own household or in a few cases went to the war, where they were introduced to eating in mess halls. It is argued that the teenager as a separate category of person requiring their own clothes, music and activities did not really appear until the 1950s (Lees and Senyard 1987; Quiggan 2000), although it is apparent that leisure activities were somewhat different for teenagers than for younger children or adults. Consequently, separation from family life usually began as a young adult, with participants usually moving out of home to commence married life, although a few remained with their families after marriage until they could afford to move out. When they left home some women learned to cook for the first time if they had not been taught by their mothers. Heather remembers:

> *Oh she taught me to make everything, cakes and sweets and main courses and that. When I got married, [I] walked out with a beautiful recipe book from my mother with everything I needed in it.*

3.2 The 1950s to the 1980s: Post-war Prosperity

3.2.1 The Adult Lucky Generation

While the Lucky Generation were raising their own (Baby Boomer) children enormous social and economic changes swept through Australia including a new sense of plenty; practical war-time vegetable gardens began to be replaced by flower beds.

Labour-saving devices began to be produced more cheaply, making them accessible to the average Australian. An American model of mechanised mass production and the resulting mass consumerism came to replace earlier, British-influenced values of thrift and self-sufficiency (Lees and Senyard 1987). Previously considered a luxury, home appliances such as the refrigerator and washing machine became accessible to the average household. An increase in discretionary purchasing power (Dingle 1998) and the use of credit led to an increase in hire-purchasing during the 1950s (Lees and Senyard 1987). Debt due to hire-purchase increased from 6 million pounds in 1945 to 350 million pounds in 1959 (Lees and Senyard 1987). New marketing styles emerged to further stimulate the consumption of mass-produced goods, which portrayed the average person as able to afford them and aimed to 'educate' women on how housework could be made easier and less tedious by the use of these appliances and products (Lees and Senyard 1987). Both the refrigerator and car had considerable influence on patterns of food procurement and storage.

Supermarkets first appeared in Australian suburbs in 1960 and were readily adopted, assisted by the increasing car ownership which escalated rapidly after the war, particularly with the local manufacture of the Holden. By 1961 there was almost one car per family (Symons 1984). With the supermarket encouraging large-scale weekly shopping, families needed a car to carry home a weekly average of 50 kg of goods per household (Symons 1984), and a refrigerator in which to store it.

Gradually, supermarkets replaced small independent grocers, as well as the greengrocer, butcher, baker, milkman, delicatessen, toy-seller, clothing merchant, and to some extent nursery, pharmacy and newsagency (Gollan 1978). Under the guise of convenience and choice, shoppers shifted to a self-service style of shopping (Lees and Senyard 1987). They relied on marketing to distinguish good quality products rather than the recommendation of shopkeepers. However, supermarkets were already expert in shaping customers' choice of purchases, via the promotion and marketing of their products, the layout of the store and product placement on shelves (Farrer 2005). The supermarket style of shopping was also thought to influence choice via the use of food images on packages (Gollan 1978) rather than by nutritional content.

The rise of the supermarket was assisted by the introduction of television, which increased the visibility of advertised food products into the household (Dixon 2002). By 1960, 70% of Melbourne homes had a TV, a staggering penetration in the 4 years since its introduction into Australia during the year of the Melbourne Olympics. The introduction had an impact on family dining, with some families making it the centre of the dining room. Betty aged 82 remembered:

> *Sunday lunchtime yes when the men use to watch World of Sport and they'd come over to our place [to watch on our TV] ... and the time would [pass] and the roast would be waiting and then [mother] said, 'right no more roasts on Sunday'.*

Australian foodways were exposed to a widening array of influences in the 1960s. Despite socio-economic and cultural changes family meals showed surprisingly little variation during the 1960s–1970s when most Lucky Generation informants were in their 1930s–1940s and their children were aged around 10–12. The most common description of the evening meal was still *plain simple food*. Jill, a 69 year-old woman recalled preparing meals at this time that were:

> *Pretty much the same* [as when she was growing up]. *Grilled chops and veggies and then I would probably have a sweet because it's like—the kids like and still like apple pie, apple sponge, stewed apples.*

Lucky Generation member Sam's account demonstrates an increasing availability and affordability of food rather than a cultural shift in attitudes to food or in the structure and content of meals.

> *Not a great deal[changed] except that there was more of it probably and perhaps a bigger variation, but more roast dinners, more roast lamb, but not a great deal had changed.*

3.2.2 Young Baby Boomers

The Luckies' accounts of family meals were supported by the childhood memories of their Baby Boomer offspring. Peter described the style of cooking as being *fairly straightforward English style cooking* and Carol said the evening meal was *meat and three veg, but we always had dessert,* while Karen noted that the meals were *very, very plain, predictable.* The thrifty habits of the Lucky Generation continued to influence their attitude to food, even in this era of increasing prosperity. Peter noted that *mum always had to be fairly shrewd with how she did things.* The British influence on Australian cuisine was still evident in the 1950s and 1960s (Symons 2007), in its emphasis on unadorned food: mainly meat and vegetables. The evening family meal remained the centrepiece, with men the main income earners and women's labour centred on provisioning and preparing food along with other domestic tasks. Sharon (aged 49) said dinner during her childhood was *at five-thirty every day, as dad walked in that door, dinner would be on.* It usually consisted of three courses still, with the table set and the whole family sitting around the table. Some Baby Boomers remembered that *...children* [were] *to be seen but not heard at the dinner table* (Peter, aged 58). There was also an expectation that children would finish the food they were served. Leanne (aged 47) stated, *you couldn't leave anything on your plate.* She hated brussel sprouts and steak and kidney pie but she had to finish her meal before leaving the table and *I remember gagging and having to swallow it.*

Although the food habits of the Luckies appeared fairly engrained, over time new habits appeared. The word casserole replaced stew, perhaps signifying a new acceptance of European culinary habits. Cautiously people adopted the food that European immigrants had introduced, such as salamis, pates, cheeses, olives, breads, continental biscuits, conserves, cured hams, and coffee (Gollan 1978), and Mediterranean vegetables and pasta became more popular (Cameron 2004). Baby Boomer Julie (aged 55) discovered spicy Italian sausages and other new foods when her family moved from the country to a multicultural suburb in Melbourne:

> *All these tastes were opened up to us. The butchers were ethnic and green grocers were from various ethnic cultures. .... My father and I really like very spicy foods so the butcher, who used to make his own small goods and stuff, he couldn't believe we were Australians because ... his sausages and things weren't hot enough. And my mum as one of her part-time jobs when I was at secondary school, she worked at the green grocers on Friday and Saturday. [The green grocer] was of Italian descent, and a neighbour. So, you know, there were different influences I guess on our life. It was no longer just, you know, good old Skips around you, Australians around ... I guess it still was fairly dominated by the meat and three veg, but my mother certainly got into ... more adventurous stuff. It was certainly far more adventurous stuff that we'd ever encountered before [moving to Melbourne].*

Some Luckies began to stir-fry their vegetables, or cook them with Chinese style sauces, rather than boiling them. Around this period and continuing over the next few decades, more diverse vegetables (e.g. avocados, broccoli, eggplant, Asian greens) were incorporated into some families' diet and some families introduced wine with the family meal. A burgeoning wine industry, mainly stemming from the introduction of viticulture by early European immigrants, made wine easily affordable and accessible (Symons 1984).

Changes to the mass production of food also began to impinge slowly on family dining during the 1940s–1960s (Farrer 2005). Despite the increasing industrialisation of the Australian food system and a marked increase in the availability of processed foods, these changes were still not much reflected in the narratives of the Lucky generation or Baby Boomer about the 1950s–1970s. While there may have been many new products on the market, the Lucky Generation appear to have fed their children very much as they were fed throughout childhood. Few mentioned products such as canned foods, although an exception was Lisa (aged 49) who described eating puddings which *probably* came out of a can. Generally the Baby Boomer generation remember food that was home-made. Laura said:

> *My mother cooked everything. There was nothing processed. We never got processed food. But it wasn't as big in those days either, not like today. My mother baked cakes, she made cordial, she pickled beetroot, she did everything. We never had anything bought it was a treat to have anything bought. You know to get a birthday cake that was bought. We were only allowed soft drink on our birthdays. So it was a real treat. .... So dinner was always meat and three veg and she would have made a sponge or an apple strudel for afterwards.*

The Baby Boomers became aware of small changes to family dining around the time they reached their early teens. Michelle observed that when her father was not present her mother and sister experimented with new foods.

> *My mother discovered broccoli and zucchini, I remember that, but it was boiled to death the same as everything else. My middle sister was more interested in food too, so we did start to play around—she started to cook things like chop suey. My Dad was a shift-worker and when he was on afternoon shift, when my mother didn't have to please him, we would sometimes have things like chop suey or chilli con carne on the odd occasion, a very Australian version. It might have had a bit of garlic in it.*

Some experimented with westernised styles of Chinese cooking. Sandra was unusual in described a shift in cooking styles occurring during her teenage years (1960s–1970s). Sandra's observation also illustrates a shift in emphasis from the cost of food to other features such as taste and innovation, which are associated with subjective experiences including pleasure.

> *Well I guess my mum was fairly advanced in the cooking food area, you know. We didn't just have meat and three veg. We would have different casseroles, spaghetti and salads and things like that. .... I used to think that everybody ate like that, and then I discovered back then, not everybody did eat like that. I mean we would have a roast a couple of times a week.* (Sandra)

Around this time, celebrity chefs introduced the idea that food was pleasurable while French cooking and dinner parties became a form of entertainment (Symons 2006) and cookbooks such as the widely sold Margaret Fulton Cookbook, first published in 1968, began including European and Asian dishes such as fried rice and boeuf bourguignon. This expanding interest in exotic foods was attributed by some to the arrival of post-war immigrants who brought ethnically diverse food and a culture of dining out to Australia while Symons proposed that increasing Australian wealth and experience gained while travelling abroad was more influential. However, he argues that much of the change that has occurred is because modern "Australian cuisine [is] essentially industrial" (Symons 1993, p. 12).

American food business models played a major role in expanding Australian experiences of sophisticated dining (Kirkby 2008). Fast food franchises began to arrive in the 1960s and early 1970s offering efficiency and meal replacement services for the housewife. However, Symons (2006) and Kirkby (2008) also observed that dining out was not widely adopted until after the 1980s. The growth in catered food outlets in the 1960s did not appear to have a big impact on the Lucky participants despite continuing to expand over the next two decades. Consequently, their children rarely ate out while growing up. At most, the Boomers described having fish and chips on a Friday night or perhaps Chinese take away and occasionally a meal at a restaurant or hotel. Carol noted;

> *Very rarely would we eat out unless it was a very special occasion like on my grandmother's 60th birthday or something like that. Then we'd go to a hotel.*

3.3 Recent Times: 1990s–2000s

3.3.1 The Ageing Lucky Generation

Because most Lucky Generation participants had already retired, they were cushioned from many of the major social and economic changes of the 1980s, 1990s and early 2000s. They had benefited financially from economic policies that favoured the young when they were young and the elderly as they aged (Thomson 1999). Most of them had dined out rarely in the past, but some now did so more frequently, reflecting their comfortable economic circumstances as well as increased opportunity with restaurants appearing in many local shopping centres. Joan, aged 78, enjoys going out often for lunch thus avoiding late nights.

> *But then twice a week we go to lunch at the local hotel, it's very good. Or there's a couple of restaurants and we go to lunch every Tuesday and Friday, we'll go this afternoon.*

Some patronised inexpensive buffets specifically aimed at seniors. It appears that dining establishments now recognised this specific market which implies a widespread change in the eating habits of older Australians. Licensed clubs have moved into this market as well, offering drinking, meals and gambling in an environment that suits older Australians (Patford and Breen 2009).

While dining out is generally viewed as a form of pleasure and entertainment (Martens and Warde 1997) some participants also were likely to adopt it for utilitarian reasons, such as to save the effort of cooking for one or two people.

Elsewhere we have argued that the habits of Lucky Generation forged in their childhood remained partially ingrained, but altered domestic arrangements (the departure of children and death of spouses) contributed to changes in their family dining patterns (Banwell et al. 2010). For example, research shows that elderly men living alone are three times as likely as men living with a spouse to have a low and limited variety of fruit consumption. Elderly women's greater interest in health appeared to have a positive effect on their partners' diets (Horwath 1988).

A growing awareness of health and diet-related concerns meant that to maintain what they considered to be a *healthy* diet of home cooked food many people cooked large amounts of food, freezing it in smaller portions, and then heating it in the microwave. The rapid rise of the freezer was in part impelled by its relationship with the microwave (Shove and Southerton 2000). Although it is argued that modern freezers are a device of convenience allowing the re-scheduling of a busy life, the Luckys often used their freezer to maintain a healthy diet and avoid mass-produced convenience foods. Being retired, they were not particularly short of time, although many lead active and engaged lives. Some men now cooked if their wives were sick, frail or had died although it was still the norm for women of this generation to do most of the cooking and taking responsibility for the family diet. Thus, changes in family living arrangements apparently had more influence on food management rather than on food choice.

3.3.2 Middle Aged Baby Boomers

The Baby Boomers began to embrace the diversifying Australian foodscape. Australians were slower to accept Asian immigrants, and their food, compared to European ones. Japanese, authentic Chinese, Vietnamese, Indonesian, and Malaysian foods took longer to influence Australian cuisine than Italian, Greek, German and French foods had (Gollan 1978). The removal of the White Australia Policy in 1973 allowed increasing numbers of immigrants from Asia and bringing with them new culinary traditions welcomed by the growing number of Australians who had travelled to Asia (Bannerman 1998; Gollan 1978; Symons 2007). Greater affluence enabled increasing demand for food variation and quality. By the end of the twentieth century Australian food was described as having developed a complex identity that now had to be described in terms of ethnic origins (Bannerman 1998).

In our interviews Baby Boomers emphasised that they cooked an increasing variety of foods while raising their children compared to the foods which they had grown up with. In particular, they ate more Asian-inspired foods, a greater variety of vegetables and less red meat. Sandra said she cooked *More Asian. A lot more Asian. A lot more stir fry and things like that.* The Lucky Generation had reserved chicken and other types of poultry for Christmas or other very special occasions. Factory farming made poultry easily affordable and available in supermarkets so that by the late 1960s it came to be eaten regularly, particularly as popular health experts encouraged people to reduce red meat consumption (Dixon 2002). *Lighter* meat was thought to be healthier.

Another noticeable difference was the loss of the predictable weekly food pattern. Leanne said *You don't have potatoes with every meal.* The idea of a 'typical' meal was no longer considered relevant by Lynette who commented that *We don't have a typical night.* The variety of food eaten for an evening meal is illustrating in Catherine's (aged 51) description of the food her family ate while her children were growing up:

Well, probably pretty much what we have now. Quite a variety of things really. We would have stir fries, we would have pasta at least once a week, BBQ's, roasts and salads... I love chicken so we have lots of chicken. .... casseroles in the winter and soup. We have a fairly good variety I suppose, probably not so much the meat and veg variety. .... so different things all the time. Not so much red meats as I used to have when I was growing up.

The Baby Boomers explored new types of restaurants, and home entertaining moved from formal dinner parties to a more casual style of dining both at home and away. Asian restaurants became very popular places to dine as they were relatively inexpensive, and people could afford to dine out regularly, which became a pleasurable leisure activity. Stephen, a 50 year-old, described this shift:

I've got to say it was probably in the mid-80s started going to restaurants, found spicy foods. I love anything spicy. I love all Asian foods, Indian, Mexican, the hotter the better. .... so that's probably the big change.

Once their children left home the Baby Boomers started to eat out as a way to socialise rather than have dinner parties at home as their parents had done. Peter explained:

We eat out or have takeaway quite a bit more. Part of that is availability and ease with my wife still working. And part of it is we have a group of friends we particularly enjoy eating out with. And as the kids are older and their partners, we enjoy all of that as well. So we don't have big dinner parties like I remember my parents having and like we tried to do when we were more recently married or early married. Now if we are having a meal with friends and they do the same, rather than having all the drama lets go out some where. And then the cook can enjoy it as well. So we eat out a bit... once or twice a week we will eat out. .... But we like to eat out now.

3.3.3 Gen Y

Typical evening meals eaten during the childhood of Gen Y became more multi-cultural, with pasta and stir-fry joining meat and three vegetables. The Gen Y's descriptions of the types of foods they ate during their primary school years were mixed. Some remembered eating a diverse range of foods. For example Sarah (aged 19) said *It would have been a roast and vegetables or lasagne or a curry, or pretty much anything.* Others, like David, aged 27, recalled mainly eating 'meat and three veg'. *Mum wasn't doing anything too fancy at that age. It was pretty stable sort of meat and three veg or whatever, that sort of thing.* Symons (1993) notes that in 1991 when the Luckies were growing up some childcare centres in Sydney were serving their charges a multicultural menu that included dishes such as borscht, sauerkraut and lasagne.

Symons (1993) differentiates between the excitement of the multicultural and diverse food available in restaurants and the conventional food which was served at home. Nevertheless, changes in domestic cuisine seemed to accelerate around the time Gen Y had reached high school. For Nicole food *got more interesting, mum got more adventurous, and started buying food magazines and things, and trying out things on her own.* She also remembers having *more exotic things* such as *mangoes and avocadoes and stuff from the deli* as she got older, perhaps because her parents had a higher income than during her primary school years. David also noted that meals began to change when he became a teenager:

> *Mum just started to get a little bit more creative with the meals. Because Nana [who is Greek] lives with us as well, she used to get involved in the cooking a bit more than she is now and when we got older our tastes changed and we could get a bit more adventurous.* So what type of things did she cook? *Stir fries and Asian stuff, even Indian stuff like curries and things like that.* What do you think sort of triggered those little changes? *Now I think back on it, dad's pretty adventurous with his food and he would have been exposed to different dinners and things like that [through work], because mum's never really been an adventurous eater. So it was probably dad's influence and then us getting to an age where we would appreciate it too.*

Other changes appeared in the Gen Y's accounts of family meals. While it was still important, the routine structured evening family meal appeared to be under pressure from a number of sources. As they grew up, the Gen Ys in particular found it increasingly difficult join the evening family meal as other activities, such as sporting, social and work arrangements impinged upon their time. Work schedules for this generation are very different from those of their parents when young. They have experienced an increase in non-standard work hours and they are more likely to be working while studying (Wyn and Woodman 2006). Their parents, too, had to cope with increased *busyness*. Thus, family meals or 'sitting down to eat', according to Christopher, sometimes became expendable. *Yeah. If I'm at work or if I'm organising stuff like the car or anything I usually just grab whatever I can eat while I'm driving or whatever yeah.*

Another fracturing force that undermined the predictability of family meals was that people's food tastes and preferences have become more individualised. For example, several participants mentioned that they or family members had become vegetarian and so the notion that everyone in the family ate the same food began to change. Stephen, a Gen Y, explained how his mother coped with individual schedules and preferences.

> *And depending on the day mum will usually ring me or [brother], my brother's a vegetarian so we just, he has to do his own. Usually mum will ring me and find out if I'm just home or if [other family members] come over I'll just cook and my mum usually just does her own thing. But if it's just us she'll usually just come home and cook something. Usually a phone call and its pre-organised who's going to be home and who is doing what.*

As many Gen Y mothers were employed, men (fathers of Gen Y) took over some of the cooking, although they were often considered to be less skillful and more inclined to purchase pre-prepared food.

> *He would do a couple of meals here and there, it was always really gross.* [This was when your mum was working full-time?] *Yeah, yeah. So probably we'd be more likely to buy the chicken from the supermarket or whatever and make up something, some sort of accompaniment with it, your coleslaw or whatever, and spag bol and that kind of stuff. So more stuff that could be frozen and brought out because of less time to do stuff.* (Emma, aged 29)

Although the Baby Boomers may have dined out less frequently during their children's younger years, eating takeaway instead of a home-cooked family meal became increasingly common with some families having takeaway weekly or fortnightly when they were busy.

3.4 Conclusion

These Australian families exemplify the changes that have occurred over the course of three generations. While we do not think that the family meal is dead, there appears to be a relaxation of routine over the three generations, from the fixed timing and content of meals, to individual members increasingly eating at different times, or dining together but eating different foods. Nevertheless, the family meal remains symbolically important to many families and they endeavour to maintain it in the face of conflicting and growing pressures. Indeed, because the evening family meal has traditionally been the main occasion when the family comes together, it is the point at which the lack of connection between work and other time demands and sociality become most apparent and may have impacts on health and wellbeing. The growth over three generations in what has been described as disordered eating has been linked to increased childhood obesity (Kime 2008).

The Lucky Generation retains a taste for the necessary but they have replaced a focus on cheap and filling food with one on food that is perceived to be healthy (Banwell et al. 2010). The early focus was probably encouraged by a lack of food variety that has been linked elsewhere with low incomes (see Charles and Kerr 1986), in addition to the regimented and somewhat hierarchical family meals. Food appears to have bolstered an ethic of egalitarianism among the Lucky Generation, where it was not noticeably associated with social and class differences despite a longstanding historical association in the literature (Germov 2008), but at the same time it made visible at the family meal the family power structures based on gender and age. In Australia and elsewhere it has been argued that class-based differences in food preferences have diminished over time but not disappeared totally, while food habits and choices have become more varied over time (Germov 2008, p. 270). This is somewhat supported by an analysis of data from the 1995 National Nutrition Survey which found that there was an association between income (as a possible marker of social class and cultural preferences), age and gender in food preferences. Fewer people with low household incomes consumed food regularly and had less varied diets. This was most marked among men aged over 50. However, it appeared that the cost of individual food items was not a determining factor in their rejection by this group of men. Young people (18–34 year-olds in 1995) and higher-income people, especially women, ate less of what were characterised as traditional foods (e.g. baked beans, brussel sprouts, peas, white bread). The authors suggested that health concerns and fashion may have influenced food choice (Worsley et al. 2003).

A discourse of pleasure in food and a growth in omnivorous tastes accompanied by a decreased concern with the cost of food appears first during the adult years of the Baby Boomers. The interest in the taste, appearance and novelty of foods has burgeoned along with the growth of food as a marker of identity and status. Food has become a form of entertainment at times and at others a functional activity where it is eaten on the run as a way of re-fuelling. The idea of pleasure taken in food has always been problematic in the history of Western thought (Conveney 2006). While the Baby Boomers were more likely than their parents to enjoy food, they displayed moralistic judgments about those who took undisciplined or immoderate pleasure in

Image 3.2 Alfesco dining in Melbourne 2012 (Source: J. Dixon)

food and were consequently overweight. Based on cross-national studies it is argued that pleasure in food (as shown by the French, who also display strong self-discipline) is associated less with obesity than a focus on health as a dominant approach to food (Rozin 2005). Furthermore, the comparatively slim French, in contrast to the populations of English-speaking countries such as the US and UK, have maintained a strong focus on commensality, sociability and ordered dining (Fischler and Masson 2009). The growth in food pleasure in Australia is associated with increasing sociality around food, but mainly at special occasions and often when dining away from home. This permits women, who are usually the cooks, to participate fully in the culinary and social experience without being required to spend time and energy in preparing it. However, when it comes to everyday dining, Australians seem to be more like the US and UK, where an individualised approach to food, employment and other activities are undermining commensality.

References

Australian Bureau of Statistics. (1945). *Year book Australia 1944–45, 1301.1*. Canberra: Australian Bureau of Statistics.

Bannerman, C. (1998). *Acquired tastes: Celebrating Australia's culinary history*. Canberra: National Library of Australia.

Banwell, C., Dixon, J., Broom, D., & Davies, A. (2010). Habits of a lifetime: Family dining patterns over the lifecourse of older Australians. *Health Sociology Review, 19*(3), 343–355.

Cahn, A. (1977). Australians in the early twentieth century. In B. Wood (Ed.), *Tucker in Australia*. Melbourne: Hill of Content.

Cameron, E. (2004). *The sixties*. Fremantle: Fremantle Arts Centre Press.

Charles, N., & Kerr, M. (1986). Issues of responsibility and control in the feeding of families. In S. Rodmell & A. Watt (Eds.), *The politics of health education: Raising the issues* (pp. 57–75). London: Routledge and Kegan Paul.

Conveney, J. (2006). *Food, morals and meaning: The pleasure and anxiety of eating* (2nd ed.). Oxford: Routledge.

Dingle, T. (1998). Electrifying the kitchen in interwar Victoria. *Journal of Australian Studies, 57*, 119–127.

Dixon, J. (2002). *The changing chicken*. Sydney: UNSW Press.

Fahey, W. (1992). *When Mabel laid the table, the folklore of eating and drinking in Australia*. Sydney: State Library of New South Wales.

Farrer, K. (2005). *To feed a nation: A history of Australian food science and technology*. Melbourne: CSIRO Publishing.

Fischler, C. (1993). A nutritional cacophony or the crisis of food selection in affluent societies. In P. Leatherwood, M. Horisberger, & W. James (Eds.), *For a better nutrition in the 21st century*. New York: Vevey/Raven Press Ltd.

Fischler, C., & Masson, E. (2009). *Six countries eating—An interview*, from http://www.lemangeur-ocha.com/fileadmin/images/actus/France-Europe-the-United-States-what-eating-means-to-us-an-interview-with-Claude-Fischler-and-Estelle-Masson.pdf

Germov, J. (2008). Food, class and identity. In J. Germov & L. Williams (Eds.), *A sociology of food and nutrition: The social appetite*. Victoria: Oxford University Press.

Gillman, M., Rifas-Shiman, S., Frazier, L., Rockett, H., Camargo, C., Field, A., et al. (2000). Family dinner and diet quality among older children and adolescents. *Archives of Family Medicine, 9*, 235–240.

Gollan, A. (1978). *The tradition of Australian cooking*. Canberra: Australian National University Press.

Griggs, P. (2006). A natural part of life: The Australian sugar industry's campaign to reverse declining Australian sugar consumption, 1980–1995. *Journal of Australian Studies, 87*, 141–154.

Horwath, C. (1988). The food habits of elderly Australians. In A. Truswell & M. Wahlquist (Eds.), *Food habits in Australia, proceedings of the first Deakin/Sydney universities symposium on Australian nutrition* (pp. 224–249). North Balwyn: Rene Gordon.

Kime, N. (2008). Children's eating behaviours: The importance of the family setting. *Royal Geographical Society, 40*(3), 315–322.

Kirkby, D. (2008). From wharfie haunt to foodie haven: Modernity and the law in the transformation of the Australian working-class pub. *Food, Culture and Society, 11*(1), 29–48.

Kociumbas, J. (1997). *Australian childhood: A history*. Sydney: Allen & Unwin.

Lees, S., & Senyard, J. (1987). *The 1950s: How Australia became a modern society, and everyone got a house and car*. Melbourne: Hyland House.

Luxton, M. (1980). *More than a labour of love*. Toronto: The Women's Press.

Mamun, A., Lawlor, D., O'Callaghan, M., Williams, G., & Najman, J. (2005). Positive maternal attitude to the family eating together decreases the risk of adolescent overweight. *Obesity Research, 13*(8), 1422–1430.

Martens, L., & Warde, A. (1997). Urban pleasure? On the meaning of eating out in a northern city. In C. Caplan (Ed.), *Food, health and identity* (pp. 131–150). London/New York: Routledge.

Murcott, A. (1983). "It's a pleasure to cook for him": Food, mealtimes and gender in some south Wales households. In E. Gamarnikow (Ed.), *The public and the private* (pp. 62–77). Aldershot: Gower.

Murcott, A. (1997). Family meals—A thing of the past? In P. Caplan (Ed.), *Food, health and identity* (pp. 32–69). London/New York: Routledge.

Patford, J., & Breen, H. (2009). Homes away from home: Registered clubs as leisure providers for older people living the tweed heads region of Australia. *Annals of Leisure Research, 12*, 172–191.

Poulain, J. (2002). The contemporary diet in France: "De-structuration" or from commensalism to "vagabond feeding". *Appetite, 39*, 43–55.

Quiggan, J. (2000). The end of the generation game. Australian Financial Review. http://www.u.q.edu.au/economics/johnquiggan/news00/Generations0010.htm/. Accessed 27 Nov 2012.

Rozin, P. (2005). The meaning of food in our lives: A cross-cultural perspective on eating and well-being. *Journal of Nutrition Education and Behavior, 37*, S107–S112.

Santich, B. (1995). 'It's a chore!' women's attitudes towards cooking. *Australian Journal of Nutrition and Dietetics, 52*(1), 11–13.

Shove, E., & Southerton, D. (2000). Defrosting the freezer: From novelty to convenience. *Journal of Material Culture, 5*, 301–319.

Symons, M. (1984). *One continuous picnic*. Ringwood: Penguin.

Symons, M. (1993). *The shared table*. Canberra: AGPS.

Symons, M. (2006). From grandmas to gourmets. *Food, Culture and Society, 9*(2), 179–200.

Symons, M. (2007). *One continuous picnic: A gastronomic history of Australia*. Melbourne: Melbourne University Press.

Teow, B., Wahlqvist, M., & Flint, D. (1988). Food patterns of Australians at the turn of the century. In S. Truswell & M. Wahlqvist (Eds.), *Food habits in Australia* (pp. 60–75). Melbourne: Heinemann.

Thomson, D. (1999). How history is failing our families. *Family Matters, 52*, 12–18.

Veugelers, P., & Fitzgerald, A. (2005). Prevalence of risk factors for childhood overweight and obesity. *Canadian Medical Association Journal, 173*(6), 607–613.

Walker, R. B., & Roberts, D. C. K. (1988). Colonial food habits. In A. Truswell & L. Wahlquist (Eds.), *Food habits in Australia, proceedings of the first Deakin/Sydney universities symposium on Australian nutrition* (pp. 40–59). North Balwyn: Rene Gordon.

Williams, M. (1985). *Australia in the 1930s*. Sydney: Trocadero Publishing.

Worsley, A., Blasche, R., Ball, K., & Crawford, D. (2003). Income differences in food consumption in the 1995 Australian national nutrition survey. *European Journal of Clinical Nutrition, 57*, 1198–1211.

Wyn, J., & Woodman, D. (2006). Generation, youth and social change in Australia. *Journal of Youth Studies, 9*(5), 495–514.

Chapter 4
How Convenience Is Shaping Australian Diets: The Disappearing Dessert

Image 4.1 Birthday party, Melbourne 1946 (Source: Museum of Victoria)

Convenient ways of eating include food that is pre-prepared and assembled or heated at home, food prepared outside of the home (such as takeaway), or catered food eaten outside the home. Its ubiquity signals the industrialisation of the pantry and of Australian domestic cooking. The range and types of foods served in Australian homes, cafés, hotels and restaurants have grown dramatically over the last 100 years, particularly beginning in the 1960s–1980s. Additionally, home-meal replacements are becoming increasingly prominent in contemporary supermarkets and delicatessens. In this chapter the replacement of home-prepared and – cooked puddings by pre-prepared sweets, together with the opportunity to consume sweet

C. Banwell et al., *Weight of Modernity: An Intergenerational Study of the Rise of Obesity*, DOI 10.1007/978-90-481-8957-1_4, © Springer Science+Business Media Dordrecht 2012

foods at any time (inside and outside the home) illustrates vividly the dietary impact of the rise of convenience foods. Another example of convenience is provided by the increasing consumption of takeaway and eating out.

4.1 The Case of the Disappearing Dessert

Desserts, sweets, or puddings are still the final flourish of the Australian family meal before tea or coffee arrives. Nevertheless, the role and significance of dessert has been transformed over the last 50 years, illustrating larger trends in family dining in Australia and elsewhere in the developed world. In the US it has been noted that desserts are becoming unpopular in restaurants due to "excessive size and inflated prices" (Siemering 2004, p. 56).

From a health perspective the disappearance of desserts is hardly a cause for concern. Surely they do nothing for people's weight, heart or blood sugar. However, we propose that the usually humble homemade pudding has largely been replaced by less nutritious and more energy-dense sweets that are no longer structurally embedded in a mealtime (Douglas 1982), and have become widely available and accessible day and night. In this regard, the replacement of dessert by ubiquitous processed sweet snack foods exemplifies the widespread growth of mass-produced convenience foods which may be more energy-dense than home-made offerings and have been implicated in the growing prevalence of overweight and obesity.

Desserts were a conspicuous feature of the Lucky Generations' accounts of family meals. The family dinner frequently finished with a pudding or dessert which consisted of sweet carbohydrate combinations such as baked and steamed puddings, rice puddings, or baked custards, with lighter desserts such as stewed fruit, jelly or junket offered in summer. Desserts were a comparatively inexpensive way for mothers to display their culinary skills and satisfy hungry husbands and children. Home-baked scones and biscuits served a similar purpose and were made for after-school snacks. Particularly during winter, English-style food patterns were maintained with puddings and desserts that were often described as heavy or stodgy. The most extreme and incongruous example of this could be seen on Christmas day, with families concluding eating the special holiday roast midday dinner with a Christmas pudding, made of flour, suet or other fat and filled with dried fruit. The inappropriateness of this dish for a hot summer's Christmas day appears to have been recognised but the tradition was nevertheless maintained to celebrate the connection with the UK (Walker and Roberts 1988) and the custom continues to this day in some Australian households. In the early part of the twentieth century Mary Gilmore recalled that people always kept golden syrup, treacle, jam, coconut, ginger and dried fruits on hand in their cupboards to make desserts and puddings (Gilmore 1934).

Factory-produced food products such as self-raising flour, custard powder and tinned fruits and vegetables were available before WWI, as was a range of biscuits, cakes and pies and over 100 varieties of confectionary (Farrer 2005; Santich 1995). The demand for short cuts in food preparation in the form of partly prepared food items increased during WWII as women joined the war effort and took on paid work (Gollan 1978). Yet few from the Lucky Generation mentioned using commercially pre-prepared products in their kitchens even though they were available.

Although commercially prepared sweet foods were widely available, the Lucky Generation ate mainly home-made puddings and desserts while growing up and they often made similar dishes for their own children. The importance of these dishes in the national diet is evidenced by the number of pages in recipes books devoted to these dishes. A book of recipes from the 1920s and 1930s contained 11 pages of vegetable recipes, 20 pages of pudding and desserts, 21 of biscuits and slices, and 21 pages of cakes (Berry and Wearing-Smith 1993). Symons notes a similar allocation of many pages in the 1925 edition of the Commonsense Cook Book to "flour-based cooking" that included bread, pastry, cakes and puddings (Symons 1984). Later recipe books from the 1960s (Country Women's Association NSW 1965; Country Women's Association of Western Australia of the Air Kalgoorlie Branch 1965) were dominated by recipes for desserts and cakes that reflected the requirement for more exact measurements and cooking skills than those needed for most savoury dishes.

Commenting on the continued importance of home-baked sweet dishes, Symons (1984) proposed that an emphasis on "daintiness" which encapsulated values such as "lightness, prettiness and gentility" in cooking and baking was valued as a feminine antidote to the gross male eating habits of the 1920s and 1930s. Significant socio-cultural emphasis continued to be placed on desserts, sweets and puddings through the 1940s to the 1960s (Duruz 1999; Symons 1984), with Duruz arguing that baking and making desserts were the "public face" of feminine identity-making in the 1950s. Failure at these could provoke a serious crisis of feminine identity (Duruz 1999). Even though these skills were so important to women's sense of being a good homemaker, research shows that men of this generation ate more sweets than women (Horwath 1988).

Around the time that Boomer children were in their teens widespread social change was underway. In 1972 in Australia, during the first wave of feminism, women won the right to equal pay for equal work. Many Lucky Generation women had worked as volunteers when their children were young and they sometimes returned to volunteer work later. A few, however, joined the paid labour force once their children left primary school. It appears that there was a period during which women juggled the competing values of paid work and those of femininity and mothering by continuing to prepare meals and desserts. Mary, from the Lucky Generation, who had taken up paid employment part-time while her children were at school, still shouldered the burden of family cooking and provisioning as was typical for women of the time (Santich 1995). Even though she was employed, her account hints at her anxiety to be a proper mother by preparing good meals and undertaking complex scheduling to be available for her daughter after school finished.

> *Well they were still getting good meals. I would prepare it perhaps before I went to work. At that point I was only working part-time and [my daughter] ... her school was at the back where we lived, so I would always take her to school and then I'd get the bus and get into, go to where I was working....And then I'd catch a bus and that would get to the school when it was time for her to get out.*

She still prepared desserts but noted that they ate lots of tinned fruit. Mary's story suggests that entering paid work put pressure on women's time for meal preparation. Some women tried to save time by no longer making desserts or making less elaborate ones, although noting that their children enjoyed them. Frieda, (aged 82) who was teaching while her children were at school, explains:

Yes, I had to cut out quite a bit of dessert making and relied on, sometimes, buying something. But also during the school holidays I used to make up a great big batch of desserts, puddings, and have them in the freezer.

Rose, a 70 year-old, observed that meals at this time were similar to those she had as a child except that she made fewer desserts. At first she first attributed her willingness to give up making desserts to her laziness but as the interview continued she acknowledged that she was juggling a number of activities. She said:

[We] probably had ice cream or something like that. Stewed fruit maybe. I was going to work all that time and had the three kids, and during that time I did a couple of uni courses.

She recounted that one child had questioned her mothering.

One of the [children] said, "Why aren't you a real mummy?" I've never forgotten this, and I said, "What do you mean?" and she said, "You know, making biscuits and hot drinks when you come home from school".

Rose's vivid memory of this exchange illustrates the potent nexus between mothering, love and food, and the difficulties mothers had in disrupting it by asking children to eat food they didn't like or by not preparing the food they enjoyed.

These stories illustrate yet another trend: the encroachment of industrially prepared food products into family dining, sometimes replacing things made at home from scratch. A number of factors came together at this time to facilitate these changes. The decades from the 1940s–1960s were a watershed for development in Australian food science as production techniques devised to feed troops during WWII were adapted for commercial production post-war. American processing techniques (which emphasised nutrition and quality control) were introduced into Australian factories preparing food for American troops (Farrer 2005). The quality of food manufactured for general consumption improved as industrial food production capacity grew post-WWII. Food canning began on a larger scale after WWII as factories switched back to commercial food production (Symons 2007), aided by the increasing mechanisation of food harvesting during the late 1940s (Farrer 2005). Canning, and eventually freezing technology, made fruit and vegetables available in the shops all year round. Home bottling, pickling, preserving, and baking were no longer essential activities and began disappearing from the home kitchen in the 1950s (Farrer 2005). Some Lucky and Baby Boomer women joined the workforce by the 1960s and 1970s (providing additional financial resources to the family) and discretionary purchasing power (Dingle 1998) rose because of high levels of employment and growing incomes.

Refrigerators began to appear in some Australian homes as mass production brought their prices down, the effects of WWII subsided and families could afford this major purchase. Even in the early 1950s, ice was still being delivered to Canberra homes (Gollan 1978). In 1955 the ownership of refrigerators differed by state, with only 67% of Melbourne homes owning an electric refrigerator, while 83% of Sydney homes did (Dingle 1998). However, by 1960 the McNair survey found that 94% of households nationwide owed a refrigerator. Initially the refrigerator was about the same size as an ice chest but larger fridges were sold as people realised that they could buy more in one shopping trip, shop less often and use the refrigerator to store supplies (Gollan 1978). The 1960s saw the introduction of refrigerated dairy cases in supermarkets and the development of new products to fill them (Farrer 2005). These developments permitted the purchase and storage of large amounts of food, and in particular a shift to dairy-based foods that previously could not be stored for long. Freezers have become items of convenience helping people "cope with the compression and fragmentation of time" (Shove and Southerton 2000, p. 315).

Ice cream was initially a high status 'special treat' taking considerable human energy to make at home and was not often bought from shops. Peter, a Baby Boomer, remembered:

> *Back in those days ice cream was significant and you didn't buy ice cream out of buckets in the shops. You made your own ice cream, so that was a bit of a treat when mum decided we were making ice cream. And me being the eldest I helped with the hand beater to make it. Makes me feel so old talking about these sort of things.*

In Baby Boomers' descriptions of feeding their children and more recently, ice cream and other pre-prepared desserts appear frequently, replacing accounts of home-made puddings and desserts. Lindsey explains:

> *I used to use the self saucing pudding occasionally. Often stewed fruit because I used to freeze it from when there was a glut, so there was always stewed fruit and ice cream. And in winter I did plum puddings and the chocolate sauce puddings.*
> Is that similar to what your mum used to make?
> *Probably. Now I think of it. She wouldn't have used the instant stuff but I did.*

4.2 Convenient Foods

In the past the concept of convenience has referred to ideas of ease, utility and comfort according to the Oxford Dictionary, but more recently has become associated with saving and juggling time (Shove 2003), particularly with regard to food purchasing and meal preparation. Warde (1999) argues that it is not only about saving time but about the scheduling of time, or time shifting so that more activities can be undertaken. With the advent of the freezer, ice cream has become an archetypal convenience food. It has the advantage of being easily stored (reducing the necessity of frequent shopping trips), it needs no preparation, it can be eaten on its own (replacing a pudding or dessert), or it can be served as an accompaniment and is readily available for between meal snacks. Consequently, it has ceased to be special. Through the 1960s and 1970s, home-cooked puddings, desserts or sweets became an infrequent feature of the family meal. Ice cream, on its own or with stewed fruit had acquired a somewhat different significance, and was somewhat less consequential or marked as a formal dessert than something home-made. Moreover, making desserts became less important to women. As they entered the workforce and feminism became influential, other identities and status became available to them, perhaps as a bread-winner rather than a cake maker (Duruz 1999). The convenience of home-stored ice cream also constitutes a weight control risk, with several members of the Lucky Generation and Boomers mentioning ice cream as the food that they found most tempting but they knew should be avoided to manage weight and health risks.

The popularity of ice cream also illustrates the shift from an English-influenced home-made diet to the American-led 'Industrial Kitchen'. In Australia, the rise of the frozen food market (mainly fruit and vegetables) was initiated by American companies, particularly Unilever's Birds Eye. Unilever bought out other ice cream companies in the early 1960s. Slightly later, the American company Sarah Lee also began producing a range of frozen desserts and cakes (Symons 1984), and in the 1970s Peters began to develop new "adult" ice creams (Symons 1984, p. 210). Supermarkets began to sell ice cream in large quantities in supermarket freezers and in containers that were large enough to last the average family a week. Yet again the rise of ice cream goes hand-in-hand with the growth of supermarkets, and the move to the weekly shop enabled by the family car. At the same time, small local suburban family-owned shops declined and home deliveries gradually disappeared.

In Australia in the 1990s, ice cream, among all the frozen foods, was sold in the highest quantities, surpassing vegetables, poultry, frozen desserts and convenience meals (Farrer 2005). As John, a Baby Boomer, observed, *I might have an ice cream a night three nights a week.*

The change from a special treat to routine consumption is described by Valerie, a Lucky Generation informant, who observed about current times:

> *But then what do you give the kids for treats if you're having all these things you know what's a treat, an ice-cream was a treat for us well now there's ice-cream in the fridge and you can have it every night of the week if you wanted to and chocolates.*

However, while domestic ice cream in 1 or 2 litre tubs has become a less significant treat, there has been an increase in the sophistication of individually wrapped ice creams that are now routinely covered in chocolate and other toppings, and are marketed to adults through advertisements evoking allure, temptation, excess, pleasure, desire, sin and sexuality. For some years Sarah Lee, the manufacturer of frozen desserts, has advertised its products as "The Nice Vice".

Biscuits, scones and cakes went the way of home-made desserts. Mainly used as between meals snacks or served with tea to visitors by the Lucky Generation, they are now rarely made at home by Baby Boomers or their Gen Y children. Instead, people eat commercially made biscuits which have a long history in Australia. Arnotts, whose products have dominated the Australian market, opened its first biscuit factory in 1865. In the 1920s and 1930s Iced VoVos were the most popular sweet biscuit made by Arnotts. Since the 1960s and 1970s they have been replaced in the popularity stakes by the chocolate covered, cream-filled Tim Tam biscuit, which has sales that increased by 19% between 2006 and 2007 and are now worth $100 million (Sydney Morning Herald 2008). Illustrating a gradual increase in serving size and energy density, VoVos are 227 kJ per serve and 1,730 kJ per 100 g while Tim Tams are 400 kJ per serve and 2,160 per 100 g. Arnotts is now owned by the major multinational food company, Campbells. In the 2008–2009 financial year the company increased its sales figures by $15 million (Sydney Morning Herald 2008).

Yet another aspect of the disappearing dessert is the widespread availability of other sweet products that can be purchased and eaten almost anywhere and at any time, completing the decoupling of dessert from the main meal. In this regard, sweet biscuits, cakes, lollies, ice creams and sweet drinks are now sold individually at supermarkets, sometimes in fridges located at the checkout and virtually any other food retail outlet, including convenience stores, in motel or other vending machines and at petrol stations. A survey of Australian supermarkets showed that many had soft drink vending machines located close to the entrance and that all supermarkets displayed confectionary, soft drinks and other snacks within easy reach of check-out counters in ways that were likely to draw upon children's 'pester power' (Dixon et al. 2006). Similar tactics are used in other retail formats.

In participants' accounts of meals, convenience is usually associated with either eating out or eating takeaway. However, Baby Boomers and their children have adopted many convenient food solutions that are barely noticed in their repertoire of provisioning and preparation. For example, the purchase of commercially prepared jams, chutneys and bottled, tinned and other preserved products increased around the time the Baby Boomers were growing up. Carol, a Baby Boomer, noted that food is now more convenient to prepare and cuts of meat are leaner due to the rise in pre-packaged, pre-cut meat products. Yet it is difficult to argue that all food purchasing and preparation is more convenient now than in the past, when products were often delivered to the home, obviating the need to go to the shops. Carol remembered:

> *And also the baker would come up the street—so it was all home delivered sort of thing. And the milkman would deliver. But I very clearly remember the grocer coming with a box of groceries on his shoulder. It was cute—to the back door and call out. It was such a different lifestyle. And then perhaps we'd go on weekends and of course the shops would shut at 12 on a Saturday, so there wasn't that convenience. [You] had to be sure to have your shopping done by midday on Saturday. And Dad used to go and get the meat, I remember, on a Saturday morning—that was when we had the car.*

A number of the Lucky Generation remembered that they had milk, bread, greengroceries, ice and sometimes meat delivered by horse-drawn cart. They enjoyed chatting to the vendors, meeting neighbours around the cart, and competing to see who could pick up the horse manure first to put on the garden. One person pointed out that there was no need to own a car because food was home delivered.

Meat was less likely to be delivered but at the shop the butcher would prepare slice, dice and trim meat to order while the customer waited. Even the cook-from-scratch Lucky Generation usually bought rather than made their bread. Modern food retailers now discourage shoppers from remembering these earlier forms of convenience by placing a high emphasis on 'choice' in their advertisements.

These earlier forms of retail convenience did not offer the same range of products that are available now but the reduction in time and labour was real.

The growth of pre-prepared, labour-saving food products accelerated during the 1970s, 1980s and 1990s. It contributed to increasing diversity in the styles of cuisine prepared by Baby Boomers and Gen Ys, so that the curries, stir-fries and other Asian and Middle Eastern dishes they describe cooking at home are easy to prepare through the use of commercially produced curry mixes, marinades and tinned coconut milk (Schubert 2009). Spaghetti Bolognese, lasagne and other Italian-influenced dishes, now a staple of many standard family meals, can be made with dried or refrigerated pasta and widely available commercial tomato paste, supporting Symons' (1993) argument that the growth in multicultural cuisines in Australia was as much about the industrialisation and internationalisation of the food system as it was about immigration.

Our participants did not discuss these sorts of convenience foods perhaps because they are now so taken for granted that they do not warrant mentioning. However, they did comment on the more high-profile convenient meal replacements (rather than specific convenient ingredients). Their accounts of family dining reported in the previous chapter show the encroachment of convenience food, takeaway meals and eating out over time and especially over the three generations. Subsequent generations have shown an increasing appreciation of convenience foods. A survey of Brisbane residents in the late 1990s found that eating food prepared by the food service industry was highest among the Gen Ys, half as likely to occur among Baby Boomers and only a third as likely among the Luckies. Within each age group, the likelihood of consuming food prepared by the food service industry was lower for women than men. Surprisingly, the likelihood was lower for those without a tertiary education. Furthermore, those who ate more food prepared outside the home ate significantly less fruit, vegetables or dairy food (Hughes et al. 1997).

4.3 Takeaway and Eating Out

In the previous chapter, we noted that the shift by middle-aged Baby Boomers to eating out at restaurants and cafés as a pleasurable social event marked a transition from their Lucky Generation parents, who at the same age and lifestage tended to hold dinner parties at home when socialising. Dining out for pleasure and sociability is different from dining out or eating takeaway to replace an everyday family meal, although both save the cook time and effort. In the latter, eating out and takeaway were seen as solutions to a time-poor and complex family life. These options were usually chosen on busy nights or at the end of the week to give 'mum' a break from cooking. Gen Y Rebecca explained:

> *Maybe I think when I was.... Year 11 we had probably takeaway once a week. And that was mainly because we were all over the place. Like [my brother] was at a sport, my dad and mum were... taking us to sport and .... mum didn't have time to cook that night so we'd have probably takeaway once a week.*

This increase in multiple and individualised activities for family members has been noted elsewhere particularly in relation to sporting activities and recreation for children (see Chaps. 3, 5, 6, 8). Middle-class families in the UK reportedly were prepared to sacrifice what they saw as the importance of a shared family meal to accommodate multiple teenage sporting and other cultural activities because these activities were seen as "contributing to social and physical health" (Backett-Milburn et al. 2010, p. 1322).

The Gen Ys appeared to have adopted both tendencies from their parents; eating out and takeaway as both a lifestyle solution and as a way of socializing with little effort. As they became teenagers they started to eat out by themselves, and this increased as they moved into adulthood. Melissa (aged 24) described eating out frequently during a couple of very busy years during her early 1920s. *I was probably eating out a lot or just, you know, grabbing something on the way to work.*

Many Baby Boomers and Gen Y participants eat out perhaps two to three times a week, especially if they do not have young children. Some had a catered meal daily, for example, with the purchase of their lunch or by grabbing a quick meal on the way home from work. Cheap, quick takeaway and eating out is facilitated by the availability of a food court in every major shopping centre, where the number and style of food outlets representing major food retail chains is dictated by the requirements of food court managers.

Baby Boomers and Gen Y participants thought of takeaway food as an easy option when they were *behind time and I was tired and lazy* (Leanne, aged 47). For Carol (aged 60) eating out is *convenient if I'm tired or something from work, we'll eat out at the hotel and have a counter tea or go out to dinner to a restaurant.*

Andrew (aged 26) believed that busyness:

> *...kills any chance of sort of eating at home... like cooking at home... I come in late at 8 o'clock or something like... there's no way I'm going to start cooking then*

The usual explanation for the growth in convenient food options such as takeaway or eating out is time shortage associated with women's 'double shift' in the workplace and at home (Schubert 2009). However, in a number of our accounts, two other reasons were also offered. One was that family members were engaging in a number of different activities that made it difficult to co-ordinate the preparation of a meal for everyone at the same time. Thus family members, particularly young people who were often juggling study, part-time work and social engagements (Wyn and Woodman 2006) would eat individualised takeaway meals at times that suited their schedule. The other explanation is that of fatigue, which is an equally compelling motive. Indeed, participants used time scarcity and fatigue almost interchangeably in their accounts.

Social dining at take-away and fast food restaurants was popular among Gen Ys who started to eat in this way when they were teenagers because it was fun and affordable. As young adults many now eat out regularly (at least once a fortnight). By the time Gen Y were growing up, the variety of takeaway and other forms of restaurants and cafés in cities like Melbourne had proliferated substantially. As Melissa said *there are so many places [restaurants and cafés] but, you know, it's a bit of a shame not to have tried all the new things there are around here.*

Although some types of dining out are still reserved for special occasions, eating out and takeaway has expanded to become part of everyday life for most Australians. In 1992, the market research group, Bis-Shrapnel (1992) cited in Hughes et al. (1997, p. 539) found that "on average, 25% of all the meals and snacks consumed in Australia were prepared by food-service establishments". Between 1985 and 1986 and 2005–2006, per capita real household expenditure on catered food rose by 30% or 1.3% per year on average (from $1,297 to $1,679). This rate of growth exceeded growth in expenditure on food overall which was 0.4% per year (Australian Bureau of Statistics 2007). Furthermore, more than half of the money spent on food eaten outside the home goes on fast food (Australian Bureau of Statistics 2000). Surveys show that the proportion of household expenditure on meals out and takeaway food has increased from 15% in 1975–1976 to 24% in 2003–2004 (Espinel and Innes-Hughes 2010).

Additionally, there has been a substantial differentiation and diversification of food outlets which are now part of (or next door to) almost every type of leisure activity venue such as cinemas, shopping malls, art galleries, bowling alleys and swimming pools. Australians can either go out specifically to eat or just grab something to eat 'on the run'. Meals no longer have to be planned since the 'when and where' of a meal is not limited.

The increase in eating out in public places has been connected to a rise of conspicuous consumption (Finkelstein 1989), with it becoming a means for individuals to satisfy personal desires and pleasures. Gen Y shared their parents' ready acceptance of eating out and eating takeaway as a solution to busy and complex life and as a pleasure, but because they are young with a relatively low earning capacity, they were limited in how often they could do so. However, compared to their Lucky Generation predecessors, both the Boomers and the Gen Ys placed much more emphasis on pleasure in food.

4.4 Food Advertising Over the Twentieth Century

Aggressive food marketing is not new but has been an important factor in the growth of all forms of convenience and industrial foods from the nineteenth century onwards. An online commentary on advertising illustrated with 20 visual images by the National Library of Australia (NLA) shows advertising to be prominent from the 1870s (National Library of Australia). It points out that following WWII "advertisements used glamour and romance to appeal to consumers affected by loss, fear and rationing". Before the advent of television, advertisements appeared in print, theatre, catalogues and on posters (National Library of Australia). The NLA's collection of images includes several advertisements for Peters ice cream dating from the 1920s which show young women in bathing suits. Later in the 1930s Peters advertised its ice cream as the "health food of a nation", employing in one example the endorsement of the famous Australian cyclist Hubert Opperman (National Library of Australia). Providing a dramatic contrast is a Peters ice cream advertisement from the 1940s. It is a sophisticated black and white photograph by Wolfgang

Sievers, of a man's hand passing an ice cream to a delicate woman's hand adorned with jewellery, implying elegance, pleasure and sex. In contrast, another 1940s advertisement for eggs returns to the theme of health (National Library of Australia). The emphasis on the health-giving properties of foods has clearly been a dominant message from the early part of this century followed closely by those of glamour and pleasure. The discovery of vitamins occurred early in the 1920s, so that by the 1930s vitamin-rich 'protective foods', including milk, eggs, cheese, meat and vegetables, had been identified and promoted to the Australian population. The population was advised to consume a pint (560 ml) of milk, 1 egg and 30 g of butter a day as part of a basic diet required for good health (Santich 2005). While the Peters ice cream advertisements do not specify why ice cream is supposed to be healthy, such advertisements presumably draw upon these ideas.

Kraft Foods' current website associated with the spread Vegemite demonstrates advertising trends over the twentieth century. It describes the product's invention in Australia in the 1920s and its long Australian history through examples of the advertisements that have been used over this time. Until the 1970s, Vegemite advertisements focused strongly on its health-giving properties, especially for children, based on its vitamin B content. As an up-to-date form of advertising, the website also enhances the notion of the product's authenticity as an iconic Australian product even though it is produced by Kraft, an international food company.

Another major theme in advertisements across the twentieth century was convenience. Even in the first half of the twentieth century magazines such as the *Australian Women's Weekly* provided advertisements and information about new and convenient industrial food possibilities. Often food advertising and recipes were co-located to promote the same foods. For example, a 1942 edition of the Australian Women's Weekly (1942) showed a full-page advertisement on the back cover for Kraft cheese with a recipe for Kraft pineapple salad. Although many advertisements drew on the theme of convenience, this was rarely mentioned explicitly. Instead, advertisements described how food products could save the busy cook time and effort (Warde 1999). For example, in the early 1920s and 1930s Bushells advertisements explained that their cocoa powder does away with "troublesome grating of chocolate" and provides a better cooking result. Bushells provided recipes for desserts such as cocoa cake, chocolate mould, and cocoa blancmange that were described as "easy" (Bushells Pty. Ltd, nd).

With the arrival and rapid uptake of television in the 1950s and 1960s a whole new medium opened up to food product advertisers who were quick to take advantage. So much so, that in the last decade or so televised food advertising, particularly if aimed at children, has come under increasing criticism because of growing levels of obesity. Compared to other developed countries, Australia has among the highest number of food advertisements shown during children's viewing times. Most of these advertisements promote industrial and convenience foods that are high in fat, sugar and/or salt (Chapman et al. 2006). The authors argue that the relative lack of "effective regulation… fails to protect Australian children from the large volumes of carefully targeted food advertising on television" (Chapman et al. 2006, p. 179). Moves in 2009 by the Australian Food and Grocery Council to "self-regulate" their advertising has done little to improve children's level of protection from this marketing (King et al. 2010). Despite promotion of products with poor nutritional content, linking food to health continues to be an important component of food advertising. In 2009 it was found that 55% of non-core foods advertised on Australian television during a set period of time contained nutritional claims sometimes ignoring other nutritionally unsound components of the food (Kelly et al. 2009).

4.5 A Rise in Health Consciousness

Once the Lucky Generation gave up making home-made puddings around the 1970s many did not return to them, even when they had more time. Among this generation, views varied about whether their consumption of puddings and sweets was good or bad for their health. Some focused on their high consumption of fruit in various desserts as positive for health. Judith argued that even the heavy puddings of their youth were healthier than modern commercially produced sweets. *I can't believe that they would do so much more damage than the rubbish that people have these days.*

And she went on to explain:

> *The fast food things. The jam tarts and chocolate desserts—it was nothing in the way of all the chocolate desserts that you have these days. Chocolate was very much ... well you couldn't get chocolate during the war, and even after the war, many years there were very limited supplies until the factories got back into it again. So, that was definitely a treat—ice-cream was definitely a treat.*

On the other hand some looked on their consumption of these traditional desserts as unhealthy. Betty recalled:

> *They had all these fattening awful things. I mean I didn't know they were awful then when I look back. Like jam roly poly and oh dear I can't remember now.*

This question of whether the replacement of home-made puddings and desserts with commercially prepared items has contributed to increasing prevalence of overweight and obesity remains unclear. Sugar, a major component of sweet desserts, has been blamed in part for the rise of obesity over the 1980s and 1990s particularly in beverages (O'Dea and Mann 2001). Sugar consumption in Australia is a complex story. Despite the increase in the last few decades of the availability of sweet foods and snacks, the consumption of cane sugar has declined from a high point of about 56 kg per capita in the early 1940s to about 43 kg in 1998–1999 (Australian Bureau of Statistics 2000). However, Australians' sugar consumption started from an extraordinarily high base, with almost the highest per capita sugar consumption in the world in the early part of the twentieth century. This probably stemmed from the colonial practice of giving settlers a sugar ration. Vast quantities of sugar were consumed in tea, where it was considered normal to have four lumps per cup in the 1930s, in beer and spirits, and in the domestic production of sweets, cakes, jams and other preserves (Griggs 2006). A strong Queensland sugar industry and the Colonial Sugar Refinery made sugar readily available. Griggs attributes the decline in sugar consumption mainly to a groundswell of concerns in the 1960s about the health effects of sugar among medicos and dentists which spread to the general population, some of whom adopted artificial sugar replacements. Another factor is important. In the 1930s and 1940s most sugar was purchased in refined form and added to home-prepared food with only 30% consumed in processed foods. This pattern was gradually reversed so that by the 1970s, 60% of sugar was consumed in processed foods. Much of the sugar that Australians consume now is invisible unless people closely study nutrition labels on food. A major form of sugar consumption occurs in carbonated drinks, which have increased in popularity from the late 1980s (Australian Bureau of Statistics 2000). While apparent national consumption data shows a decrease over most of the twentieth century, nutrition surveys based on self-reported data indicate that sugar consumption rose slightly from the 1980s–1990s (Australian Bureau of Statistics 2000). Thus the story of the disappearing dessert together with the decline in national apparent sugar consumption displays the limitations of simple explanations for obesity prevalence.

The growing health awareness of the Lucky Generation is shown in their accounts which provide a retrospective examination of their childhood diets from a health perspective. When they were growing up, the emphasis was on food's ability to keep the family feeling satiated, satisfied and healthy or able to perform hard work (Banwell et al. 2010). But as many of the Lucky Generation observed, views about what is healthy food have changed dramatically under the influence of the rise of health consciousness with moral overtones.

> *We used to eat meat with fat on it, we thought that was pretty good. What meat we had. I cut all the fat off the bacon. I am very good. I used to like the rind on the bacon. I don't do that anymore. I am very good.*

While talking about their recent health and weight problems, the Lucky Generation often volunteered that they now monitored their diets due to concerns about health problems such as high cholesterol or blood pressure.

This increasing focus on health among the study's participants is reflected more widely. A discourse analysis of food advertisements and articles in the *Australian Women's Weekly* sampled between 1951 and 2006 shows that emphasis on healthy food choices for the family grew from 1951–1971 (Schneider and Davis 2010). By 1981 the focus on family health had been replaced by what was described as "the emergence of the healthy food consumer", in which the focus shifts from the family to an individual (often female) located within an unhealthy Australian population that is likely to suffer from chronic diet-related diseases. In general, in *Australian Women's Weekly* articles, individuals are instructed to take "responsibility" for their own health by actively engaging in dietary change, guided by self-examination (Schneider and Davis 2010). The changes noted in the content of the magazine are reflected in the increasingly individualised and detailed concern with diet, evident later in the life of the Luckies, and to a greater extent in the Baby Boomers and the Gen Ys at increasingly early ages.

The use of diet to manage health was often triggered when an individual faced a health crisis either directly or via identification of increased risk of potential future ill-health. This was particularly evident in the life narratives of the Lucky Generation as many of them began to experience age-related health problems. As Minnie from the Lucky Generation commented: *...I watch more what we eat now rather than back a few years because we weren't as health conscious I don't think.*

However, even some of the younger Baby Boomers, particularly men, had been forced to change their diet when they were found to have high cholesterol or had experienced a heart attack. Although Gen Y did not undertake dietary changes for current health issues, a few did so because of the perceived future risk they faced given their family health histories. For example, Andrew's partner has *got quite a lot of diabetes in her family... So she's trying to cut down on sugar.* Nicole (aged 45) believed she needed to reverse years of poor eating habits as her health was now suffering. Participants of all ages related the prevention and management of chronic diseases to more than nutritional issues, also changing their eating to manage food intolerance and mental stresses.

While the Lucky Generation's functional approach to food revolved around providing fuel for work, subsequent generations took a more scientific approach to nutrition to enhance sporting performance. As a keen golfer Julie (aged 55) believed that *if you eat shoddily, you get shoddy output.* Gen Y David, who has competed in sports at a state level, has a particularly functional view of food in which it broken down into nutritional components such as proteins to provide the physical outcome that he was seeking. *When I was weight-training protein would support my diet as well and give me that extra bit.*

Participants from all three generations reported that they had reduced their consumption of red meat due to health concerns, mainly related to weight and cholesterol. Their diets are reflected in long-term trends in apparent consumption of foodstuffs showing a fall in meat consumption from over 100 kilograms (kg) per person in 1938–1939 to below 73 kg per person in 1998–1999 (Australian Bureau of Statistics 2007). However, poultry consumption has more that trebled since the 1960s. Fruit and vegetable intake has also increased dramatically over the same period (although this is unlikely to include domestic or backyard produce). Egg consumption has dropped, as has fat intake, particularly of butter (Australian Bureau of Statistics 2007).

Thus, growing concern for health by our three generations is apparent in their accounts of their own eating habits as well as in national consumption figures. As we have observed already, messages about health have been an important selling point for food advertisers for most of the twentieth century. As convenience has become a more dominant concern for the younger time-pressured generations, it is not surprising that health and convenience would be brought together in newly processed and packaged food.

4.6 A Modern Yearning for Convenience and Health

Convenience food, particularly in the form of takeaway, fast or junk food, is strongly associated with high fat, highly processed ingredients, and is considered by most study participants (including those who eat it) to be both unhealthy and fattening.

Yet there has been a clear shift to solving the problems of time scarcity, family flexibility, and the family cook's fatigue through the use of industrialised and convenience foods. Individuals and families undertake considerable negotiation to reconcile these two contradictory forces: the need to maintain family eating rituals and standards in a time-pressured environment. One result is that all generations, but particularly Baby Boomers and Gen Ys, have become skilled in distinguishing between convenience foods on the basis of their apparent healthiness. Most fast foods are seen to be unhealthy, although some convenience foods are viewed quite positively. Restaurant-produced Asian meals are considered to be reasonably healthy in contrast to a standard meal from a chain takeaway restaurant. Indeed, many convenient food products enable the production of a speedy and reasonably healthy meal through the use of items such as tinned chickpeas, lentils, tuna or mass-produced curry pastes and pasta. Much of the production of these foods is driven by the retailers' search for market and consumers' desire for longevity, increased performance and avoiding disease (Dixon et al. 2006). The move from red meat to chicken meat is an example. Dixon argues that through technological innovation supermarkets have used existing consumer perceptions to buttress their own self-promotion as experts on, and purveyors of, healthy convenience. The cool chain is used to produce conveniently chilled (rather than inconveniently frozen) chicken. They have also promoted chicken meat as healthy and acceptable to the whole family including children and even sometimes vegetarians, and convenient because its pre-prepared forms are quick to cook (Dixon and Banwell 2004). A more extreme example is the production of functional "phoods" which has become a growth industry, marrying the modern requirement for health with convenience by adding "nutraceuticals or a bioactive ingredient to deliver health benefits" (Dixon et al. 2006, p. 639). This market has produced convenient take-home products that address a range of health problems, from the restoration of healthy gut flora, the perceived need for vitamins, minerals and other supplements, along with salt – and fat-reduced foods. The desire to manage weight is one of the dominant drivers of convenient functional foods. Some people purchase 'slimming' products from supermarkets while others sign up to slimming programs providing pre-prepared meals. For example, one Baby Boomer participant bought herself several week's worth of calorie-controlled catered meals (three per day) when she found herself putting on weight, arguing that this saved her time while she lost weight. She considered it well worth the additional cost compared to cooking at home.

4.7 Conclusion

We have argued elsewhere (Banwell et al. 2010) that the Lucky Generation's taste for the necessary (Bourdieu 1984) developed during the food restrictions of their youth has been maintained to some extent into their later years in the form of health-related diets and a limited uptake of convenience foods.

Over the course of the Lucky Generations' lives and those of their children and grandchildren, a discourse of healthy citizenship has developed (Davis 2011), encouraging individuals to show responsibility by monitoring and managing their food consumption and undertaking health-promoting physical activities. Our two younger generations certainly recognise these exhortations, and strive to adopt them to a greater or lesser extent. Yet increasing Australian obesity (Walls et al. 2009) suggests that a generalised concern with health and diet does not necessarily lead to slimmer bodies. Indeed, the more influential drivers of Australians' dietary patterns and ultimately people's weight may be the widespread availability, accessibility and adoption of commercially prepared, convenience foods which are often energy-dense. These drivers have arisen as women and men have moved into a flexibilised and deregulated workforce. The Australian population has sought a range of convenient and (sometimes) healthy foods as a solution to their busy, fragmented lives. The story of the disappearing dessert exemplifies these changes over three generations.

Image 4.2 The dessert aisle at the supermarket, Melbourne 2012 (Photo: J. Dixon)

References

Australian Bureau of Statistics. (2000). *Apparent consumption of foodstuffs, Australia, 1997–98 and 1998–99* Cat. No. 4306.0. Canberra: ABS.

Australian Bureau of Statistics. (2007). *Australian social trends – 2007 4102.0*. Canberra: ABS.

Australian Women's Weekly. (1942). Advertisement for Kraft cheese. *Australian Women's Weekly, 9*, 48.

Backett-Milburn, K., Wills, W., Roerts, M.-L., & Lawton, J. (2010). Food, eating and taste: Parents' perspectives on the making of the middle class teenager. *Social Science & Medicine, 71*, 1316–1323.

Banwell, C., Dixon, J., Broom, D., & Davies, A. (2010). Habits of a lifetime: Family dining patterns over the lifecourse of older Australians. *Health Sociology Review, 19*(3), 343–355.

Berry, J., & Wearing-Smith, H. (1993). *Proud tradition of Australian cooking: A collection of inherited recipes from the 1920s and 1930s*. Roseville: Simon and Shuster.

Bis–Shrapnel Pty Ltd. (1992). *The Australian foodservice market* (Vol. 3rd). Sydney: Bis–Shrapnel.

Bourdieu, P. (1984). *Distinction: A social critique of the judgement of taste*. London: Routledge and Kegan Paul.

Bushells Pty. Ltd. (nd). *Bushells cocoa cake recipes*. Sydney: Bushells.

Chapman, K., Nicholas, P., & Supramaniam, R. (2006). How much food advertising is there on Australian television. *Health Promotion International, 21*(3), 172–180.

Country Women's Association NSW. (1965). *A dessert for every day of the year*. Sydney: Country Women's Association.

Country Women's Association of Western Australia of the Air Kalgoorlie Branch. (1965). *1965 recipes: Tested recipes from the C.W.A. of the air*. Kalgoolie: C.W.A. of the Air.

Davis, A. (2011). *Healthy citizenship in an obesogenic environment*. Canberra: Australian National University.

Dingle, T. (1998). Electrifying the kitchen in interwar Victoria. *Journal of Australian Studies, 57*, 119–127.

Dixon, J., & Banwell, C. (2004). Heading the table: Parenting and the junior consumer. *British Food Journal, 106*(2/3), 181–193.

Dixon, H., Scully, M., & Parkinson, K. (2006a). Pester power: snackfoods displayed at supermarket checkouts in Melbourne, Australia. *Health Promotion Journal of Australia, 17*(2), 124–127.

Dixon, J., Hinde, S., & Banwell, C. (2006b). Obesity, convenience and 'phood'. *British Food Journal, 108*(8), 634–645.

Douglas, M. (1982). Food as a system of communication. In M. Douglas (Ed.), *In the active voice* (pp. 82–113). London: Routledge & Kegan Paul.

Duruz, J. (1999). Food as nostalgia: Eating the fifties and sixties. *Australian Historical Studies, 29*(113), 231–250.

Espinel, P., & Innes-Hughes, C. (2010). *Apparent consumption of selected foods and household food expenditure. Monitoring update*. Sydney: PANORG.

Farrer, K. (2005). *To feed a nation: A history of Australian food science and technology*. Melbourne: CSIRO Publishing.

Finkelstein, J. (1989). *Dining out: A sociology of modern manners*. New York: New York University Press.

Gilmore, M. (1934). *Old days, old ways: A book of recollections*. Sydney: Angus & Robertson.

Gollan, A. (1978). *The tradition of Australian cooking*. Canberra: Australian National University Press.

Griggs, P. (2006). A natural part of life: The Australian sugar industry's campaign to reverse declining Australian sugar consumption, 1980–1995. *Journal of Australian Studies, 87*, 141–154.

Horwath, C. (1988). The food habits of elderly Australians. In A. Truswell & M. Wahlquist (Eds.), *Food habits in Australia, Proceedings of the first Deakin/Sydney Universities Symposium on Australian Nutrition* (pp. 224–249). North Balwyn: Rene Gordon.

Hughes, R., Harvey, P., & Heywood, P. (1997). The food–service industry, dietary guidelines and change. *Australian and New Zealand Journal of Public Health, 21*(5), 539–544.

Kelly, B., Hattersley, L., King, L., & Flood, V. (2009). Smoke and mirrors: Nutrition content claims used to market unhealthy food. *Nutrition and Dietetics, 66*(1), 62–64.

King, L., Hebden, L., Grunseit, A., Kelly, B., Chapman, K., & Venugopal, K. (2010). Industry self regulation of television food advertising: Responsible or responsive? *International Journal of Pediatric Obesity*. doi:10.3109/17477166.2010.517313.

National Library of Australia. *Slideshow Trail: Advertising Australia*. Retrieved July 6, 2011, http://www.pictureaustralia.org/slideshow/Advertising+Australia

O'Dea, K., & Mann, J. (2001). Importance of retaining a national dietary guideline for sugar. *The Medical Journal of Australia, 175*, 165–166.

Santich, B. (1995). 'It's a chore!' women's attitudes towards cooking. *Australian Journal of Nutrition and Dietetics, 52*(1), 11–13.

Santich, B. (2005). Paradigm shifts in the history of dietary advice in Australia. *Nutrition and Dietetics, 62*(4), 152–157.

Schneider, T., & Davis, T. (2010). Fostering a hunger for health: Food and the self in "the Australian women's weekly". *Health Sociology Review, 19*(3), 285–303.

Schubert, L. (2009). *Diet and domestic life in 21st Century Australia: An exploration of time and convenience in family food provisioning*. PhD thesis. University of Queensland.

Shove, E. (2003). Converging conventions of comfort, cleanliness and convenience. *Journal of Consumer Policy, 26*(4), 395–418.

Shove, E., & Southerton, D. (2000). Defrosting the freezer: From novelty to convenience. *Journal of Material Culture, 5*, 301–319.

Siemering, A. (2004). Cooking globally eating whenever: The future of dining. *Futurist, 38*(3), 51.

Sydney Morning Herald. (2008, August 14). Back to the Tim Tam future, *Sydney Morning Herald*. Retrieved from http://www.smh.com.au/business/back to the tim-tam-future-20080813_3v14.html

Symons, M. (1984). *One continuous picnic*. Ringwood: Penguin.

Symons, M. (1993). *The shared table*. Canberra: AGPS.

Symons, M. (2007). *One continuous picnic: A gastronomic history of Australia*. Melbourne: Melbourne University Press.

Walker, R. B., & Roberts, D. C. K. (1988). Colonial food habits. In A. Truswell & L. Wahlquist (Eds.), *Food habits in Australia, Proceedings of the first Deakin/Sydney Universities Symposium on Australian Nutrition* (pp. 40–59). North Balwyn: Rene Gordon.

Walls, H., Wolfe, R., Haby, M., Magliano, D., de Courten, M., Reid, C., et al. (2009). Trends in BMI of urban Australian adults, 1980–2000. *Public Health Nutrition*. doi:10.1017/S1368980009991455.

Warde, A. (1999). Convenience food: Space and timing. *British Food Journal, 101*(7), 518–527.

Wyn, J., & Woodman, D. (2006). Generation, youth and social change in Australia. *Journal of Youth Studies, 9*(5), 495–514.

Chapter 5
From Sociable Leisure to Exhaustion: A Tale of Two Revolutions

Image 5.1 Drouin schoolboys playing cricket, Victoria circa 1944 (Source: National Library of Australia)

5.1 The First Revolution in Leisure Activities

The leisure and physical activity opportunities of late nineteenth century Australia, when the parents of the Lucky Generation were growing up, were characterised by social status and gender distinctions. For working-class Australian women during this time, leisure was confined to home-based games, reading and excursions on Sunday and public holidays or family picnics; while middle-class women had a wider repertoire: taking part in drama and music productions and visiting libraries,

C. Banwell et al., *Weight of Modernity: An Intergenerational Study of the Rise of Obesity*, DOI 10.1007/978-90-481-8957-1_5, © Springer Science+Business Media Dordrecht 2012

galleries and museums (Parker and Paddick 1990; Timms 2008). Working-class and middle-class men played weekend sport, and the latter had their own clubs.

As the Lucky Generation were becoming young adults, life in Australia was changing dramatically with profound consequences for leisure, sport and social life more generally. The nation gained a reputation as the 'social laboratory of the world', in large part because it introduced legislation enshrining the 8-hours working day in the early 1920s (Lewis et al. 2006), explicitly invoking Robert Owen's dictum from 1817 that there should be 8 hours work, 8 hours leisure and 8 hours rest. The national government introduced a family minimum wage and Australian women were among the first to be given the vote. Trade union and social reforms led to improvements in working and living conditions which resulted in higher disposable incomes and an increase in leisure time. One effect was to provide the middle and working classes with more opportunities to participate in sport, and to enjoy the entertainment aspect of amateur sports as they were becoming increasingly organised.

These developments also had a profound effect on the relationship between parenting and children's leisure and recreation. As children's employment on farms and in factories declined, they too gained more leisure time, and concern developed around how they used their new-found freedom. For much of the nineteenth century relationships between parents and offspring had tended to centre around children's moral and physical wellbeing more than their personal development (Timms 2008). As various professions, including psychology, started to focus on the raising of children, new social standards emerged in relation to child-rearing, which ceased to be seen as a private matter. By the early twentieth century, sport was being re-framed in the US and elsewhere as 'character building'. As a potential way to educate, sport could train the body for work and the mind for achievement and loyalty (Coakley 2008). Although a part of this ethos was new in that it was animated by producing fit bodies for labour market participation, much of it echoes periodic assertions made over 2,000 years by philosophers and religious figures regarding the symbiosis between a virtuous polity and society, with an engaged populace resulting from routine, disciplined physical exercise (Porter 1999).

A countervailing force to physical exertion also appeared on the horizon at this time. Few families of the Lucky Generation owned a motor car, but for those with access to one, it began to open up new leisure activities: participation in bushwalking, for example. Gradually outdoor activities became democratised with the mass-production of cars and motor-cycles, improvements in railways and roads, and the production of cheap bicycles (Parker and Paddick 1990). The purchase of a car was often associated with being able to go on holidays. However, the car played little role in helping people take part in sporting or leisure activities, regardless of class background. Public transport, the bicycle and walking provided most people's access to daily or weekly leisure activities.

When the Lucky Generation were children, the 'activity environment' was characterised by three features: home-based entertainments which were largely free and based on creative play; the emergence of diverse forms of mass culture, including spectator sports (Fabian and Loh 1980); and the gradual rise of school and club sports. The second and third of these trends operated to undercut the socially stratified nature of physical activity that had prevailed for their parents.

5.2 The Sociable Lucky Generation

5.2.1 The Childhood Years: 1920s–1930s

Typically, the narratives of the Lucky Generation's childhoods were portrayed as being simple, full of freedom, physically active, and reliant on imagination and self initiation. Our interviews resonate with assessments that forms of nineteenth century leisure continued as major sources of leisure when they were in primary school: people made their own entertainment (Timms 2008, p. 81) and children still made their own fun at home and in the neighbourhood (Fabian and Loh 1980).

As many lived in the country or in suburbs which were semi-rural, children had access to vast areas to explore for unsupervised adventures. According to Arthur,

> *Rosebud (in rural Victoria) was a child's paradise, particularly if you had a 12 gauge shot gun which I had when I was about ten. Go out in the wintertime and just go out in the backyard and shoot rabbits. The backyard was three acres.*

They described riding horses and bikes, catching tadpoles and frogs, running wild, and walking long distances. Peggy continued the theme about the importance of the outdoors:

> *... at school and after school we'd ride bikes to one or other places and continue games like hide and seek and all the usual things that children play. Outside games, definitely outside games. And in the winter ... we played board games.*

This generation often noted the lack of available technologies for entertainment. As Alice put it:

> *I think life was a bit tougher than today.... We didn't have any method of entertainment so we entertained ourselves which was mind games, like the made up games...*

Barbara's description reflected the inexpensive and outdoor nature of play, and captured a wide array of activities:

> *I was always turning somersaults on the lawn. If it was good weather we were outdoor playing. ... you'd meet friends when we came home from school. I can remember playing whip-top in the middle of the bitumen road ... run away when the odd car came along. We used to make our own things. My sister and I used to play together well, and play under my grandmother's wattle tree, and scoop up all the things to make rooms for our dolls house and all that.*
>
> *So games of imagination?*
>
> *Yes. .... We had a little shop in the old chook house. Mum used to save us all the packets she opened, and we would make the money out of her piece of cardboard, and cover it with a bit of silver foil for our coins... Then, as you get older, you play a bit of cricket with the boys down the paddock.... Then we had board games for inside. We had a table-tennis thing .... We used to have young people from the church in the clubs every Sunday night and come and have tea with us and play table croquet and things like that. .... but I suppose you would call it just an average childhood. I collected stamps and went about swapping that, and ... later on, as I got to a teenager, fifteen I suppose, we had a bike, so I would ride a bike ... and go looking for boys, I suppose. No, we had a very normal childhood. The only thing I regret—we weren't encouraged to do a lot of reading. No. Mum and dad weren't readers ...*

Outside play was not strictly gendered, and more than one woman described herself as a tomboy. In Edna's case:

There weren't any other girls around so I went out with the boys catching tadpoles and frogs and played football and got a dog one Christmas. I didn't want a dog, I wanted a football so I was a real tomboy. Of course when I got older we had horses and everything and I would go riding and things like that. I had my own horse ...

In contrast, there was a clear gender dimension to hobbies. We heard from the men about their childhood hobbies based on purchased toys—model trains, photography, meccano sets—as well as 'making things with their hands', including woodwork, electronics and radio sets. They saw riding a bike a long distance as entertainment. Learning to play the piano, reading, knitting and sewing featured strongly in the women's childhoods, with some describing dancing lessons and baking. They regarded spending time with friends as a hobby or pastime.

5.2.1.1 Entertainment Possibilities Abound with Mass Culture

The Lucky Generation said that their parents had had few leisure pursuits, but during their own childhood important new forms of leisure became available with the arrival of cheap music sheets, mass-produced musical instruments, mass-circulation newspapers and cinematography (Parker and Paddick 1990). A handful of the Lucky Generation talked about the cinema as one of the few out-of-home entertainments their parents could afford. Richard remembered:

Their week consisted probably of going to the movies, once or twice a week. You didn't have a car, you didn't get out. You walked to the nearest picture theatre and where we lived we had access to three. So you could walk in three different directions and get to a movie. It was quite a decent walk.

A cinema matinee was a relatively inexpensive form of escapism and amusement, although attendance declined during the Depression (Whimpress 1994). Picture theatres replaced travelling picture shows in country towns by the 1930s (Williams 1985), and 'talkies' were offered in luxurious movie 'palaces' with cheap admission (Kociumbas 1997). For those who could afford a ticket, weekly newsreels were an instant success when they were introduced in 1931 as they provided news from around Australia and abroad (Williams 1985). During the 1940s and 1950s many children would have visited 'the flicks' weekly (Fabian and Loh 1980), with Edward telling us:

My parents had very little... or virtually no outside activities except the home. I can recall going to the films with mum and dad probably in the latter part of primary school I suppose that would be, yes, Saturday night pictures...

The second form of mass culture to become accessible for working people from the 1920s onwards was the wireless (Fabian and Loh 1980). Initially a novelty for the wealthy, it was soon transforming home leisure as production rapidly grew and prices dropped (Williams 1985). By the 1930s the radio industry was well established with stations set up around Australia and in many large country towns. Paid entertainment was out of the reach for many during the Depression, and even other forms of home entertainment such as having friends over became hard for some people. However, wireless sets continued to sell well (Fabian and Loh 1980), as they were a free form of entertainment once the set had been bought and the annual licence fee paid (Williams 1985). Charles described how he *always had a family meal, school lessons after the homework, a bit of wireless, then bed.* Like other 'mod cons', including the telephone, families did not have to own a wireless to access one because according to Edna they *used to go next door.*

Radio involved the simultaneous transmission of information and entertainment.

> [It] quickly brought the decline of the living room musicale. More than just operetta or popular songs, the wireless offered news, stories, game shows and a raft of other entertainments, and it had the huge benefit of immediacy: for the first time the family sitting at homes could hear what was going on in the outside world, more or less as it was happening, and that was thrilling. (Timms 2008, p. 83).

The radio also made it possible to listen to sporting events at home, creating a new dimension to sport spectatorship. The Australian Broadcasting Commission (ABC) first broadcast cricket in 1932, which became hugely popular. Games played in England were relayed across Australia, often with studio sound effects such as the crack of the bat on the ball to make them more realistic (Williams 1985).

Australia developed very few sports of its own—the exceptions being Australian Rules Football (AFL) and the handicapped horse race enshrined in the annual and globally recognised 'race that stops a nation', the Melbourne Cup (Adair and Vamplew 1997). The radio helped to spread their appeal, both for at-home 'spectators' and those who could be present at the sporting oval or race course.

The AFL featured in the stories of about one-fifth of our Lucky Generation respondents, who were initiated into its ways by their fathers. Minnie said about her father:

> *He liked working in the garden, that was his main thing... And he loved his football... I remember he started going to the football when I was about five years old... [he would go] with his father and all the family together.*

As with going to the picture theatre together as a family, the football was a family occasion: *We used to take the children to the football every Saturday... they weren't terribly interested in it* (Elizabeth).

Playing football in winter informally on the streets and empty residential blocks of land was a staple pastime for affluent and poor children alike. Played in this way, football provided more than physical exertion because it offered access to a large neighbourhood tribe, as reflected in this quote from Brian:

> *We'd kick a football and break the electric wires. Then if the police came down and caught you, they'd take the football away and you wouldn't have a football. So you'd get a paper then, a newspaper, and roll that up and tie that up and that was your football.*
>
> *[Or] you would go up to the Carlton football ground and speak to one of the players and that and they'd say, now, you get behind the goals out in the street, so you'd go out in the street and all of a sudden over would come a football. Off you'd go. But they knew what they were doing, but we didn't, you know.*
>
> *Mickey Crisp, he was an insurance agent and he played for Carlton. And one day I trapped him and... I said,' how about a football, Mr Crisp', you know, and he said, 'well, you come up such and such a night' and then, boom, boom, he'd kick one over the fence. So you'd grab it, put it under your arm... and then, of course, you'd [tear off].*

For some, including Maureen, 'catching up at the footy' persists with family or with neighbours:

Well when I was a child we lived ... just up from the football ground. My father was a keen Bulldogs, or Footscray, supporter in those days, and we just [continued to follow] from the time the babies were born, and we encouraged them to be Bulldogs ... And we meet again at the football, we all have seats at the football and we meet again with my son. That's another catch-up of family.

Going to the cinema and the football were weekly outings; for children and adults alike, daily leisure activities continued to be centred around the home and in neighbourhood streets throughout this period.

5.2.1.2 The Rise of School and Club Sports

As with food, the early waves of settlers to Australia used sports to maintain links with Britain. Participating in the 'motherland's' sporting traditions fulfilled three functions: it offered the new colony a way to evaluate itself since beating Britain at its own sports was taken as a sign of colonial maturity; it helped to make Australia a familiar setting to British migrants; and the wealthy and free settlers could distinguish themselves from convicts via the class distinctions present in British sports (Adair and Vamplew 1997; Vamplew 1994).

British sporting traditions—cricket, croquet, cycling and tennis—were popular at this time, and many children played cricket and some tennis formally at school and informally after school and on weekends. Charles remembered:

We did have rounders as a school sport and there'd be swimming as part of the school sport too. .... I can remember playing cricket with my brothers not far from our house.

Swimming was one of the few sports promoted by government schools at the turn of the century, largely because of the safety factor involved in learn-to-swim and lifesaving classes (Phillips n.d.).

The range of sports available at school appears to have varied greatly, with many interviewees talking about either having no sport at school or a very limited variety.

A few, including Norma, mentioned that they did not have free time to play sport outside school hours because they had to do homework and household chores:

We'd come home from school and you'd have to bring the cows in, milk the cows and do our homework and no, there was only lunchtime to do sport. We used to go with the family to a tennis match on the weekend and yeah, not much time. Oh, we used to play sport at school.

Others did not participate in organised sport because they did not have access in part because of the cost, or because they lived in the country. For Edward, *To play sport in those days, who could afford to buy a tennis racquet, a footy*? Alice reflected on how constrained her sporting opportunities were, as well as foreshadowing family involvements in the sports of Gen Y:

Oh well we didn't have any sport. The only thing is I loved running. ... if we went to picnics there was always races in those days... and I always won them ... I was about fourteen I think, I ran in a race down at Bentley Football Club .... and a trainer approached dad and asked could he train me. And you know my parents are too busy, they've got younger children, and they said 'oh if she wants to do it she can do it but she had to get herself there'. Well getting myself there meant riding my bike back and forth and I was terribly shy and so I didn't do it and I've always regretted that ... I have a granddaughter now who's a really good runner so I'm reliving my life through her.

Our male interviewees had more school opportunities to play organised sport. George said:

On Wednesday afternoon, we'd go to Prince's Park and kick a football, and get exercise, we did that in primary and secondary school. .... Secondary school, I did two sports there. I did boxing and ... I played lacrosse. I enjoyed boxing or sparring. I thought that was a great .... until I got belted and got hurt.

For boys attending private schools, the range of activities was almost as extensive as it is today. Indeed this situation had pertained since the 1870s, with private schools promoting strenuous activities (Phillips nd). As Kevin explained:

There were extra-curricula activities at school, there was dancing lessons and so forth, this was in secondary school, we went up to the girls' school and had dancing lessons one night a week in the winter term. There was always after school sport to either watch or partake in ... You were forced, at that secondary school anyway and probably generally at that time, ... to try and if you weren't in a team you were expected to come out on Saturdays and watch the team and all that kind of thing, which didn't thrill me very much .... They had these activities every year, they had house boxing and rowing, I had my best success at rowing.

Kevin, whose parents had matriculated, was one of very few who also described club-based sporting activities:

I was in a church tennis club at weekends. .... When I could, I was in the Scouts and we had Saturday afternoon activities apart from a weekly Scout meeting .... We'd do a bit of hiking because of that association with Scouts. That was a popular activity, bushcraft and all that Baden Powell kind of stuff. ....

The 1920s and 1930s were decades when women's and sporting lobby groups agitated for greater opportunities for women, riding the wave of successful women cyclists and swimmers. From our interviews with Lucky Generation women, these efforts, combined with the National Fitness Council's promotion of a nation that should be full of sports-minded children (Fabian and Loh 1980), appear to have taken several decades to translate into a widespread trend.

Eight of our 111 respondents talked about being fat as a child, and one said that as result she did not like physical activity. The overwhelming majority liked 'being physical', although several did not like school sports if they felt they were not good at it. These children knitted or read or played musical instruments, although finding the latter difficult might be a deterrent to persistence.

5.2.1.3 Unsupervised Play

While Doris described fond memories of playing with her father, parents rarely featured in descriptions about how this generation filled in their spare time. Children appear to have had a large amount of unsupervised play, and a few described their mothers as not having time to play with their children. Edna reported that:

I would have loved my mother to have had the time to take me out as mother and daughter but that didn't eventuate because mum was very busy.

Charles also described a desire to have greater attention from his mother:

I always liked reading and I'd want to read to my mother and she'd say she was too busy and I'd walk around behind her reading to her ... and I'd get in a cupboard and pretend I was a gramophone and things. Then when she'd be polishing the floor my younger brother and I would sit on the back while she was on her hands and knees polishing the lino.

Other than the country children who had 'yard chores', especially looking after and feeding animals and helping out in the vegetable garden, not many children helped in the house. Running errands was common for city children and drying up dishes appeared to be the most common inside 'chore'. The lack of children's involvement is striking considering how much household labour their mothers were doing.

In a portent of what was to follow with the Baby Boomers, Lucky Generation Kevin described being involved in his children's extra-curricular activities in the following terms:

.... well we were shunting the children around a lot to camps and I helped with the Scouts at that time too, so I was driving—I helped with the Scout group by going down to the meetings and giving them games and trying to organise the group. I got involved in weekend camps sometimes and excursions and hikes and so forth.

While an atypical description, it reveals the unfolding of major changes over the second half of the twentieth century in parental involvement in their children's leisure time.

5.2.2 The Teenage and Early Adult Years: 1940s–1950s

Dancing was encouraged by the arrival of radio and cinema (Fabian and Loh 1980). As teenagers, Lucky Generation boys and girls started to attend dances organised by churches, clubs or private dance instructors. There were many commercial dance halls, and people often met their life-partners at the dances. Indeed its popularity among our Lucky Generation and Baby Boomer respondents is such that we explore further its importance in terms of physical activity in the next chapter.

Dancing was not the only activity to integrate social and physical activities. Tennis was hugely popular, often beginning in childhood as an unorganised activity played in the street or against a wall, progressing onto numerous suburban tennis courts (that have since disappeared through higher density residential developments). Tennis shared similar attributes with dancing: highly orchestrated moves requiring appropriate attire, interpersonal etiquette, and several of our respondents also met their spouse playing tennis. Along with golf, tennis was considered an appropriate sport for women because it was not too strenuous or highly competitive: in other words, it was not too 'manly' (Vamplew 1994). Joyce played tennis at school, and on giving up work to have children she played *married ladies tennis*, keeping it up for many years. Squash was also considered suitable for women, and

Ivy *used to play squash on Monday night and tennis twice a week. Take all the kids along.* Those not playing would take turns to mind the children.

The importance of tennis in the lives of many women was supported when others made a point of saying that they did not play tennis. Peggy said she was not interested in *joining tennis clubs and things like that at all. I mean you seem to get plenty of activity walking the children here there and everywhere, shopping and all the housework and things like that.*

A few women referred to playing netball, with Doris noting *and then the babies came and I gave it up.* According to Phillips' (nd) *History of Women in Sport in Australia,* netball became a force for social change when its popularity meant that venues had to open after hours (6–11 pm) to accommodate all the women who wanted to play.

Young men maintained hobbies alongside their paid employment, especially 'working on' a car or a bike, followed by long bike rides. However, when they married, city respondents often relinquished club and social activities to build or renovate a house. Half a dozen mentioned building a house with a tennis court. Major weekend family activities were going to the beach, picnics in parks, and games.

Doris was an early user of gyms with child minding:

> *When I say a gym, not the ones today. You know, a church hall with an instructor and you'd turn up ... and if you were lucky you got a cup of coffee, and it probably cost, I don't know, the equivalent of probably $2 today. But it was still a gym and it kept you fit and you talked to people.*

It sounds as though the church hall gym experience was a bit of a substitute for [not being able to play sport] after you were married?

> *Yes. My eldest daughter had started school and my youngest one was still in the pram, so I used to wheel the pram and do my half hour or hour gym.... She'd either lay there or go to sleep and then I'd walk back home.*

As the Lucky Generation's children got older, there were more references to driving them to activities, but not to school because children invariably rode their bikes or used public transport as Chap. 7 describes.

Some women, including Betty, resumed tennis as their children became teenagers: *Well I played tennis and golf and of course we went out to a lot of dinner dances and ...there was always something going on.* As they gained more time on weekends, men took up or resumed golf. Tennis and golf were justified because they were enjoyable social (rather than solitary) pursuits, with a hint of competition. However, winning was less important than spending time with friends outside of paid employment and household duties, and these two activities were recognised as helping interviewees to 'keep fit'—a phrase that crept in when our respondents were discussing their later middle age and senior years.

5.2.3 The Senior Years: 1980s to Present

For men and women alike, the list of 'retirement' activities was extensive and many judged themselves to be doing more in the retirement years than at any stage in the lifecourse. This observation accords with a study of older New Zealanders, who talked about ageing both slowing them down (so that activities would take longer to complete) but also expanding available leisure time as they were released from employment and familial responsibilities (Annear et al. 2009).

A few commented that they were not a sporting person when young, but they began to appreciate physical activity as they got older, often under the influence of a spouse. Indeed, the influence of partners over particular pursuits was profound, with men particularly mentioning their wife's encouragement to become more active. This was noted with changing dietary patterns too. They were not always successful, however. Jill reported that her husband who retired from his business a year earlier at age 71 was finding it hard to settle down but she could not entice him to do volunteer work.

Fred said that his wife got him involved in running op shops, and hospital visits to elderly patients.

> *... and we work at the Flying Doctors... we're professional envelope stuffers and Christmas card stuffers, but I also do a few odd jobs at the office, help them out if something goes wrong... and I'm still working around home, and I've got a mountain bike that I still go out and ride around the creek.*

Connie, an extremely active woman, detailed how she has moved from involvement with young people through being a Girl Guide Commissioner, Brownie leader and Sunday School teacher, to joining the Board of Management of an aged care facility. Over a period of 15 years, Connie estimates that she has helped to raise $10 million which has been used to extend and update the buildings. She is now writing a history of the facility. As well as becoming volunteers for non-government organisations, women reported supporting family members by providing childcare and elder care.

There was a clear cleavage in our sample regarding volunteering for community or church organisations. About half the sample appeared to be heavily involved while the rest were not: and there were few in between.

For a sizable number, one or more activity continued throughout their lifetimes. Men kept on with gardening and home maintenance as well as with hobbies like woodwork. Women kept on knitting. About a dozen were still playing tennis at the time of interview. Part of its attraction beyond the socialising was relative cheapness because it did not involve buying a meal although there might be a post-match coffee. As bodies 'gave out' and knees 'went', a handful of former tennis players moved on to golf or bowls. After having a heart attack Edward (aged 79) gave up golf *because I couldn't do 18 holes*. Then once his wife retired, they both took up lawn bowls together and found it to be a *tremendous game*. Even though Ruth was playing golf three times a week, she said that she missed *the social life* of tennis. Then when their bodies could not withstand the demands of golf or if they did not like to drive long distances (necessary to transport golf clubs), they walked daily to stay fit.

Many said how they preferred to walk over using the car, and that they felt unhappy when they could no longer walk long distances. For them, walking was an ongoing expression of independence, while for others it was a social affair. About half of the sample walked around their neighbourhoods either alone or with their spouse, and when visiting a holiday shack or caravan they would go on long hikes with one or more family members as part of the overall holiday experience. Others belonged to walking groups organised by clubs such as Probus. Some of the walking groups would take trains to country towns, so as to *really make a day's outing*. Their explanations resonated with other findings that while older people may initially be motivated to walk by individual health concerns, the pleasure of being in organised walking groups mattered for continued participation (Copelton 2010). Several joined church-sponsored or YWCA exercise groups, like the Prime Groovers, in order to do *exercise in company* (Alison), and a number augmented social exercise routines with home-based exercises suggested by a health practitioner.

A New Zealand study of people over 70 years sheds some light on a possible motivating factor for being physically active: most participants held a belief that for their older body to maintain a good level of functional ability, it must be a *busy* body (Grant 2008). In this sense, pervasive cultural understandings of health and activity are critical to behaviour, as are individual capacities to adjust to new cultural norms: from growing up at a time when older people were told to take it easy (Grant 2008) to the current refrain of use it, or lose it. A majority of our study participants appear to have made the successful transition to stay active, while about a quarter have resisted adopting a view that it's time to slow down. The remainder expressed frustration that physical health is now limiting their activities.

5.3 Baby Boomers: The Sandwich Generation

5.3.1 The Childhood Years: 1950s–1970s

When the Baby Boomers were growing up, there were more continuities than discontinuities in the activity environments that prevailed pre- and post- World War II. From the 1950s onwards, neither the increasing access to a car nor the advent of television appeared to dramatically change the nature and extent of physical activity by young Baby Boomers. The car certainly did not alter how they got to school, with bike-riding, walking and public transport being the norm.

The Baby Boomers described a childhood that was remarkably similar to their parents, one that they experienced as carefree and involving a lot of time spent outdoors. They had unstructured playtime, and they could 'muck around' with other kids and explore their local area without adult supervision. A number talked about living in rural or semi-rural areas, and suburbs which still had nearby paddocks, creeks and green spaces. Peter explained:

> *You'd jump on the push bike and go around to a mate's place and go for a ride here or there. Go down the creek yabbying and all that sort of rural pursuits really because it wasn't as heavily built up as it is here.*

Their after-school activities also contain strong echoes of their parents' accounts of *making your own fun* (Stephen) and *neighbourhood play. You didn't actually go anywhere* (Leanne). From Carol we heard that spare time was spent

> *Mostly around home. I think I had a couple of girlfriends just around the street that I went to school with and so my spare time was more going to their house .... But there was a bit of tennis, things like that and I was a bit of a tom boy because there weren't many girls in our street .... You know I'd be playing marbles and things like that with the boys, or we'd play monopoly ....*

In these respects—simple home and neighbourhood, low-cost entertainments and self-initiated activities—Baby Boomers regularly reflected that they saw their childhood as being quite different to their own children's. As Leanne put it, *It was just more low key* and Carol reflected, *Really unsophisticated life compared to what the kids get up to these days.* Elizabeth expressed it as:

> *We had a sort of fairly basic childhood, there's wasn't a lot of money but that was the norm but we had lots of fun and life was fairly free, we would just go out and mum would say come home when the street lights are on and we would come home. There wasn't the threat of bad people in the community .... You'd never say to your parents, can you take me here or can I have some money. It was all very low cost and self sufficient.*

5.3.1.1 The Consolidation of Organised Sports

One incremental change involved education departments emphasising the importance of all children participating in team-based sports, with British sports continuing to dominate Baby Boomer childhoods. Stephen recalled:

> *I've got to say there wasn't many [organised clubs or sporting groups] around in those days ....or we didn't have access to it. The only sports or team sports we played was at school ... just football and cricket. None of the soccers or anything like that.*

As with the Lucky Generation, Baby Boomer girls played a different and narrower range of school sports to boys: netball, tennis and hockey if they attended private school and little athletics featured if they did not. This was despite a view promoted by a range of groups and movements in Australia from the 1960s onwards that 'female weakness' should not prevent women from competing in male-dominated sports (Vamplew 1994), and despite an increase in access to sports competitions for women organised at the regional, state and national levels (Howell and Howell 1987).

For boys and girls alike, though, church youth groups provided sporting opportunities and, compared to their parents' generation, we heard more references to Scouts, Brownies and Girl Guides. Laura's account was quite typical.

> *I was in the Girl Guides for 10 years. Brownies, Girl Guides, Rangers. And I played netball for a couple of years as well. .... I remember being in a church group when I was very young but not for long, we are not religious.*

Some did numerous activities, including Peter who said:

I was very much involved in scouting and the church youth group and the tennis team. .... Cubs started at age 8 and then it was scouting. Tennis probably came in about age 15, and I did judo from about that time. But from the 10–15, it was bikes and billy-carts.

Respondents proffered accounts of participating in organised clubs and church groups in answer to our question regarding 'hobbies'. There were fewer references to more solitary pasttimes undertaken by the Lucky Generation, like knitting and building things. However along with their parents, children listened to radio serials and read a lot. Carol told us:

We had homework to do during the week and in those days, with radio, lots of kids liked listening to the serials on the radio. Yeah so it sounds very simple now. And we did, you know, lots of reading as well—much more reading I think pre-TV.

5.3.1.2 The Advent of TV

Television arrived in Australia in 1956, in time to allow Australians around the country to view the 1957 Melbourne Olympics Games (Lees and Senyard 1987).

This new form of mass entertainment reorganised the living room, centring it around the television set (Timms 2008). It also acted as both a new product and a powerful advertising medium, opening up new possibilities for sports spectatorship (Parker and Paddick 1990) and targeting marketing to the primary household consumer, women (Lees and Senyard 1987). Despite initially being expensive at £200 they proved popular (Lees and Senyard 1987) and television set ownership reached 55–60% in Sydney after only 3 years (Campbell and Keogh 1962; Frey and Eitzen 1991).

Like the radio, television provided a cheap form of entertainment for families who were still struggling financially despite the increasingly affluent times. Similar to the cinema, it offered a form of escapism. Michelle's recollection resembles those of the Lucky Generation, except TV has replaced radio.

Ours was a working-class family so there wasn't a lot of spare cash around. I suppose I spent a lot of time watching television. ... There wasn't money for hobbies or sports—we weren't a particularly sporting family. I think mainly family events and watching television. My family were great card players and, you know, we got together and we played games like charades—not on a really regular basis, but Christmas and that sort of stuff when you get together as a family and do that sort of thing.

The effect of television on both physical activity levels and food consumption has been a major element in recent debates over the causes of obesity. However, concerns over the impact of television have been expressed since its inception. The report *Television and the Australian adolescent: a Sydney survey* highlights how Australians were already worried about its effects on adolescent leisure activities, family relations, neighbourhood relations (Campbell and Keogh 1962). Interestingly,

Table 5.1 The sporting binary

Sport as play	Competitive sport
Lucid, playful activity pursued for its own sake	Used for extrinsic purposes
Entry & exit free, voluntary; rules emergent & temporary; fantasy permitted, result uncertain. Outcome no serious impact beyond activity. No formal organisation	Rules formal, enforced by official regulatory bodies; outcome impacts on individuals and organisations not actually participating; winning valued above participating
Control with player/participant	Control with manager and audience
Morality and ennoblement, play	Spectacle and entertainment, display
Playing skill important	Attracting spectators & media sponsorship; profit & market important
Principles of play and enjoyment guide sport	Ethics of business and the corporate world guide sport

(Adapted from Frey and Eitzen 1991).

the Lucky Generation did not seem to reflect critically on the role of TV in the lives of their own children, but we heard often from the Baby Boomer parents about their concerns regarding the impact that TV and other screen-based activities was having on the sedentary behaviours of Gen Y.

For Baby Boomer teenagers, television's significance related less to its contribution to hours spent in passive entertainment and more to its role in consolidating the transition between sport as play and sport as competition. According to Frey and Eitzen (1991), twentieth century American society could be interpreted through a sociology of sport lens as comprising two eras separated by the introduction of television. They juxtaposed the eras in the following way (Table 5.1).

Parallels have been documented for Australia (Dixon and Winter 2007). In our interviews we began to hear the phrase representative cricket or football or other sports, even when Baby Boomers were describing their early secondary school years. This notion of playing for your school, state or country is integral to competitive sport.

In terms of the allure of spectator sports, Baby Boomers inherited a love of following a football team from their parents; and like the Lucky Generation they delighted in talking about attending football games with their parents. It was quite common for fathers to induct their sons into club-based football because fathers would move from playing into coaching and umpiring roles as part of their service to the school or community.

5.3.1.3 Rising Parental Involvement

A few Baby Boomers described how their parents became involved in their sporting and leisure activities as they got to secondary school. This may have been due to changes in parenting styles that promoted children's participation in organised activities as increasingly important for their development. It also could be attributed to the televised Melbourne Olympic Games, which positioned Australia as a successful modern sporting nation, and where great pride was attached to competing at elite levels.

However, it was rare for Baby Boomers to be negative about their parents' engagement, in contrast to how some Gen Y participants criticised close parental supervision of their sporting activities. Baby Boomer Lisa described having both a sense of freedom and parental involvement in her leisure time while she was growing up:

> *Mum and dad did president and secretary for the swimming club so we did a lot of swimming. I trained until about 14 at 6 o'clock in the morning a couple of days a week until I didn't want to do it anymore. .... Mum and Dad were involved in everything we did pretty much.... So I think our childhood was on one hand structured with that sort of stuff that mum and dad organised like swimming and Brownies or whatever we were in....in that you could be out doing stuff with a whole pack of kids under very little adult supervision.*

5.3.2 *Bringing Up the Children and to the Present Pre-retirement Years: 1980s to Mid-2000s*

There were two defining physical activity trends as the Baby Boomers were entering the workforce in the 1970s. One related to a decline in occupations that required physical exertion or relatively high levels of incidental activity that accompanied jobs (like storemen). The second was the rise in body consciousness that had emerged for a range of reasons in the 1960s and 1970s, and was rapidly commodified by the fitness industries. They were countervailing forces: having to pay to become fit in order to counteract the creeping sedentariness of everyday life (see Chap. 6), whether in paid employment or through the use of labour-saving devices, including the car (see Chaps. 7 and 8).

5.3.2.1 Team Sports Give Way to Individualised Gym Routines

Most Baby Boomers described playing team sports after they finished secondary school until when they began to have children. Popular sports were netball and swimming for women and football and cricket for men. Some gave up exercise altogether when children arrived, while others used the child minding services of gyms to continue to exercise.

Women also reflected how they successfully negotiated child care responsibilities and physical activity. Catherine explained how she manages:

> *I love playing netball. I love taking the exercise classes. ... I play netball at a time that suits the family rather than suits me. So you work it into the family. The walking with the dog has to fit in with the work commitments. So we usually go first thing in the morning. So it has to work around the daily routine and it has to be something you enjoy doing.*

Some also took advantage of their growing children's exercise routines to play sport as a family, although supporting their children's activities was more likely to rob parents of exercise opportunities as the quotes below indicate. Leanne explained that the:

children... did Cubs, Scouts, Guides... tennis, we were involved in the tennis club because they were playing tennis at that stage. And school activities. ... Oh and my daughter did ballet.... And their tennis became very time consuming and they would have coaching two or three nights a week, play every Saturday. They played juniors Saturday mornings and while they were younger they also played seniors on the same day. And we also played seniors so sometime we were on the same teams together. And as they got better they would play tournaments. So that would have involved going away to country towns for the week-end. So that just took up all our spare time.

A recurrent rationale was 'giving the children opportunities'. Peter summarised it as follows: *But we basically committed a 20 year slab to the kids—which I have no regret about as they have all grown up quite adjusted and we are proud of the three of them.*

Having sport injuries was a common refrain, especially in relation to the gym and team sports. The anecdotes are supported by survey evidence from the middle 1990s (see Table 5.2) when many of our Baby Boomers were heavily involved in both. Although the most common reason given was lack of time, nearly 21% of survey respondents said they stopped playing sport because of a sports-related injury.

Common scenarios involved bursts of activity or dipping in and out of different activities. For Denise:

Since my mid 20s I've always had something going on. Whether it's teaming up with some-one and going for walks or doing some sort of yoga or squash. But it just tends to peter off after 12 months. Then usually you pick something else up 12 months later but.... it's often not the same thing. ...Like with yoga I've kind of been doing it off and on again for 5–10 years. And in the last year my exercise has dropped off absolutely completely.

However for a few (more in keeping with the Lucky Generation), the same activ-ities lasted years as in Michelle's case:

I swam for many years. Even when I was separated I would drop my daughter off before school program at 6.30 or something and go swimming three times a week before work and kept that up. Really I was very determined to keep it up as one of the stable things in my life...I did continue it for a long time and then I think I just got more and more unwell and couldn't sort of fit it in with everything else and so I let it lapse. And I started going to the

Table 5.2 Main reason for discontinuing organised sport, 1996–1997

Reason	Men (%)	Women (%)
No time/too busy	30.9	23.7
Injury/health problems	20.7	20.8
Moved away from club	13.9	8.6
Lost interest	10.3	10.2
Too expensive	6.8	10.7
Change in employment	3.8	2.7
Child care problems	0.5	3.5
Other/don't know	13.2	19.7
Total discontinuing sport	9.090.000 1.8 million	9.037.000

Australian Bureau of Statistics (1999)

gym—I think I was still swimming at the time when I started going to the gym and couldn't fit both in so I started to use the gym rather than swimming.

Gym-based activities were often described as displacing team-based activities because of their flexibility. They allowed people to schedule physical exercise around other daily and weekly activities. This theme is elaborated in the following chapter.

5.3.2.2 Community Involvement

As their children were growing up, our Baby Boomer respondents typically became active in one or more community services. The Church figures strongly as does fundraising for different organisations like the Country Fire Authority, Royal Flying Doctors Service or major service clubs. From Peter we heard:

I've been very community orientated. I am a life member of Apex, I am a foundation member of the State Emergency Services unit, I served in the Army Reserves for a number of years and ... I am still in the Masons Lodge doing community work.

There were a few whose activities straddled volunteering and a passionate hobby. Sandra described:

Now I volunteer at Birds Australia, mostly office volunteer work—stuffing things into boxes and things like that...and you get involved in the research. Putting out the traps at night and going around in the morning and seeing what we have caught. Or going around plots of marked out ground and seeing what is growing. And going with ornithologists and seeing what birds are there.

Carol exemplifies a person who has assumed care responsibilities for her parents as well as extensive community involvements. She helps out at:

the mother's club, assisting with the catering for weddings in the community and all that kind of thing, involvement in the church, participating in the services, you know, readings and all that stuff... and then, in recent years, when I finished my teaching career, that was in 2000,.... I got involved in voluntary work ... supporting families and I trained as a chaplain in the nursing hospital which was very interesting and personally fulfilling sort of work and then my last two years I've been working as a community support person—community carer... And of course recently I've been involved with supporting my ageing parents. I mean they are very active for their age, 82 and 83, but they can't keep going forever and they like the contact.

The decline in older forms of incidental activity—household provisioning, active transport and physically demanding occupations—contributes to Baby Boomers feeling under pressure to schedule physical activities into already busy lives.

Sandra described the benefits of having a car: *I was driving people, taking them shopping. That was [for the] Multiple Sclerosis Society*. While the Lucky Generation also used the car for community outreach purposes in their senior years, the Baby Boomers express a deep commitment to investing time and energy in family times up and down the generations—earning them the nickname of the squeezed sandwich generation—and also to supporting community endeavours.

5.4 Generation Y: Perform Hard and 'Hang Out'

5.4.1 The Childhood Years: 1980–1990s

For Gen Y as children, play, sport and leisure consisted largely of organised activities based at schools and clubs, and sedentary forms of home-based leisure. Compared to the Lucky Generation and Baby Boomers, unstructured play with other children appears less common. When asked what out-of-school activities her children were involved in, Baby Boomer Deborah replied:

> *Well at the moment they are both at gymnastics two hours a week. They play tennis for half and hour. That is all. .... see their life is much more structured, than ours. To have someone come over and play with them, you have to know what child does what... so that you can line up your child with their child to monitor their play. Very tricky.*

A reliance on home-based settings for play appears as strongly with this generation as it did with the Lucky Generation, but for different reasons. Instead of lack of affluence and limited alternatives being the underlying forces to physical activity, other factors were at work during the 1980s and 1990s: a parenting style oriented to supervised childhood development (Banwell et al. 2010); rising fear for children's safety playing on the streets due to stranger danger and traffic (Timperio et al. 2004); and an increase in the number of forms of technology-based leisure available in the home (such as TV, PCs, video games etc.). By their very nature, and compared to constructing playthings from the garden, shed or house, they can encourage a more sedentary way of being.

The last quarter of the twentieth century saw a huge proliferation in screen-based products. By 1985, 93% of households owned a colour television; by 1997, 99% of Australian households owned at least one television while 56% had more than one, 82% had a VCR, 36% had a personal computer, and 11.6% had internet access (Australian Bureau of Statistics 2001). With all of this technology available, it is not surprising that in 1997, the Australian Bureau of Statistics reported on Australia's preferred leisure pursuits as watching TV, talking, socializing, listening to the radio and reading. In the late 1990s, almost half of the estimated five free hours of daily leisure was spent on watching TV and videos (Australian Bureau of Statistics 1999).

The presence of numerous technologies for amusement and entertainment was indicated by the multiple remote controls in households. When asked how many remote controls they had in the house Sarah said:

> *I've probably got four, but the household has probably got like eight. Crazy, because I've got air conditioning, TV, VCR, DVD, a high definition thing and I've got my own bloody surround sound and stuff so it's probably more close to 20.*

The Baby Boomers described monitoring their children's television viewing, and sometimes went on to reflect on their parenting abilities. For example Karen mentioned *My kids watch far too much TV. .... slack mother—watch TV! And now they are in their 20s. Yes they watch far too much TV.* John talked about how he and his wife regulated their son's television:

> *... we have a diary for how much TV is allowed. For my son, if he could, he'd sit there for ages so we have a daily limit on how much TV is allowable. .... he works hard at school and he does all his sport and he comes home and he just flakes and that flaking occurs on his favourite chair in front of the television so we don't mind him having a bit of time to do that but he also has to know there are limits.*

Gen Y described varying levels of television watching. For example David, who characterised himself as being quite 'sporty', said he was not interested in TV or computer games when growing up:

> *We weren't restricted on how much we could watch, but because we were always doing so much sport and there were three of us boys, we didn't watch a hell of a lot of TV anyway. Myself and my brother, if we weren't at soccer training or athletics training it would be outside kicking a ball, playing basketball. We just didn't watch much TV so never really had to have restrictions placed on us.*

When asked about computer games, David said *I've never been into that. None of us really have been.* In contrast, Adam described more regular use of TV and the internet especially in colder weather. During primary school he used to *come home, watch TV and then I used to do stuff, in the summer like, I'd play cricket at my friends.... and then winter when you're cooped up we'd watch TV.*

5.4.2 The Teenage and Early Adult Years: 1990s to Mid-2000s

5.4.2.1 Screen-Based Activities

As Gen Y entered their teenage and early adult years, their parents observed relatively greater use of technologies, such as computers, compared to previous generations. Peter believed that:

> *All of [my children] would be lost without laptops. They would be lost without mobile phones. They also have play stations or X-box type things for playing car races together.*

Karen noted differences among her children:

> *My youngest one gets on the internet a lot. But [my other child] isn't interested in computers as all. .... [My youngest child] pays for it and it's in his room so I am not really privy to it. But I think he spends a lot of time chatting [online].*

It was not simply the presence of the technologies but their use that changed approaches to everyday life as Baby Boomer Denise observed:

> *Well I mean I suppose things like mobile phones and that it's just opening up a whole lot of new possibilities and that's very different to when we just had the black phone that you picked up. So that phone technology and that connectedness is very different. ...I mean I've seen one of them with the laptop, the Xbox and the TV on a different program so you know it's just that's sort of quite different the multitasking I think.*

Moreover, the trends are not uniform even within families, with Lucky Generation Shirley describing different predispositions among her grandchildren:

My grandson, for some reason or other, is not—he seems to be more into playing the games. He's got to be dragged off the PlayStation or the Nintendo or the computer games. He doesn't get out much and play with the mob. Bit of a loner.... Likes reading. Ashley is definitely the outdoor—she's the athletic type, she plays basketball, she plays netball, she plays cricket in the season and she swims, and does well at whatever she takes on... He's more the indoor type.

We discuss intra-familial differences further in Chap. 9.

5.4.2.2 Parental Support for Extensive and Intensive Involvement in Sport

Typically, from starting school at 5 years of age, all respondents nominated one or more sporting activities that they were involved in until the senior years at school. Athletics and calisthenics were the most common primary school activities, with hockey, basketball and netball beginning in high school. One respondent reported body image issues as making her hate sport, but then (as we report in the next chapter) she took up social dancing.

Since the 1980s, Australian children's lives have been described as increasingly busy and highly structured, with after-school activities, including organised sports, leaving precious little 'free' time. However, between 1985 and 1997, when Gen Y was growing up, the National Health and Fitness Survey showed that the proportion of boys aged 10–13 years who participated in at least one sport declined from 87–76% and for girls the decline was 80–71%. The same survey results also indicated that these children had observed a drop-off in sporting participation by their parents. There could be a link between the two results, given the reported role of family members as sporting role models (Martin et al. 2005).

Indeed among our respondents, involvement in sports and exercise varied considerably between participants as they left school. Five out of 12 respondents had been or were still participating at elite levels, while two were not doing any sporting activity or gym exercise. Andrew said he walked as part of daily routines for exercise, contrasting himself to his brother who was 'sport-mad'. The other told how he rode his bike as a child and continues to do so.

While acknowledging a biased sample, our interviews reveal that those who engage with sport in their teenage years and beyond do so with quite extraordinary vigour. They are driven to excel in order to compete at the highest levels. Unlike the more egalitarian impulse emerging around leisure activities a century ago, the emphasis on winning and excelling at sport sets up new social distinctions based on a performative body.

Elite or competitive sports generally entailed heavy contributions in the form of financial and practical parental support. Sarah described swimming at age one. Under the influence of her parents, she then proceeded to do Tae Kwon Do for 9 years until she was 15. She had lessons three times a week after school, competitions were on the weekend and grading would occur once a term. Over the same years, she did calisthenics on alternative days. Calisthenics involved five competitions a year. *I always wanted to do dancing and my mum did calisthenics when she was little so I got into that.*

Generation Y spoke of themselves as either 'sporty' or 'not sporty', with the former group describing how they spent hours disciplining their bodies through training so that they could compete at national or even international level. Reports of numerous and repeated sport-related injuries were noteworthy. One of the more extreme accounts of injuries came from David who had aspired to becoming a professional athlete.

> *From age five I was doing athletics and stuff like that.... I had some serious injuries through sport that put me out of action for that part of my life ... That was around age 17 and 18... A stress facture in my back, two stress fractures in my shins and hamstrings, tearing my hamstrings. I was riddled with injuries, because I used to do a lot of sport... I just had to take some time out and my world got busy and I didn't get back to it.*

This young man described the arduous routines in high school:

> *[At 17] I was competing in the under 21 world championships and from there that's when my injuries went from worse to worse. I was training about 10 times a week at that stage and I was only doing three subjects [at school] so that I could commit more time to my sports. Soccer finished up at age 15, because it got too hard with pre-season athletics and so they were overlapping, but I was playing for the Victorian soccer team at the time as well. So I had to choose. It was getting to a level where I couldn't realistically do both..... Athletics was something that I just loved doing for the thrill of it all, to being a real job, constant physiotherapy just to maintain my body to try and continue competing, ... and it became more of a chore. I lost the thrill out of it when all I was trying to do was keep my body up to scratch. So by the time I left I was disgruntled.*

The story was more positive for Nicole, a hockey player at state level in Victoria, who continued to play and to coach.

> *[Before starting under 16 hockey for a top league], I played netball and I did athletics. I think I did athletics since I was probably 9 or 10 till about 13. Then I played netball. ... I started hockey while I was doing netball and sort of had to decide whether I would continue with the netball or just continue with the hockey.*

She was driven in her pursuit of excellence in all sports that she joined, as illustrated by her account of running professionally over the summer to keep fit for the other sports. Other aspirant professional sportsmen and women had jobs (nursing, restaurant waiting and shop assistant) that entailed being on their feet all day, which they viewed as part of their training regimen.

Generally the 'sporty' interviewees would have more than one sport at which they excelled, and the training schedules were onerous. Sports training often entailed also gym work-outs to keep fit.

There were numerous references to Baby Boomers watching their offspring play competitive and elite sports, and travelling overseas to support them if playing at the national level. The stories we heard from the Baby Boomer and Gen Y respondents revealed how hard they worked to combine family times with sports and exercise. Our material also supports the findings of another qualitative study conducted in Melbourne with four families. In that study, family leisure time was underpinned by two discursive undercurrents: the dedicated pursuit of health, and calculations of risk and benefit around both health and personal safety (Fullagar and Harrington 2009). The findings indicated how family leisure has become 'purposive leisure'; a term which can be usefully applied to our Baby Boomer and Gen Y respondents in contrast to the Lucky Generation, for whom leisure was being around the house together in an unstructured way or going on a very occasional social or entertainment outing.

5.4.2.3 'Hanging Out' with Friends

As only one Gen Y had a child and their main responsibility was to themselves, Gen Y did not express the same difficulties in maintaining exercise as the Baby Boomers. Additionally, half were still studying and living at home with their parents. However, Gen Y still described being busy, which was often due to taking part in sports and maintaining study, socializing and part-time work.

For GenY, unstructured sport had been replaced by competitive team sports which were considered laborious, and akin to study and paid employment. For this generation, leisure and entertainment involve pursuits in which you don't push yourself physically. This means meeting up with friends, going to the 'pub', or simply *hanging out* at home. They described little in the way of hobbies (exceptions being playing a musical instrument or tinkering with racing cars) or community involvement: life seemed to oscillate for the majority between pushing themselves in sport, study and paid employment. There were numerous references to the toll that shift work takes and *doing nothing* becomes the way of balancing the demands of working life and study.

The elite sportspeople rarely went out with friends or had a social life. Gen Y reported a schism between socialising and their physical activities, which centre mainly on competitive team sports or individually oriented self-improvement activities in the gym. Performativity is crowding out pleasure. Hockey player Nicole quoted above explained:

> *I go out with my friends sometimes, movies, just out to a club. Yeah that's pretty much it.... but I don't have much time for much else with all that. And work, and the work, my shifts are all over the place so it's hard to....Yeah it was really hard to get used to doing the shifts. It nearly took a year a half before I actually started getting into that and I still get very tired after doing like a 2 o'clock to 10 o'clock a night and then having to get up for a 7 o'clock in the morning ... get about 5 hours sleep so. And then I go straight to hockey some nights after the then don't get home until 9.30, 10 so yeah. It does get really tiring but...*

The young men said their bodies could not handle the drinking that went with going out with friends, so they rarely did this, preferring quiet Saturday nights and evenings with their families. Perhaps due to the lack of social activity, the Gen Y accounts did not resonate with the sense of enjoyment at recalling leisure time as did the accounts of the Lucky Generation. Indeed, there was a resigned air in many of the accounts of social life: one man reflected he had to be physically active to have energy in reserve for socialising, but he was always too tired to become fit through exercise.

The practice of technology-based sedentary pursuits which sets Gen Y apart from their parents, and certainly their grandparents, allows this generation to stay in touch with one another through social networking when face-to-face friendships are hard to maintain given their multiple demands. Giving up elite sports seemed in the main to be a relief, not the least because it allows more social activity to be fitted in, and diminishes the constant time-consuming attention to injuries.

5.5 Conclusion: A Second Revolution Is Underway

What happened at the turn of the twentieth century was a freeing-up of leisure: there was both an increase in the time that could be devoted to not being in paid employment and the types of possibilities expanded significantly. In contrast to the comparative lack of positive affection/emotion that Lucky Generation members expressed for food and food occasions, they were highly positive about their physical activity over the lifecourse. Despite the relative absence of commercial entertainments and organised sports, the reported levels and mix of activities—sports, hobbies and leisure activities—undertaken by the Lucky Generation in their early and senior years is notable. The Lucky Generation combined entertainment with physical activity pursuits of a largely social nature: dancing, tennis, golf and walking groups. There were clear continuities with one or two pastimes that often spanned lifetimes, perhaps interrupted when their children were growing up. As the older generation aged however, they expressed increased anxiety around getting enough exercise. Exercise has become for them something one has to manage for the sake of one's health or for the wellbeing of a partner.

In 2005–2006, at around the time of our interviews, one third of Australian adults reported not participating in any sports or physical activity in the 12 months prior to being interviewed, while 29% reported regularly participating more than twice a week and 36% participated up to twice a week (Australian Bureau of Statistics 2007). This does not seem from our interviews to be by choice. Our Baby Boomer respondents in particular expressed frustration at not being able to maintain the exercise and leisure opportunities they had enjoyed during their younger years. The reasons for this are many, including paid work (see Chap. 8), but additional pressure comes from supporting their children to succeed in sport and other facets of their lives. Indeed, Baby Boomer parental involvement can add to a feeling of pressure by Gen Y to be engaged and successful in competitive sports.

For Gen Y, the highly organised and extrinsic nature (motivated by 'being the best' and selection for elite competition) of their sporting and preferred pastime involvements has had the effect of displacing leisure time spent on non-competitive activities like hobbies, and has also diluted associations between pleasure and being physically active. Social life is not as lived through being physical for the Baby Boomers or Gen Y, and there appears to be less enjoyment pulsing through their physical activity: it is hard work for the majority, and exercise is punctuated by sport and gym-induced injuries. At the turn of the twenty-first century, there is a sense that leisure time and opportunities have diminished. A state of leisure is confined for

Gen Y to *collapsing* in front of television, or socialising with friends over drinks or a meal.

This is a profound turn of events. If physical activity has lost its association with pleasure then it follows that younger generations may not sustain their activity routines, unless they obtain financial reward or fame from them. This situation has health consequences in light of the Lucky Generation and Baby Boomer accounts of weight gain once sport and active leisure pursuits ceased.

The following chapter lingers on social dancing and aerobics as a reflection of one of the more pronounced differences between the older and younger generations: the Lucky Generation's capacity to enjoy being physical through the entwining of social and physical activity, with fewer dilemmas about their bodies until illness (mainly heart disease for the men) and ageing-related wear and tear (for both men and women) set in. As with their appreciation for a rather simple diet, their valuing of sociable physical activity began when they were young and has been maintained.

Image 5.2 Girl playing on computer, New South Wales 2001 (Contributor: P. Gostelow. Source: National Library, Australia)

References

Adair, D., & Vamplew, W. (1997). *Sport in Australian history*. Melbourne: Oxford University Press.

Annear, M. J., Gildlow, B., & Cushman, G. (2009). Neighbourhood deprivation and older adults' preferences and perceptions of active leisure participation. *Annals of Leisure Research, 12*(2), 95–123.

Australian Bureau of Statistics. (1999). *Australian social trends, 1999: Recreation: How Australians use their free time*. Canberra: Australian Bureau of Statistics.

Australian Bureau of Statistics. (2001). *Australian social trends, 2001: Household amenities*. Canberra: Australian Bureau of Statistics.
Australian Bureau of Statistics. (2007). *Australian social trends, 2007: Participation in sports and physical recreation*. Canberra: Australian Bureau of Statistics.
Banwell, C., Dixon, J., Broom, D., & Davies, A. (2010). Habits of a lifetime: Family dining patterns over the lifecourse of older Australians. *Health Sociology Review, 19*(3), 343–355.
Campbell, W. J., & Keogh, R. (1962). *Television and the Australian adolescent: A Sydney survey*. Sydney: Angus and Robertson.
Coakley, J. (2008). *Sports in society: Issues and controversies in Australia and New Zealand*. North Ryde: McGraw-Hill.
Copelton, D. (2010). Output that counts: Pedometers, sociability and the contested terrain of older adult fitness walking. *Sociology of Health and illness, 32*(2), 304–318.
Dixon, J., & Winter, C. (2007). The environment of competing authorities. In J. Dixon & D. Broom (Eds.), *The seven deadly sins of obesity* (pp 126–147). Sydney: New South Wales Press.
Fabian, S., & Loh, M. (1980). *Children in Australia: An outline history*. Melbourne: Hyland House.
Frey, J. H., & Eitzen, D. S. (1991). Sport and society. *Annual Review of Sociology, 17*, 503–522.
Fullagar, S., & Harrington, M. A. (2009). Negotiating the policy imperative to be healthy: Australian family repertoires of risk, leisure, and healthy lifestyles. *Annals of Leisure Research, 12*(2), 155–171.
Grant, B. C. (2008). An insider's view on physical activity in later life. *Psychology of Sport and Exercise, 9*(6), 817–829.
Howell, R., & Howell, M. (1987). *A history of Australian sport*. Sydney: Shakespeare Head Press.
Kociumbas, J. (1997). *Australian childhood: A history*. Sydney: Allen & Unwin.
Lees, S., & Senyard, J. (1987). *The 1950s: How Australia became a modern society, and everyone got a house and car*. Melbourne: Hyland House.
Lewis, W., Baulderstone, S., & Bowan, J. (2006). *Events that shaped Australia*. Sydney: New Holland.
Martin, M., Dollman, J., Norton, K., & Robertson, I. (2005). A decrease in the association between physical activity patterns of Australian parents and their children; 1985–1997. *Journal of Science and Medicine in Health, 8*(1), 71–76.
Parker, S., & Paddick, R. (1990). *Leisure in Australia*. Melbourne: Longmann Cheshire.
Phillips, S. (nd). History of women in sport in Australia. http://www.activeaustralia.org/women/history/htm. Accessed 10 Mar 2010.
Porter, D. (1999). *Health civilization and the state*. Oxon: Routledge.
Timms, P. (2008). *Autralians at home since federation*. Carlton: Melbourne University Publishing.
Timperio, A., Crawford, D., Telford, A., & Salmon, J. (2004). Perceptions about the local neighborhood and walking and cycling among children. *Preventive medicine, 38*, 39–47.
Vamplew, W. (1994). Australian and sport. In W. Vamplew & B. Stoddart (Eds.), *Sport in Australia: A social history*. Melbourne: Cambridge University Press.
Whimpress, B. (1994). Australian football. In W. Vamplew & B. Stoddart (Eds.), *Sport in Australia: A social history*. Melbourne: Cambridge University Press.
Williams, M. (1985). *Australia in the 1930s*. Sydney: Trocadero Publishing.

Chapter 6
Fitness Marginalises Fun and Friendship

Image 6.1 Couple dancing, Melbourne circa 1940 (Source: State Library of Victoria)

C. Banwell et al., *Weight of Modernity: An Intergenerational Study of the Rise of Obesity*, DOI 10.1007/978-90-481-8957-1_6, © Springer Science+Business Media Dordrecht 2012

> Maybe I'm old-fashioned … I hope so … because I still feel that ballroom dancing in all styles is, dollar for dollar and mile for smile, the best exercise and social bargain yet devised (Essex 1968, p. 21).

Three qualities are said to underpin the leisure and sporting activities undertaken by older adults in Western nations: fun, friendship and fitness (Dionigi 2004; Grant 2001). For our Lucky Generation participants, the intertwining of physical activity with sociability is notable. The quote above from Russ Essex, an amateur dancer interviewed by the mass media in the 1960s, sums up the spirit towards physical activity amongst the Lucky Generation.

In this chapter we expand on our view that leisure and sporting activity have become progressively de-coupled from social activity over the last 50 years, with competitive activity and gym-based fitness coming to dominate the public imagination about what it means to be physical. This trend is exemplified by the different generations' descriptions of dancing and by the rise of gym-based activities, which this chapter describes in turn.

6.1 The Antecedents of Social and Competitive Dancing in Australia[1]

European forms of social dance arrived in Australia ten generations ago with the First Fleet of ships in 1770. According to Mrs Lilly Grove writing in 1895, "It is said that Captain Cook (who planted the English flag on Terra Australis) thought dancing was most useful to keep his men in good health during a voyage. When it was calm, and the sailors had consequently nothing to do, he made them dance—usually the hornpipe—to the sound of a fiddle, and to this he attributes much freedom from illness on his ship" (Andrews n.d., p. 17). Within two decades, the English royal family's appointed governors were organising balls featuring the waltz and Scottish reels. The following decades were a period of dance innovation, and Andrews reports that European styles were heavily influenced by another genre, folk dances, popular in country Australia. We see in Andrews' descriptions and elsewhere the physical strength and stamina required for dances, such as a "rollicking waltz" (Cannon 1973, p. 259). Not only was fitness required for the dancing which often went on until daybreak, but people's daily activities were physically arduous and some rode long distances to attend. Dance historians claim that the hybrid of European social dancing and folk dancing, newly popular in the cities, contributed to a more egalitarian ethos than in Europe.

Andrews (1997) maintains that after the 1850s Gold Rush, Melbourne became Australia's dancing capital, with numerous public dance halls being established there and throughout country Victoria. Writing in 1862, Clara Aspinall visiting from the

[1] Much of the material for this section comes from archival material located at the National Library, Canberra. Often the sources are personal notes and records kept by key individuals involved in the dance scene in Australia, and they are missing dates and page numbers.

UK noted about her time in Melbourne that "the ladies and gentlemen are the most indefatigable, and I believe the most accomplished, in the world. Dancing is the accomplishment which is most cultivated in the colony" (Andrews 1997, p. 184). In his detailed account of Australian daily life in the nineteenth century, historian Geoffrey Blainey (2003) reported on the importance of dancing to the lives of many urban and rural Australians who were the parents to our Lucky Generation. "Successful ballroom dancing" was seen as a "fast growing social asset" (Chowne n.d.).

By the early twentieth century, modern ballroom dancing had emerged in Europe and North America, and rapidly spread to Australia. In her account of life in Sydney at this time, Matthews (2005) argues that social dancing along with visits to the 'picture palaces' signalled a simultaneous embrace of both romance and modernity. She describes modern dance forms as an early manifestation of a flirtation with global culture: "[b]orn in Buenos Aries, developed in Paris, marketed from New York, mechanically produced in Hollywood, embraced in Sydney and danced everywhere, the tango became a sign of cosmopolitan modernity" (Matthews 2005, p. 4). Everywhere dance hall proprietors were assisted by Hollywood cinema, including Rudolph Valentino's rendition of the tango in the 1922 film 'The Four Horsemen of the Apocalypse', which garnered thousands of tango devotees.

According to Andrews (1979), World War I soldiers brought back dances they had learned overseas from the Americans, and The Charleston swept Melbourne from the late 1920s. The Grand Leggett's Ballroom of Melbourne was built in 1920, with nightly dancing continuing at this Melbourne institution until it was destroyed by fire in 1976. After Phil and Beryl Leggett saw a private screening of 'Flying Down to Rio' with Fred Astaire and Ginger Rogers, they copied the dance and introduced it in costume with "eight couples from the staff doing the Argentine Tango in formation … This made a wonderful spectacle and was filmed by Fox Movietone" (Leggett 1991, p. 52). They introduced new dances, giving annual exhibitions of the latest steps from London, such as the Modern Waltz, Quickstep, Slow Fox Trot and Tango. Teaching staff mingled with dancers while Phil explained the steps over the microphone, and "within 15 min everyone could do the latest steps from overseas" (Leggett 1991, p. 52).

The Leggetts, who taught dance in Melbourne for 50 years, organised dancing competitions, balls, novelty nights, exhibition dancing and floor shows (Leggett 1991). They included circus nights, magicians, a commercial carnival. For World War II troops, they held the Patriotic Ball, June, 1942. At this time they were teaching 50,000 people a year to dance. They held appeals for bushfires, donating all funds because they kept nothing "after expenses". Phil Leggett reports that he let people in for free or little. "I'd put on a gramophone and boys and girls could dance to that for nothing" (p. 27). During World War II, the ballroom was made free of charge to the Air Force.

Dance halls were present in major country towns too, and Colin Silk remembers that during the 1930s "People who were 70 when I was about eight or ten were excellent waltzers and masters of the Highland Schottisches, Mazurkas" (Silk and Silk n.d., p. 27). Free buses ran in and out of Bendigo town to the country balls two to eight miles out. As prosperity increased, debutante sets grew in appeal, and young people generally became more involved with ballroom dancing.

This condensed history of dancing indicates how accessible dancing was for many young people: physically, through a combination of public transport and the great spread of venues; socially, through the low cost involved and the free on-site tuition; and emotionally, through the cinema legitimising heterosexual romance being negotiated in the public dance hall. These were highly sociable and sensual occasions.

6.2 Dancing: Social or Competitive?

6.2.1 The Lucky Generation: "I Love It"

When our Lucky Generation participants recounted their memories of what constituted leisure times for their parents, they nominated dancing as well as movies (described in the previous chapter). They were often introduced to dancing by their parents. Joyce told us:

> *Mum was a very keen dancer and dad taught me to dance. I wasn't allowed to go to the public dances. I was allowed to go to social dances at dad's lodge and things like that, but I wasn't allowed to go to the Town Hall dances.*

Lucky Generation boys and girls started to attend dances as teenagers, which they viewed as both a hobby and leisure time activity. Especially for Catholic and Baptist children, ballroom dancing was something that parents felt was an acceptable form of mixed sex social activity. Edith remembered *Mum was pretty strict. I was only allowed to go to the church dances, not to the public dances. We would do that of a Saturday night or go to the pictures. It was one or the other.*

Private school participants attended dances organised between single sex schools, often on a Friday night. Dances were also put on by service clubs. Barbara described a soldier's camp where:

> *there was a dance on the Friday night, and of course the soldiers came in and they needed partners, so we would all just go in as a group of girls and never sit out a dance. It was sometime during that time, or just after that I met my husband ... and then we also went to dances and other things, as you do, as a couple.*

Barbara was not the only one to describe meeting her spouse at a dance. George remembered that:

> *... every church, every school had their social activities and they had dances, and we did it. We did a lot of dancing, ballroom dancing, 50/50 it was called, 50% old time, 50% modern, so we thought why not. And I enjoyed it, and [my wife] enjoyed it.*

So many of the descriptions were of cinema and dance—*that's what you did then*—echoing Matthews' (2005) argument that a modern citizen danced and went to the movies to participate in a romantic way of life.

Some travelled far and wide to attend dances, and the travel itself required physical exertion. Richard described:

> *I think I was just fifteen and from then on, yes I used to go off with the boys to dances and we used to .... probably an hours walk and dance all night and walk back. Then [my friend] and*

> *I used to go dancing twice a week, at least twice a week. We didn't think of the travel: from Preston, jump on a tram and go to St Kilda or Heidelberg. Big bands, very enjoyable.*

Edna mentioned catching the bus and train to Leggetts, *or to the Empire Ball, there used to be a little ballroom there and the floor was just beautiful. It was so slippery.*

Social dancing was heavily ritualised at one level, and yet it was multi-layered: with equal focus on the suppers, dress, and highly gendered and mating behaviours. Women were encouraged to display cooking prowess. For example, at Sadie Hawkins' Grove Ballroom in Malvern on Sunday night "the ladies" compete a bit "by bringing along sandwiches, cakes and savories" (Dando n.d.). UK magazine *Danceland* contained useful advice on husband-hunting in dancehalls: "Watch out, for instance, for 'the fellow who takes you home from a dance in his car and flies round corners and tears along streets at a mile a minute … [he's] often hiding intense hostile, aggressive feelings'" (Patton 1928). It provided insight into dance etiquette: "Good [tango] dancers have mastered their steps. This seems to apply to the man; the woman has simply to let herself be led while looking 'cool as a cucumber'" (Patton 1928, p. 4).

In a development highly pertinent to our Lucky Generation female participants, and one which was to challenge the idea that women should be cool and collected, the Women's League of Health and Beauty entered Australia from England in 1935. Operating for the next 40 years, the League's motto was 'Movement is Life', and it was aimed at business women and busy women with some independent income "to enable them to conserve and improve their physique. It started in the firm belief that pride of body is an essential foundation on which to build life and character" (cited in Matthews 1990, p. 25). Modern social dancing fitted the Women's League of Health and Beauty ethos well—"symmetry of the body was thought to reflect physiological—even spiritual fitness" (Matthews 1990, p. 25)—while still embodying widely accepted views of feminine characteristics: flexibility, grace and co-ordination (Vamplew 1994).

For some, dancing was addictive. Edna said:

> *I danced a lot. Nearly every night of the week and then the other two nights I went to the movies. [I did] ballroom and then jive and jitterbug and everything like that. I loved it …In fact I got up at my grandson's 21st and asked him if I could have a dance and he looked at me stunned and I got up and there is this modern dancing going on and they played a rock on and he said 'can you do this nanna' and I said 'oh yeah'. I'm spinning around.*

Like Edna, others were proud about mastering the temporal and spatial routines both when young and later in life. While the Lucky Generation often stopped dancing when they had children, for many dancing resumed in their 50s and 60s or they took up new forms of dance. Joy described her current dancing and activity routines:

> *I go line dancing. I go clogging, which is over-emphasised tapping … you know, with big taps on your shoes and making a big lot of noise to country music. I love it. And I belong to an entertainment group, so we're doing like movement all the time and we put on displays … I love the dancing, I really do. And I still walk… I walk everywhere I possibly can … It's for the exercise, yes. As I say, I haven't been back to tennis, I haven't been back to golf, or bike riding.*

For about a dozen, dancing remains important. Widower George told us: "*I'll walk into Camberwell and meet Debbie and have lunch and then do dancing for 2 or 3 hours, then I'll go dancing Wednesday night as well. … take out my ballroom dancing and take out going into the market and the kids, then I've got nothing*"

Like the early sports played in Australia, time spent dancing for the parents of the Lucky Generation continued links to Britain. However, 60 years later, there are Lucky Generation devotees for line dancing, swing, the South American salsa, tango and samba, alongside the more European-inspired two-step and fox-trot. Those who attend regularly become knowledgeable about the origins of their particular dance style, and in this sense the pursuit takes on the qualities of a hobby. Participants discussed dance history (both long-past and contemporary), key dance exponents and the best venues and 'occasions'. For example, George talked at length about

> *a distinctive difference between ballroom tango and Argentine tango. Tango started in the brothels .... It's a mixture of the native dance and the African-based. Because it's the pimp showing off the girl... and there's a love-hate relationship between the two of them and ... she wouldn't have any partner if they couldn't do the tango... They weren't interested. ... it was quite common for men to dance with men. ... So when ...the French and the English [discovered it],... they sanitised it because it was too risqué or what have you...*

Some noted that they danced when they travelled, and that the practice of well-defined dance styles provides a lingua franca, allowing people to move around (locally or internationally) and to 'fit-in' effortlessly with other dancers. The capacity to do the dancing is the only calling card necessary.

The dancers among our interviewees reasoned that dancing confers numerous health promoting advantages beyond physical activity: opportunities to get out of the house and for shared enjoyment; pleasure from being regarded as attractive to the opposite sex, especially in their old age; and a quiet self-confidence from experiencing mastery over activity that not everyone can do. The necessity for body-mind coordination has been described elsewhere by regular dancers. Winnie, 70, and her husband Arthur, 71, went dancing every Tuesday and Sunday night and every other Saturday during the 1980s at Sadies. "Dancing is the one thing Arthur and I both enjoy together. It makes you use the body, but if you take it up properly it also makes you use the brain". Winnie and Arthur started taking lessons at 45, with Winnie preferring the gracefulness of old-time dancing: "a sequence set to a chorus of music ... You not only use your feet, you use your whole body—the arms, legs, head, everything. If you do it properly, it's very good for deportment and gracefulness, and you get that lovely feeling that you are part of the music" (Dando n.d.).

Dancing was resumed in part to keep fit, but the social occasion was the major attraction. Lindsey explained:

> *when I retired my wife decided that I should socialise because I'm not a social animal and we took up dancing, So we now do ballroom dancing. That keeps me occupied at night time. [We go] on an average three times a week regularly. Occasionally we get a fourth session in about twice a month... it's a good three hours to four hours each night... I find if we don't keep dancing I get very stiff.*

For our widower respondents, taking up dancing appeared to be the equivalent of internet dating. Helen reflecting on her parents, said:

> *Well mum doesn't exercise. ... My parents separated probably 15 years ago and since then [dad] has had to make his own social life. So he took up ballroom dancing and golf. And he has given up the golf now but he still does the ballroom dancing. In the last few months he has gotten a bit less energetic but he is super fit. For an 82 year old you just wouldn't believe it.*

Within a context of obesity and diabetes prevention, the World Health Organization recommends that adults undertake a mix of moderate and vigorous exercise each day. This is easily achieved by men and women who participate in Modern and Latin American dance sequences (Blanksby and Reidy 1988). Moreover, there are numerous other self-reported health and wellbeing advantages of dancing for the over-60 age group. The conclusions from a UK study are amply supported by our study.

> [Social dance] can provide continuity within change. It offers an opportunity to be sociable and have fun in ways that both reflect, and avowedly move beyond, the dancers' teenage years. It promotes a welcome sense of a community spirit. It is a way of becoming visible and aesthetically pleasing, and it bestows a sense of worth and achievement in skills learnt through dancing. Last but not least, dancers can experience the joy of a fit and able body in both real and mythic senses (Cooper and Thomas 2002, p. 689).

To these benefits preventive health experts add bodily balance, flexibility and neuro-plasticity that accompanies having to coordinate multiple tasks. Gerontologists recommend that senior centres investigate the potential of tai chi and social dance as 'promising' to prevent fall-related disabilities (Judge 2003). Lay experts, in the form of dance teachers, are quick to add their views on the health benefits of dance. For example, Nena Pavey who runs a tap dancing school on the Gold Coast, Queensland, says that her 70 year-old pupils are "a lot stronger and healthier than most people their age, or even younger". She also notes that they "come out of their shell" and are less self-conscious about their bodies (Gilltrap 2004, p. 43). Many of her pupils grew up during the Depression and Second World War and had neither opportunity nor money for dance classes. The unofficial mascot of her school was Terri Kirkpatrick, aged 80, who did not begin dancing until "later in life". Now competing round the world, she practices every day: "If I die tomorrow, I'll die a happy woman" (Gilltrap 2004, p. 144).

6.2.2 The Baby Boomers: "It's a Little Bit Difficult to Fit in"

One magazine, *Australian Dancing Times (ADT)*, is a particularly rich repository of the influences on social dancing circulating during the 1960s when the Baby Boomers were in their teenage years.

Television began to play the role that cinema had played for their parents. For example, Carlu Carter became a well-known Channel 10 dancer and choreographer whose shows prefigured the current rash of TV dance shows. The reasoning behind TV adopting dance programs was simple: "It is always enjoyable to see ballroom dancing done" (ADT May 1967, p. 5). Watching dancing was more than a voyeuristic undertaking and could function as an inexpensive form of tutelage.

Augmenting the celebrity teacher was a rise in professionalism and a sense that teaching dancing was an industry like other educational domains. It was during the mid-1960s that the Country Ballroom Dancing Federation (Australia) advertised positions for professional dancing teachers to be based in "schools outside an area of 100 miles from any capital city … [providing] the opportunity for Professional Examinations and Amateur Medal Tests" (ADT October 1967, p. 30).

Contrary to the idea that dancing could simply be done for enjoyment, there was a new push that people needed recognition and awards, increasing the prominence of competitive dancing: illustrated by the St Kilda Palais de Danse deciding to present an 'Academy Award' to the person who had done the most for dancing the previous year (ADT July 1967, p. 6). These Australian developments were following in the wake of the international emergence of Dancesport, a term adopted to describe competitive ballroom dancing first broadcast on English television in 1960. Under the lobbying of the International Dancesport Federation, DanceSport became recognised by the International Olympics Federation in 1997 (see DanceSport Australia. http://www.dancesport.org.au/ Accessed 26.11.09); and like other Olympic sports it is subject to anti-doping laws.

As with organised physical activity more generally (see previous chapter), the Baby Boomers were introduced into dance as children through school, church and private tuition in after-school activity. Catherine explained:

> *I was doing ballet and tap dancing… from about age 4 or 5–12, and when I was about 16 I did ballroom dancing".*

As for their parents, church-run dances were important.

Carol described *Once I got to Bendigo I made a … couple of girlfriends and we played tennis. It wasn't sort of until a bit later that I started going to the Church dances and that sort of thing, because my parents were very strict about socialising with the boys, especially if they weren't a Catholic.*

Unlike many of the dance styles to have emerged in the last 40 years, which allowed individuals to move in unscripted ways without recourse to another person (only one Baby Boomer referred to attending discotheques), the dancing that our generations referred to in this chapter was highly orchestrated.

First shown on television in Australia in 2004, *Dancing with the Stars* was used as a reference point by three Boomers when describing the quality or standard of their dancing skills. It was also mentioned in a context of the competitive dancing that couples were doing. Catherine told us:

> *I met my husband through ballroom dancing and we started doing dancing together competitively… my husband was doing dancing before we met so he knew a lot of people in the dancing industry. And we used to go to places like a theatre restaurant, something that had entertainment and a meal. …. And we did lots of championships… Not quite up to Dancing with the Stars. But we won a couple of championships and we did that … probably for 5 years. And then it was just getting so expensive and we were trying to save for a house and everything like that so we gave it away then.*

The Baby Boomers inherited from their parents the phrase, "I loved dancing". We heard it frequently; and we also heard that as young adults fitness was secondary to the enjoyment. Judith summed up the dancing spirit of her cohort when she said:

> *when I was a younger adult, particularly with the dances I was involved in, it was more a social event. Dancing, I really enjoy it but it wasn't "I really need to get some exercise, oh let's go and do some dancing!" It was more "Oh I really enjoy dancing" and I just got the exercise.*

There were exponents of a large range of dance styles. Tap dancing was popular, and folk dancing and Morris dancing were also mentioned. More often than not, though, the love of dancing was in the past tense. This was the case for ardent devotees, like Judith who described how she had danced:

on and off over the years. I did a year of tap dancing about a decade ago. Mainly for getting fit. But I really enjoyed dancing but I just don't do much these days.

Occasionally, dancing had been displaced by gym-based exercise as is described in the second part of this chapter. However this is not always the case, as Margaret illustrated:

I do Scottish country dancing which is very nice.... No it's not a performance thing. The country dancing is different from highland dancing. It's sort of like community dancing so they have regular socials. The thing I go to on Tuesday night is a class and then they have socials where I guess people are more inclined to dress up and they don't explain the dances, they kind of expect that you already know how to do them so often it's more of a social occasion. ... I go to all the ones that Box Hill run which is three or four times a year but they tend to be on a Saturday night and [my husband's] not involved in it so I tend not to go too many ... But every fourth Tuesday is a social rather than a class and I always go to those.

As with their other activities, the Baby Boomers found it hard to continue dancing given the other demands on their time. Catherine expressed this rather poignantly:

We still love going out dancing socially .... for my 50th birthday mum ... said "here you go, now that you have turned 50 you can join the seniors tap dancing" and I said "you know what, I would really, really love to". But because it's in the city and the travelling backwards and forwards, and it's only on Saturday morning. So there are things you'd like to go back and do but it's a little bit difficult to go and fit it all in. So may be I'll wait until I am 60.

Baby Boomer mothers showed a keen interest in introducing their daughters to dancing, and wanted them to perform at a high standard. However, for similar reasons given by Gen Y in relation to dropping competitive sports (see previous chapter) they did not always meet the expectations. For example, Carol explained that her daughter:

worked at Safeway and she was an Irish dancer and, you know, her study and so on and so [she gave up]. She did very well. Like with the Irish dancing, she got to the National level and all that.

Other mothers were mindful of the competing pressures in their children's and their own lives. Patricia described how:

they are picked up from school and taken to a dancing lesson. And then they will go from dancing lesson to a quick meal and then they will be off to hockey or what ever. And then they will come home and they have homework. To me ..., once a week doesn't hurt, but everyday is quite strenuous. It's strenuous on the parents too.

Sharon recounted with pride how her children became competition ballroom dancers, but that the gowns were costly. Other Baby Boomers said that the cost of dancing was a deterrent to their own continued involvement, and yet this was not voiced by the Lucky Generation as a constraint for their generation. Certainly the archival material by the dance hall proprietors of the first half of the twentieth century reveals that they were only 'making costs'. They were running quasi- public services because they too enjoyed the substance of what they were doing. Theirs was a very different ethos to today's 'dance studios' located in large gym facilities, and run by fitness chain franchisees.

6.2.3 Gen Y: Dance as Televised Sport

By the time that Gen Y was growing up, what has been called the 'sportisation of pasttimes' was well and truly underway (see Table 5.1). According to Forsyth (2005), activities are transformed into sport through acquiring three features: extrinsic rewards/recognition by others; emphasis on winning; and bureaucratic oversight with technologies for enumerating and assessing progress and setting standards regarding drug use. Along with Dancesport, celebrity dancing of the 2000s shared these particular three features. Instead of Ginger Rogers and Fred Astaire who became famous for their dancing prowess, film and other celebrity figures could attract huge audiences for allowing themselves to be filmed learning how to dance, being ranked on their performance and subject to elimination.

According to the Australian government-supported AusDance peak body, dance as entertainment is extremely popular (Ausdance n.d.). In 2007, *Dancing with the Stars* Series 6 dominated the 20 Top Ten most watched programs. The popularity of these types of programs is further illustrated by figures showing that the 2008 premiere of *So You Think You Can Dance* was Channel Ten's highest rating summer premiere since rating agency OzTAM began collecting data in 2001. The 2008 finale was watched by over 1.8 million people, making its overall audience ranking that year at number 14. Two sporting events come in at numbers 1 and 2: The Beijing Olympics' Opening Ceremony (where dance was a major feature) and the AFL Grand Final. Perhaps ominously, a year later no dancing program appeared in the Top 20, with Master Chef rated number one.

However, young Australians are not simply watching dance performed by others. In 2005–2006, more than 330,000 children participated in organised dance activities outside of school hours, making dance a more popular activity for children than soccer or AFL (personal correspondence: Julie Dyson of AusDance). Our Gen Y females spoke of dancing, commencing in their school years, learning a mix of styles: Jazz, Latin and Irish, with the latter being the more popular.

In high school, Melissa was doing music, drama and Irish dancing.

> *I sort of got into it, you know, when Riverdance came out ..., and my dad [has] an Irish heritage and [he] was really keen to ...have some connection with that...He was so encouraging. ... he would take me to all the competitions ... I mean most of the other dancers had their mums there, but my dad was always there. ...So instead of a dancing mum, I had a dancing dad, which was really interesting... I used to... competitively dance, but when I hurt my foot a couple of years ago, I didn't get back into it because it was just, ah, too much pressure actually. Yeah, ... I used to compete in the states, in the nationals; and then we used to have to road trip ... to wherever we were competing, but the lead up to the actual big competitions was really, really intense...*

Melissa went onto tell us that when she stopped dancing, she became *really unfit, extremely unfit. When I stopped dancing was when I put on a fair bit of weight.*

Interest in dance has never wavered. The reasons for its popularity adapt themselves to the times, as they have since the 1800s. As has been the case from the early days, social dancers continue to be judged on numerous criteria: personal appearance, clothing, charisma, and knowledge of the routines. And while there has long been a competitive edge, what is new is the prominence of professional dancers who behave like any professional sports person. Thus it may not be sufficient for some parents and young people if dancing is undertaken for purely social and fitness reasons. Today's ballroom dancers have additional status and performance pressures courtesy of televised dance programs, modern dance touring companies and Olympics Games inclusion.

Melissa is the only Gen Y to continue to dance, having found a more relaxed and forgiving setting:

> *there's a few like mums of the little dancers, they come along just for a laugh and do fun stuff… I've sort of been getting back up to the level that I was at when I was competing and [the new teacher is] trying to keep the balance between pushing you to do more, to do better and not pressuring you…*

Her story resonates with the observation that: "the more outcomes take on importance in leisure and recreation, the less the importance of enjoyment" (Forsyth p. 129). This axiom certainly resonates through what has become of social dancing, and also the exercise regimen subscribed to by the Baby Boomers, namely aerobics.

6.3 Commodified Fitness: Gym-Based Aerobics

We have provided ample evidence here and the previous chapter to establish that by the end of the twentieth century, physical activity had become something that people had to schedule into their week in the form of 'exercise', and this had to be conducted in personal leisure time. Due to the disappearance of incidental exercise, what was required were 'labour making devices', often in the form of gyms or health clubs (Glassner 1989). This is the context for the post-1970s evolution of commercial fitness programs in Australia through gymnasiums, aerobics and yoga classes. This is evident in Australia and a range of OECD societies (Frew and McGillivray 2005; Glassner 1989; Sassatelli 2001).

The discourse of fitness is a defining feature of the Baby Boomer activity environment, one which has a hybrid progeny. The 1960s and 1970s were decades in which a host of critical social movements arose to challenge the shibboleths of modernity: the power of technology, the efficacy of modern medicine, the wisdom of modern lifestyles with attendant crises in cardiovascular disease and stress-related conditions. The critique of modern culture had a well documented effect of turning people's attention to self-help (Rader 1991), to individualise and tailor-make solutions, and to adopt what were considered 'alternative' to the mainstream approaches (Sassatelli 2001). At the same time as some fitness discourses could appeal to those eager to embrace social movement principles, other fitness discourses harkened to associations with long-established political philosophy, of Athenian democracy and personal liberation through demonstrations of moral fibre. These would have appealed to traditional middle-class values of self-control and self-determination (Sassatelli 2001). As Glassner (1989, p. 187) noted, "The consumer of fitness is working towards a 'mosaic of physical, emotional, economic and aesthetic transformations, a potpourri of ends-and-means". This characteristic makes it an ideal market-based commodity because its very ephemeral nature is mainly appreciated by, and affordable to, those with steady incomes. Furthermore, unlike many sports which seem to be located within a natural life stage—vigorous sports when young, gentler team-based sports and activities with age—fitness is a never-ending enterprise, and thus is an ideal commercial venture.

Indeed, industry was quickly responsive to the desire by large numbers of modern consumers to improve physically and grow spiritually (an aspiration that affected the culinary culture too), and the post-Fordist economy aimed its myriad and endless novelties to the 'worried well'. Pandering to the link between health and fitness at this time, a raft of commercial service providers emerged: health clubs, diet food manufacturers, vitamin shops, and health magazines. Commercial approaches to fitness were legitimised further by large corporations hiring other firms to provide employee fitness programs (Falkenberg 1987).

One of the most popular and enduring commercial activities to have emerged out of these social and economic conditions was aerobics. In the 1970s, the television with its advertisements and broadcasting of fitness programs, along with the rising household ownership of video recorder/players, were critical for popularising the commercial products and services that were springing up to help women in particular gain mastery over their bodies and life.

While aerobics was 'invented' by two women in the US, it only became a mass movement through movie celebrity Jane Fonda. By 1986, one-quarter of American participants were involved via aerobics videos, allowing young people and housebound women to implement an aerobic exercise program at home (Kegan and Morse 1988). With her movie persona, Fonda performed a similar duty to Ginger Rogers by entwining glamour with physical activity; further, she appealed to those concerned about ageing. Closer to this part of the world, and broadening the appeal to men, was New Zealand world aerobics champion Les Mills. Such exponents of fitness appeared in the mass consciousness at exactly the time that physical activity from incidental and sports-based activities had become problematic.

According to Brabazon (2000), aerobics is a mass participation activity, exercise and elite sport rolled into one. It had multiple origins—the gymnastic tradition, dance culture, martial arts, yoga and weight training. In the late 1970s and 1980s, it embraced choreography, and gyms installed mirrors leading to women usurping men in participation levels; and by the late 1990s, aerobics was second only to swimming as the most popular general participation sport for women in Australia. Some gendered analyses of aerobics have portrayed it as about narcissism, beauty and youth, but Brabazon argues that aerobics also contains narratives of strength, flexibility and competence, as well as positive social and political benefits. These include beneficial psychological outcomes from women spending time together in a non-competitive way. All sorts of women can meet, mingle, and talk; a 'new style women's club' (Matthews 1990, p. 102), much akin to the Women's League of Health and Beauty of the 1930s (introduced in the previous chapter).

The parallels with the League's philosophy is particularly striking when one considers the pedagogical function performed by aerobics, in that it teaches physical coordination, fitness, and how to combine individual and group goals. As the walls of the Fitness First chain of gyms pronounce, 'a strong mind starts with a fit body'. Arguably the League's philosophy also resonates with today's devotees of social dancing, and there are several nuanced parallels between modern social dancing and aerobics. Numerous commentators have observed, for example, that participating in aerobics and other active forms of exercise under the watchful eye of a teacher/trainer and others has robbed people of mastery over their time: they became ever more conscious of what could be achieved in a minute, an hour, a set of routines. Many who write on the fitness era comment about its many temporal dimensions, from slowing the ageing process ('stopping the biological clock') or at least sculpting a desirable ageing body (Kegan and Morse 1988), to paying for time to exercise (Sassatelli 2001), to acquiring physical capital in order to perform for longer periods whether in work or leisure (Frew and McGillivray 2005). For Brabazon (2000, p. 100), aerobics is a speedy way of getting fit: it is "the McDonalds of the fitness industry: fast, ubiquitous and cheap".

6.4 Baby Boomer and Gen Y Experience the Flexibility of the Gym

A few of The Lucky Generation described involvement in clubs, which ran gym-based exercises. Their participation appears to have taken place at both ends of the lifecourse: as teenagers and young mothers and then again in the senior years. The different phases of involvement carried different meanings: companionship was important at the young life stage while keeping fit became particularly important later on. Nevertheless, 'social exercising' was a consistent motivation.

Social exercise appeared as a motivator for young mother Baby Boomers too; and gyms often presented a most supportive opportunity for these women to get exercise beyond the minimal exertion involved in today's household duties. When taking children to sports, mothers could get involved in parallel activities organised for parents. Denise explained the chain of events: *At one stage when I took them swimming I'd do the aqua aerobics because it was on at the same time and it worked out.* She continued that she also *started pilates … before [my son] was born and did a prenatal pilates class. And then after he was born everything pretty much went to the dogs.*

Indeed it appears that one appeal of the gym is that it has always allowed Baby Boomers to dip in and out of exercise routines as everyday life circumstances dictate.

For Judith:

> *the gym is so more accessible because its flexible... I would really like to be doing regular dance classes but I just don't have the time to fit in. So it's time and opportunity...I've had a*

regular membership for a number of years [at the gym]. When I am travelling I will get there on the weekends.... Actually ... going in patches. Like, I've got a really good incentive at the moment. I am going on the holiday of a lifetime in January so I need to get reasonably fit.

A few Baby Boomers mentioned that the absence of social support in the form of child care or a dancing partner could be a barrier to ongoing participation. Gyms, on the other hand, often provide child care and they are venues where the individual is welcome. These combine with long opening hours and the many suburban facilities to make them relatively accessible.

As with team-based sports for the Baby Boomers, gym-based injuries are a recurring issue that interrupts exercise routines. For example, Michelle replaced swimming with the gym because she could not fit both in, but:

I injured my shoulder and so I think I stopped for a couple of years, but I've been back for a couple of years now....Go, three times a week now...do weights and bike. And my husband and I also walk every morning.

Family members had a marked influence on commencing particular activities as young and older adults. *My husband, at the time, was a fitness fanatic. He would nag me* (Michelle). And, ... *mum retired just before [my daughter] was born and she used to go to a Fabulous 50s class. And a few times I went along with her I thought this is fabulous* (Catherine). Such psychological pressure is possibly supported by the practical fact that many gyms offer family memberships with reduced joining and monthly fees if more than one person signs up.

Sometimes, there was a degree of obsessive behaviour in gym participation, and a few interviewees used the language of addiction to describe their involvement. Stephen elaborated:

Well [aerobics] really started out as necessity. I wanted to ski, if I wanted to ski well and enjoy it, I'm the first bloke on the mountain, I'm the last bloke off the mountain so you had to get fit to do that. If you wanted to go and catch waves and surf all day, we used to go out three to four times a day, you had to be fit so I've always just maintained that. I did it for so long it just gets to be the longest campaign of my life.

And Sharon explained her devotion in this way:

...yes, started with water aerobics and met a girl there, an older lady than me, we became competitive. And then I went to land aerobics and I became, not a gym junky, [but an aerobics junky] .... And until I got this job I used to go three to four times a week. ...I'd do aerobics and pump. I'd do like a step class and one of my other best friends does that, he was one of the instructors. .... Certainly became very health conscious when I turned 40. ... I do step 'cause it's contained, It's in an hour and you don't have to look beautiful. And pump 'cause it's all muscle toning work. So I try and do a mixture of pump and step. I think my aerobics instructors are really, really good.

For Sharon getting rid of fat influenced her beliefs about exercise. She had become highly regimented in her approach.

I've been doing pump now for over ten years and I have not really increased my weights and people say well that just silly. But the thing is I maintain my tone and fitness but to increase more I injured my shoulder and that's just silly. So I see people going really big weights and

I just laugh 'cause they are not using technique and they are certainly not doing it right. So you learn that through your instructors. So tomorrow I will do a double class because I haven't done anything for nearly a fortnight so you need to shock the body to start again to get you into that burning body calories.

For Gen Y, the issues are almost identical to their parents. Gym services afford flexible scheduling of exercise: an important attribute even for young people, when competing priorities from school work. A recent study of teenage girls in Melbourne found that time pressure was a major factor in their ceasing sporting involvement (Craike et al. 2009). When Sarah began studying for the High School leaving exam she dropped both her sports, and began at a gym to keep fit:

[it] was more flexible. I could go when ever I wanted to. I could go by myself, I could go with my aunty. It was sort of different. I was getting sick of Tae Kwon Do because I wasn't the best. ... the injuries just not good. And calisthenics I had been doing that for 10 years and I was getting sick of it. So it was something different, my aunty made me go because she is like a health Nazi. ... I joined her gym and started going with her 3–4 times a week.... oh she is horrible, she really is. ... she has always been like "you have to look fantastic. I look fantastic and I am 45".

Once again, we see the influence of a family member encouraging their favourite exercise pastimes. Rather than mass culture being the sole culprit in pushing particular body images, family members may be mediating cultural norms regarding what constitutes an aesthetically-pleasing body. In large epidemiology studies, the role of social networks comprising family members and friends has been associated with smoking and eating behaviours, and this same social contagion may also apply to physical activity. Social networks are considered to be agents of change through inducting members into new social norms which govern behaviours (Christakis and Fowler 2007, p. 370). Contact and friendship or familial ties have been described as important in the case of obesity because they "change...an ego's general perception of the social norms regarding the acceptability of obesity" (p. 378).

The main reason Jessica goes to the gym is because her friends go: *I don't really like to go by myself... I've got one gym friend in particular and a lot of the time that I go, will depend on her.* However, describing the gym as a space for friendship was exceptional; otherwise it was mainly about the pursuit of fitness, and even for Jessica, fitness was imperative if she was to keep up on physically demanding family holidays.

It is striking the extent to which social dancing and gym-based exercises are beginning to resemble one another. To remain relevant (and it certainly has), social dancing comes in myriad formats these days. Dancers can enter competitions but they can follow them keenly either online through the many dance style websites or they can travel several hundred kilometres to attend a dance congress in a football stadium. On these occasions, they can join a class or simply 'show-off' their prowess to thousands of other dancers without officials judging them. Equally, as with the early days of Jane Fonda aerobics videotapes, they can dance at home using the numerous dancing programs as free tutelage.

Likewise, aerobics has been heavily influenced by dance: choreographed movement to music. Routines, time-controlled movements, and exact mimicry are present. However, it departs from dancing in the degree to which social interaction is missing. Other people may be in close proximity but their behaviour has little bearing on the person nearby, except for informal competition trying to do better than the girl on your left. Interpersonal etiquette is not necessary (with the exception of flatulence) and in this respect aerobics might be experienced as more liberating.

Our research has led us to conclude that the rise of fitness regimens from the 1960s onwards means that becoming and staying fit has replaced the beneficial psychosocial and emotional states gained through leisure opportunities, which Mann (unpub) identifies in her Australian research on young people as being associated with the following qualities:

- the weekend, break-up the monotony of the norm: time for challenge through keeping things interesting and enjoying the end product
- maintain sanity, downtime, having own space, time, freedom
- relaxation, feeling fresh, feeling good
- enjoyment, having fun, happiness, time for social outlet

Generally, gym-based activities do not hold these qualities for our participants. Indeed GenY needed leisure times to recover from, or compensate for, their fitness training.

Gyms certainly do not share many features with the Women's League of Health and Beauty, available to Lucky Generation women. Matthews (1990) asserts that the League's exercise classes were characterised by "moments of escape, of autonomy, of excess, when women took pleasure in themselves, had fun". To be more precise, excess (in terms of workouts) is present in today's gyms, but the elements of autonomy and pleasure are always in the future and elusive (one contemporary gym wall slogan reads 'Go nowhere fast'); and if moments of escape are present, it can be assumed that the gym user is not working hard enough. While the manufacture of desire is omnipresent, it is not aimed at immediate gratification as much as at individual striving for what could be termed success-based health. Social dancing is becoming suffused with an elusive and future orientation too; and perhaps it will come to appeal more to those with a performative rather than a sociability ethos.

6.5 Conclusion

The qualities of fun and friendship, which were so integral to the leisure activities of the Lucky Generation, appear to have become less pronounced for Baby Boomers. For this generation, the flexible scheduling of fitness sandwiched between family and work commitments is becoming increasingly pertinent. Although some

Boomers did enjoy social dancing when younger, and saw the health aspects as secondary to the social benefits, they began to devote more time to individualised workouts in the gym as family and community commitments took over. Gym-based exercise appears from their accounts to be a more efficient and effective means of getting and staying fit.

In contrast to pursuing activities that bring pleasurable sociability (whether in leisure or as volunteers), Gen Y described gym-based exertion, often in order to excel at competitive sports. While their sports were often team-based, they did not provide a key signifier of leisure: time out from other more arduous activities. The material from Gen Y suggests that dance as an enjoyable pastime/leisure time activity has been overtaken by pressures to excel in sport, school and life. Sport is something that one devotes many hours to each week and that often entails significant injuries. Like sport and gym work-outs, dance is considered to be demanding of time, commitment and discipline.

And while a competitive ethos has been present in social dancing since the Depression era, the pressure to be a highly accomplished dancer seems to have escalated perhaps in tandem with televised dancing programs and with "the sportisation of pastimes". Unlike their grandparents, Gen Y did not learn to dance in a woolshed or dancehall with their more chaotic learn-by-osmosis approach. Often it begins through calisthenics and ballet, both highly structured and assessable activities, with strong parental encouragement and possibly pressure to succeed. They watch the competitive television dance programs and visit the international touring Riverdance shows where fame, high-level skills and extravaganza meet. Success in this environment is extrinsically defined—winning medals and accolades—whereas for the Lucky Generation it was meeting a partner and the intrinsic rewards of having fun and being good enough to have the confidence to keep dancing.

Today, aerobics and modern social dancing share an emphasis on the ideal body. There is little chance of here-and-now satisfaction. Delayed gratification in the pursuit of fitness has sidelined fun and friendship. It prompts us to ask whether the decoupling of fitness from other more sociable qualities might be an obesity risk factor akin to solitary eating (Rozin et al. 2003). Eating alone has been associated with weight gain in part because it is thought to encourage dis-inhibited food consumption, eating large amounts and types of food that are socially disapproved, and eating at a speed which precludes early satiety. Social eating goes hand in hand with more socially acceptable eating, which is a good thing when this is healthy eating, much less undesirable when household members share a taste for energy-dense, nutrient-poor diets. Similarly, solitary exercising could have healthy or unhealthy effects: it could encourage people to use an exercise video at home and to 'work out' in a comfortable setting getting exercise they otherwise would not, or it could encourage over-exercise, resulting in unnecessary injuries and exercise fatigue. Putting aside the conjecture, what our Lucky Generation teaches us is that moderate levels of enjoyable exercise, experienced over the lifecourse, predispose people to lead long and contented lives.

Image 6.2 Fitness fanaticism, Melbourne shop, 2012 (Source: J. Dixon)

References

ADT (Australian Dancing Times), (1967). Issues for July, October National Library of Australia collection

Andrews, S. (1979). *Take your partners, traditional dancing in Australia*. Melbourne: Hyland House.

Andrews, S. (1997). When Australian folk danced so expertly and energetically. *Australian Folklore, 12*, 181–185.

Andrews, S. (n.d.). Australian traditional dance, Part two http://www.australian-heritage-dance.com/andrews2.html/ Accessed on 20 Nov 2009.

Anonymous. (1928). How dancers can keep cool. *Danceland News, 3*, 4.

Ausdance. (n.d.). *Dance factsheet*. Canberra: Australian Dance Council.

Blainey, G. (2003). *Black kettle and full moon, daily life in a vanished Australia*. Camberwell: Viking.

Blanksby, B., & Reidy, P. (1988). Heart rate and estimated energy expenditure during ballroom dancing. *British Journal of Sports Medicine, 22*, 57–60.

Brabazon, T. (2000). Time for a change or more of the same? Les mills and the masculinisation of aerobics. *Sporting Traditions, 17*(1), 97–112.

Cannon, M. (1973). *Life in the country*. Ringwood: Viking O'Neill.

Chowne, F. (n.d.). *Standing up to your dancing*. Ernest Hoskin Papers, (MS 9517). Canberra: National Library of Australia.

Christakis, N. A., & Fowler, J. H. (2007). The spread of obesity in a large social network over 32 years. *The New England Journal of Medicine, 357*(4), 370–379.

Cooper, L., & Thomas, H. (2002). Growing old gracefully: Social dance in the third age. *Ageing and Society, 2*, 689–708.

Craike, M. J., Symons, C., & Zimmermann, J. A. M. (2009). Why do young women drop out of sport and physical activity? A social ecological approach. *Annals of leisure research, 12*(2), 148–172.

Dando, M. (n.d.). *My Melbourne: Winnie baring, ballroom dancer talks to Mark Dando*. Papers of Shirley Andrews, (Articles XIII, 10/13). Canberra: National Library of Australia.

Dionigi, R. A. (2004). *Older people and competitive sport*. Degree of Doctor of Philosophy Ph.D. The University of Newcastle, Newcastle.

Essex, R. (1968). Rus Essex (quoted in the Daily Press). Reproduced in *Australian Dancing Times*, April, p. 21.

Falkenberg, L. E. (1987). Employee programs: Their impact on the employee and the organization. *The Academy of Management Review, 12*(3), 511–512.

Forsyth, C. J. (2005). Discerning the symbionic relationship between sport, leisure, and recreation: A note on the sportization of pastimes. *Sociological Spectrum, 25*, 127–131.

Frew, M., & McGillivray, D. (2005). Health clubs and body politics: Aestheteics and the quest for physical capital. *Leisure Studies, 24*(2), 161–175.

Gilltrap, A. (2004). *Strictly dancing*. Sydney: ABC Books.

Glassner, B. (1989). Fitness and the postmodern self. *Journal of Health and Social Behaviour, 30*(2), 180–191.

Grant, B. (2001). 'You're Never too old': Beliefs about physical activity in later life. *Ageing and Society, 21*, 777–798.

Judge, J. (2003). Balance training to maintain mobility and prevent disability. *American Journal of Preventive Medicine, 25*(3), 150–156.

Kegan, E., & Morse, M. (1988). The body electronic: Aerobic exercise on video: Women's search for empowerment and self-transformation. *TDR, 32*(4), 164–180.

Leggett, P. (1991). *Select your partners*. Prahran historical series, No 11, (MS6000, Box 14, Folder01/17). Canberra: National Library of Australia.

Mann, K. (unpub). The role of the commodification of leisure in the obesogenic environment in Australia: Enabling and inhibiting healthy levels of physical activity. NCEPH, March 2008.

Matthews, J. (1990). They had such a lot of fun: The women's league of health and beauty between the wars. *History Workshop Journal, 30*, 22–54.

Matthews, J. (2005). *Dance halls & picture palace. Sydney's romance with modernity*. Sydney: Currency Press.

Melbourne shop, 2012 http://www.australian-heritage-dance.com/andrews2.html. Accessed 20/11/2009.

Patton, M. (1928). *How dancers can keep cool, Danceland 3*(8). Ernest Hoskin Papers, (MS 9517). Canberra: National Library of Australia.

Rader, B. (1991). The quest for self-sufficiency and the new strenuosity reflections as the strenuous life of the 1970s and the 1980s. *Journal of Sport History, 18*, 255–266.

Rozin, P., Kabnick, K., Pete, E., Fishcler, C., & Shields, C. (2003). The ecology of eating: Smaller portion sizes in France than in the united states help explain the French paradox. *Pyschological Science, 14*(5), 450–454.

Sassatelli, R. (2001). The commercialization of discipline: Keep-fit culture and its values. *Journal of Modern Italian Studies, 5*(3), 396–411.

Silk, C., & Silk, I. (n.d.). *A life time, dances in the Geelong area mid-late 1930s*. Shirley Andrews Research Notes, (Folder 9/19., MS6000, Box 12). Canberra: National Library of Australia.

Vamplew, W. (1994). Australian and sport. In W. Vamplew & B. Stoddart (Eds.), *Sport in Australia: A social history*. Melbourne: Cambridge University Press.

Chapter 7
The Rise of Automobility

Image 7.1 Family picnic, family picnic, Melbourne 1935 (Source: Museum of Victoria)

The automobile can inspire romantic accounts of speed, freedom, independence, status and excitement. Such an optimistic view is reflected in the statistics that show rising rates of car ownership over the last century, and the considerable economic and geographic change that has supported car use in that time. These perspectives might suggest that the growing popularity of the automobile was virtually undisputed during the twentieth century.

A more sinister counterview of the automobile has been posed by researchers and activists. They juxtapose the ubiquity of the car against an underbelly of global

---

With major input from Sarah Hinde

C. Banwell et al., *Weight of Modernity: An Intergenerational Study of the Rise of Obesity*, DOI 10.1007/978-90-481-8957-1_7, © Springer Science+Business Media Dordrecht 2012

industrial geopolitics, social inequality, injury and death, pollution, environmental degradation and climate change. In a more personal sense, the car is implicated in the acceleration of daily life (in spite of the grinding effects of traffic congestion). Australians' heavy dependence on the motor vehicle was nominated by our Delphi experts (Banwell et al. 2005) as one of the most important trends contributing to rising rates of obesity. They explained that car reliance had displaced active transport and underpinned a range of obesogenic social trends.

Our intergenerational study allowed us to track the phenomenon of car reliance from its origins to the present day through the eyes of everyday Australians. The respondents from the Lucky Generation have borne witness to the almost the entire trajectory of the automobile's rise: although cars were first introduced before their time, private automobiles were not widely adopted until well after our Lucky Generation were born. Insights from our interviews with people across the three generations demonstrate that Australians didn't necessarily embrace the automobile as unquestioningly and enthusiastically as the contemporary situation might imply. Australia's adoption of the motor vehicle might be better described as open-minded and incremental.

7.1 Paving the Way for the Lucky Generation—Melbourne's First Decades

Because Australia was settled by British colonialists in the nineteenth century during the industrial age, the key economic drivers for its cities were manufacturing from agricultural and mining inputs, public utilities and suburban development. Transport, communication and the requirements of industry were therefore central concerns for urban planners. The development of land, housing and services—and therefore a labour supply—was promoted in close proximity to where factories were built (Davison 1978; Forster 1999).

The inner suburbs of Melbourne began as unattractive landscapes. They were flat, swampy, and prone to flooding. The rivers were used for waste disposal. These unpleasant spaces were deemed worthy only of factories and the homes of factory workers. The industrial activity made the areas even more offensive, fostering social and health problems such as poverty, pollution, injuries and labour disputes (Davison 1978). By the 1880s, "the inner core of working-class suburbs had become a region synonymous in public estimation with dirt, disease and poverty" (Davison 1978, p. 150). Clear geographical inequalities and class divisions had already clearly emerged in the Melbourne landscape.

British town planning values about the health benefits of escaping the dirt, disease and poverty of city life underpinned a fervour for suburbanisation. Suburbs offered hope for a happy, peaceful existence in clean, friendly surrounds. Melbourne's skilled workforce was the first to realise this dream of detached housing away from the urban core, and they led the way to new suburban frontiers (Davison 1978).

Railway lines were deployed for their symbolic and practical support of commercial pursuits. Rail was viewed as a guarantee of successful suburb development and tracks were constructed. The government introduced the so-called 'Octopus' Railway Act in 1883, which facilitated the installation of 900 miles of track the following year and ongoing construction in subsequent years (Davison 1978). At the same time, a private consortium joined with inner city municipalities to form the Tramways Trust. The tram system was built between 1886 and 1891, and displaced horse-drawn vehicles in the inner areas (Mees 2000).

Increasing residential sprawl led to a growing separation between where the labour force lived (in the outer, low-density suburbs) and where they worked (in inner city factories and commercial or administrative enterprises in the central business district) (Davison 1978). However, during the boom years of the 1880s, industry strategically shifted to outer suburbs where the labour force lived. Factory villages were established and the number of factories in the north-western sector of Melbourne quadrupled (Davison 1978).

Melbourne was the first place in Australia where automobiles were first observed driving on the roads (Knott 1994). The first commercially produced automobile in Australia was built in Fitzroy (Fredman 1975) and one of the first vehicles to be driven in Melbourne was seen at the beginning of 1897 (Tranter 2005). Still, rail remained the potent symbol of progress and prosperity. People were suspicious of the motor vehicle and nearly a half-century elapsed before the automobile was widely embraced.

7.2 Learning to Drive

As some Melbournians began to adopt the automobile, there was growing community concern about the increasing use of the car. These concerns included worry about the dangers of fast-moving vehicles and the rising number of fatalities they caused, ambivalence about the accelerating pace of life, anger about the impact of the automobile on traffic conditions, resentment towards the upper-class (the main owners and users of these ostentatious and aggravating contraptions), and dubiousness about the 'foreign' origin of automobiles, which were mostly imported from Europe (Knott 1994).

One of the Lucky Generation respondents, George, described his father's reaction to driving in a memory that captured this ambivalence.

> *He got in the car and we drove in, and he drove around the block and I was sitting with him, God it was scary, he came back, parked it, and he said "That's it, I'll never drive again. I'll keep my license, it might come in handy in an emergency. I'll keep it, but I won't drive again. I can't think fast enough—I'm used to getting on a horse, slapping it on the rump, say 'home', three miles an hour—I can't at 25 miles an hour". I always thought of that and I think that's a great philosophy.*

Around a decade after the first cars approved on Melbourne streets, the first *Motor Car Act 1909 (Victoria)* was introduced. The community concern about motor vehicles led to a prolonged period of parliamentary debate and indecision before the legislation was passed (Tranter 2005). The Act was focused on licensing and registration of automobiles, rather than curbing or preventing their use, which might have been more attuned to community concern (Tranter 2005). Tranter (2005) argues that politicians regarded the adoption of motor vehicle as an inevitable part of 'progress.' The role of government was therefore conceived as regulatory—to facilitate what was bound to happen—rather than as an active decision-maker in the future of Melbourne's transport.

Formal acceptance of the automobile triggered industry development and began to change the urban landscape. In the second decade of the new century, plants were established in the outer western suburbs (such as Yarraville and Altona) to import and distribute petroleum products. Subsequent decades brought a huge concentration of oil refining activity in this area (City of Footscray 1984; Lack and Ford 1986). Ford and General Motors had set up vehicle assembly factories in all the Australian states except Tasmania by the 1920s (Sperritt 1987). Depression-time employment programs provided labour for road construction in the western parts of Melbourne, facilitating the influx of workers and residents to this area as industrial and residential development intensified (Lack and Ford 1986).

Although the city, its laws and economy were beginning to be transformed by the advent of the automobile, the children of the Lucky Generation continued to walk, ride a bicycle or use public transport to get themselves to and from school, to sport or social events, or to visit friends. As George described it: *cycling was a way to get around—it was the alternative to the car, because nobody had cars so the only way was to ride the bike.* Joyce commented that she either walked or cycled to school—*I don't think I was ever driven to school in my life.*

As Richard put it, walking, cycling and public transport gave them mobility and freedom which gradually diminished as the car started to take over Australian streets.

> *The bike was the form of transport I suppose. I rode a bike everywhere and so did all my mates. We used to get on the bikes and just ride. I remember once we put packs on our backs and went out and camped... for the weekend and used to ride down to Williamstown to watch the car racing on the air strip down there [and] across to Coburg lake to have a swim. So mainly it was things that you could reach and do on a push bike. Football in the street, cricket in the street... Yeah, all the kids played on the streets. Can't do it these days [because of] traffic.*

In his teenage years Richard used to walk for an hour to attend dances twice a week, where he would dance all night and then walk another hour to get home. He would *not think twice* about taking a long tram ride to see the big bands in St Kilda. To get to dances or parties further away from home, the Lucky Generation used multiple modes of transport, such as a bus and train. However, their transport plans did not always work out, as Charles remembered.

> *I can remember a party out at ... a market garden and apricot orchards where we had friends. So we went out there and we were going to leave and catch the last bus into Essendon to catch the train and tram home ... We missed the bus at [the market garden], walked into Essendon, missed the train from there, walked into town, walked from town down to [home]. You wouldn't do it these days.*

Joyce recalled walking to visit her cousins. She felt that the concept of a long walk has changed over time, and that during her childhood people were willing to walk longer distances. She said *we walked a lot further in those days than we do now, didn't we?*

Transport was more problematic for parents than children. If there was no home delivery, shopping was hard work for many mothers who had to walk or cycle to the shops and carry the shopping home. Alice explained:

> *The shops were miles away. My mum had to ride a bike or just walk... The shops would have been I don't know four or five k's away. There and back and carrying.*

During World War I and the interwar period, cars were expensive due to high tariffs. In 1929, 70% of General Motor vehicle purchases were financed by instalment (Conlon and Perkins 1999). Running costs were also significant. It is estimated that, compared to today's consumers, the automobile owner in the 1920s was paying four times as much for registration, double for insurance, and petrol was six times more expensive (Knott 1994). These costs, combined with economic hardship and petrol rationing, contributed to great public demand for affordable public transport. The Melbourne and Metropolitan Tramways Board was initiated in 1919 to manage centrally all of Melbourne's trams. Ongoing investment in trains continued, and a disorganised system of bus services was evolving (Mees 2000).

This was an era when cars were often shared within extended families. Barbara described how their family used her grandmother's car before her father owned his own vehicle.

> *It was my grandmother's car that we had as a child. She lived next door and she bought the car in 1936 .... When she made other arrangements, Dad must have endeavoured to get his own. We had two or three old bombs from time to time, so that was an upgrade for our working-class family... we had family holidays in the car ... due to the car.*

Whilst most families did not have a car, they may have owned or had access to other forms of transport such as a truck, motor-bike or horse and cart. Edna believed that driving a horse and cart for many years had given her "a good road sense" when it came to learning to drive a car. For Alice's family a new truck brought great time saving advantages.

> *[My parents] didn't have anything. I suppose the truck would have been [exciting] when they first got it... although we never went much in the truck... that was a big asset because before that it was horse and cart. And [the] time-saving with a truck was amazing.*

The car was adopted for limited uses—mainly for getting their fathers to work, and for visiting relatives or having a day out on the weekend. Typically, the mothers of the Lucky Generation did not drive. Richard described the excitement of purchasing one of the first cars in his family:

> *I came home with a car and [my wife's] parents were there for dinner with us and she said, 'oh whose car are you driving'. I said, 'oh it's ours'. She didn't believe me, went into a great panic, dinner got turned off. We all had to go for a drive. It was a very old ex-taxi actually, it was all I could afford but it was our car.*

This gradual acceptance and adoption of the motor vehicle led to a startling increase in the rates of car ownership and use during the 1920s. In the period 1922–28, Melbourne's population increased by 22% and motor vehicle registrations increased 255%, reaching a ratio of one car per 11 people. At this time, small motorised vehicles claimed 62% of road journeys. Over the same period, there was a steady decline in the number of tram and rail passenger journeys per head of population (Metropolitan Town Planning Commission 1929).

Still, for most of the Lucky Generation driving was not the main form of transport used—the majority of their families did not own a motorcar. Pedestrians walked down the middle of the street, and only a few cars were on the road.

As young adults, Lucky Generation men might have owned a motorbike or scooter before they progressed to owning a car. One respondent noted that she *was never interested in a boy unless they had a car*. Buying a car often coincided with having children. When Martha was married, her husband had a motorbike and installed a sidecar for the family to travel with him. She explained, *I got in first, my eldest daughter got in next and my youngest daughter got on top and that's the way we went to football*. They then progressed to a truck in about 1953, followed by a 'ute' and a car some 10 years later.

Peggy got a 1928 Chrysler a year after they were married, when they had a baby. They lived in Geelong, where there was no public transport. But still their car was not used much.

> *The children were picked up by a school bus just a few yards away and the butcher called, the baker called, the grocer called, the milkman came. There was no need for such great expeditions in a car. My husband rode a bike to work, he didn't need a car.*

Although many did not own an automobile, and those who did considered it had limited uses, in the midst of an economic depression following World War I the Australian Government felt the development of the automobile industry was crucial to stimulate Australia's economic recovery. The Australian Government pursued an agenda of establishing an Australian-owned and operated car manufacturing industry throughout the 1930s (Conlon and Perkins 1999, 2001). The business sector's reluctance to engage in such small economies of scale in Australia led to threats by the Prime Minister to establish a government-owned plant. General Motors eventually led the way with the introduction of the Holden (Conlon and Perkins 1999, 2001).

Awaiting the introduction of the Australian vehicle, consumers of the 1930s continued to purchase vehicles that had been cobbled together sometimes from ill-fitting parts that had been imported or manufactured by any of the numerous, small-scale Australian operators. Conlon and Perkins (1999) argue that the high tariffs for assembled vehicles introduced after World War I were an important factor causing the fragmentation and inefficiency of Australia's auto sector in the 1930s. Automobiles were expensive and poor quality by international standards.

A number of the Lucky Generation described their first cars as *bombs* and referred to the regular repairs and modifications that they had to perform to keep their cars operational. A man from this generation relayed to us how his first vehicle *broke his heart.*

> *If I remember, [it was] a 1927 Chrysler. I paid £100 for it... It broke my heart as well as my pocket... The fan came off and busted up the radiator, and we drove it back from Wagga back to Parramatta and I had it by that time. It ended up I sold it for £50 to a junk yard. That was the first one. Then I had a'37 Graham. That wasn't too bright either, it had an aluminium head, and of course it cracked.*

Melbourne's transition to a more car-centric city began to occur during the early adulthood of the Lucky Generation. Despite the fact that cars were expensive and poor quality, vehicle ownership rates rose and peaked in 1939 at one car per four families, before declining again during World War II (Sperritt 1987). Measures such as permits and petrol rationing curbed the uptake of the automobile during World War II (Davison 2004), and car use rates dropped to levels similar to those observed over a decade earlier in the late 1920s (Sperritt 1987).

As Charles described, *not many places had cars... so it wasn't used for daily types of thing*. Families who did not have a garage next to their house might garage their car some way away. Petrol rationing during the war also limited car use. Consequently, the Lucky Generation's experience of cars was associated with special occasions. Kevin described how his father would save up petrol ration coupons during World War II so the family could go away on holidays:

> *There was petrol rationing then and [my father's] father had a car and ... we used to borrow it for holidays and occasionally for some special occasion... he hoarded the ration coupons so we could get enough petrol to go on holidays and we always kept a few drums of petrol ... They were sort of tucked away in a corner of the garden out of the way so they wouldn't be a fire risk. So that was the kind of thing you had to do during the war to have enough petrol to drive.*

Some of the Lucky Generation talked about the experience of becoming a car user, and how the car became a necessity. Edna didn't enjoy driving, saying *I only drove because I had to. I won't say I loved it but it was a necessary thing*. Barbara first learnt to drive when her children were very young *only for emergencies* but once she became competent at driving, she said, *you couldn't keep me home then.* Joyce also referred to the car as becoming *a necessity of life*. For many of the women of the Lucky Generation the car also represented independence (Davison 2004). This independence operated in a practical or material way rather than symbolically, which is the pitch of contemporary car marketing. It meant that women could shop more easily and take children to appointments.

For some men, 'working' on the car and bike was a hobby. As Joyce told us, her husband had a car when they first met.

> *His pride and joy: his Citroen. It ended up on my finger. He sold it when we got engaged. He and all his mates messed around with bombs of cars for years, you know, and he'd just bought this Citroen when I met him.*

There was a symbiosis between cars, life events and the lifecourse which helped to weave the automobile into the fabric of people's lives. Joyce described how they had used their automobile as they gradually built their home, and eventually the car had become a fact of life for the family.

> *We were building our house and we had enough money to buy the block of land and pay to have the frame put up. Then we got married. Then we came back from our honeymoon and we decided to buy the [1934] Plymouth because each week when I got my pay, [my husband] worked Saturday mornings but I didn't, so I'd take the car up to the local joinery and spend my pay in weatherboards. Bring them home to mum and dad's, and prime them. Then Sunday morning we'd go up and nail them on. That went on for weeks and weeks and weeks... Then we've sort of had a series of cars since then over the years, because it gets so that it's a necessity of life. As a matter of fact we both have a car now, but I haven't driven mine for about three years.*

The car could offer excitement and pleasure, save time and effort, and offered a means for reaching destinations outside of walking distance or places where public transport did not go. At the same time, concerted efforts by lawmakers, government and industry meant that Australia's cities were increasingly shaped by the automobile. The distinct usefulness of the motor vehicle became increasingly apparent as public transport systems were poorly planned, while public and private investment in the automobile continued to expand.

By the time the Lucky Generation became parents, the motorcar had taken root in Australian cities. Their children—the Baby Boomers—grew up in an environment where the car was a common feature. During their lives, there were always cars on the road, cities were sprawling, and new car-reliant cultural and economic activities emerged.

7.3 Baby Boomers—The Car Consumers

The years after World War II brought a growing focus on the automobile in Australia. The congestion of public transport and general material deprivation during wartime seems likely to have predisposed Melbourne residents to adoption of the automobile (Davison 2004) once austerity eased. Although cars were not a necessity during the 1950s, the comfort and convenience they provided was soon embraced by the public (Lees and Senyard 1987).

As the public were feeling appreciative of the merits of car travel, the government, industry and city planners were also throwing their support behind this transport mode. These decades after World War II were characterised by the concentration of auto-related industry, removal of government taxes and regulations, and the active incorporation of the automobile into cultural events and settings. A dramatic transformation of the urban environment began, with the demolition of residential and green space to install freeways and large-scale car parks.

Mass production of the automobile began after World War II. With prompting from the Federal Government, various companies announced plans to produce Australian vehicle, but the most significant entrant to the car market was the Holden, manufactured by General Motors in Adelaide and Melbourne (Davison 2004).

Oil refining also accelerated during this time. For example, Petrochemical Refineries Australia established in Altona in 1949 and over the ensuing decade grew into a large oil processing complex (Lack and Ford 1986).

Changes to Australian Government policy also facilitated the uptake of the motor vehicle. In 1949, the Labor government was compelled by a successful court appeal to lift import regulations on cars, thus permitting an influx of vehicles from other markets (Davison 2004). In 1950, petrol rationing was abolished and by that stage, a General Motors Holden survey suggested ownership was already as high as 50% (Davison 2004). Although cars became a more common household possession during the post-war decades, for those respondents whose families did manage to acquire a car at this time, it was considered a big occasion because, as Doris explained, *not everyone had cars*.

Despite the growing popularity of the automobile, the significant costs of purchasing a car may account for the class and gender differences in adoption of the automobile at this time. One in three professional and managerial males owned a car; one in five white collar workers; one in ten semi-skilled and unskilled workers; and just one in 20 women (Davison 2004, pp. 13–14). Baby Boomer Patricia, who lived in a rural area, commented on the class differences of car ownership:

> *We were in a very small country town, and there were lots of quite poor people, and lots of people didn't have a car. And only two people had a TV and we were one of them... [and] we did have a car.*

Families tended to have one car, which the husband would use to travel to and from work. When wives had a driver's license, they might occasionally access the car in order to do the shopping or take children to appointments. Joyce's husband would usually drive the car to work *because where he worked public transport wasn't readily accessible*. But she said that *if I absolutely had to have the car for any reason*, such as taking the kids to an appointment, *I'd drive him to work and then go back and get him in the evening*. Other mothers did not drive and it was rare that children were driven to school or other activities.

In Michelle's family, her mother didn't drive and *dad had use of the car for his own purposes*. On weekends, Michelle said her family may have occasionally used the car to go for a picnic but generally *he wasn't a person who drove us around, like even to get to youth group and stuff. It would be a rare occasion*. It was a similar experience in Leanne's family:

> *My mother never drove so we would walk to school; walk to do the grocery shopping that sort of thing... I don't think [the family used the car] a great deal during the week when we were young. [My father] would use it for work. He would drop me at the bus stop when I went to secondary school. Church on Sunday, visiting our grandparents, family, weekend family activities, little athletics, things like that... I would catch the bus after school to the training oval [for little athletics].*

By the 1960s, car ownership was no longer seen as a luxury and had become viewed as a necessity for business and families (Davis 1980). Cars became important objects in the family. Family portraits around this time were often taken in front of the family car. The car fostered social change by facilitating access to a wider range of leisure activities, including the Sunday family drive (which displaced the weekly trip to church), shifts in youth culture, changes in the daily lives of women, a growing appreciation and investment in the aesthetic qualities of the motor vehicle (Davison 2004).

The car also became the centrepiece of new popular cultural events. Drive-in cinemas appeared in the suburbs (Lack and Ford 1986). In 1946, a speedway opened at Maribyrnong, accommodating 8,000 spectators who came to watch Australians compete with other countries in dirt bike races (Lack and Ford 1986). When Melbourne hosted the Olympics in 1956, a Grand Prix race was held at Albert Park (Davison 2004). These events caused conflict in the community between those in favour, and those who objected to the ill-effects such as noise, pollution and crowds—indeed, such events continue to cause controversy (Tranter 2003).

During the 1960s, Melbourne's urban landscape also changed dramatically to accommodate the car. Lack and Ford (1986) describe the changing local environments, as services such as petrol garages began to appear. The petrochemical complex in Altona expanded, prompting further private and government investment in housing, and the western suburbs grew. At this time, houses and land were demolished for the construction of the Tullamarine Freeway, Princes Highway and Western Highway.

Another way in which the geography of Melbourne was transforming during the 1960s was the increasingly apparent class divisions between suburbs. The inner suburbs began to be 'gentrified' as the 'slums' were demolished for high-rise public housing, and low-income residents were displaced by wealthy young people who bought and renovated houses in the area (Birch 2003; Logan 1985; Sandercock 1990). There was growing recognition of the disadvantage accumulating in the western suburbs, giving rise to a 'Deprived West' social movement in the 1970s (Lack and Ford 1986; Sandercock 1990).

Even as the motor vehicle was transforming the landscape, economy and culture, not everyone could own a car and class divisions in car ownership were persisting. Not only did people need sufficient financial resources to acquire a car, but also enough proficiency in English to pass a driving test (Lack and Ford 1986). Families living in outer suburbs had relatively limited access to services and opportunities, due both to distance and having fewer transport options compared to those in the inner areas of Melbourne.

Still, the growing dominance of the automobile had not fully filtered down to the transport experiences of children during this era. The Baby Boomer respondents described their childhood transport habits and many explained that they walked to primary school. Elizabeth said that during her primary school years, *we'd walk, just walk, without our parents, just local neighbourhood kids, we'd all just walk in a group.*

As teenagers, the majority of the Baby Boomer generation caught the bus to and from high school, and some caught the train or cycled. Only two participants said they were driven to school, but this did not happen all the time so they also used

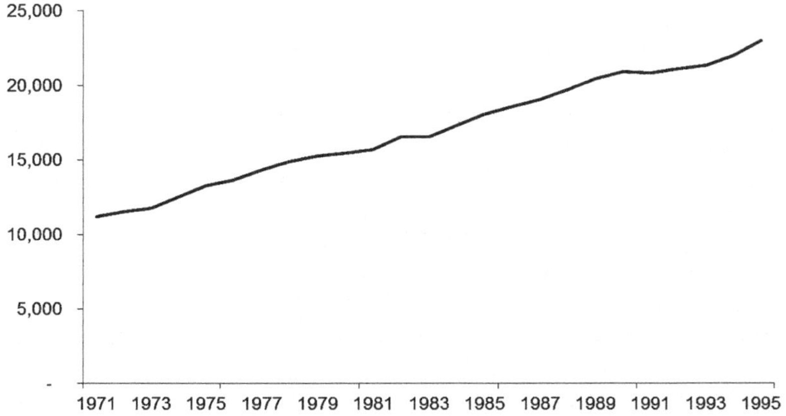

Fig. 7.1 Urban passenger vehicle-kilometre estimates 1971–1995, Melbourne (Source: Bureau of Transport and Resource Economics 1998)

public transport. Elizabeth *either walked or rode a push bike, so [I] didn't get driven like [children] these days*. Laura recalled:

> *[When I was at] primary school, my mother walked me [to school]. It wasn't that far, it was just crossing a main road, so she walked me. It was probably only a seven minute walk. High school, that was much further away but it was zoned so you didn't get a choice where you went. So I caught the bus. And when I didn't spend my bus money, I [also] caught it home. Otherwise I walked home, like all teenagers would have done, scoffing lollies.*

The Baby Boomers generally walked or cycled to travel to out-of-school activities, such as sport or socialising with friends, just as their parent's generation had done. Peter said *it was bike up to scouts, bike off to tennis*.

However, as the Baby Boomers entered adulthood cars came to be used more routinely. Support and planning for public transport systems declined further, and the car virtually displaced the other modes for most parts of Melbourne, except the innermost suburbs (Mees 2000). Figure 7.1 illustrates the growth in car use in Melbourne, as measured by the number of vehicle-kilometres travelled each year for the three decades from 1970. The chart shows a steady rise in the distances Melbourne cars were travelling during those decades.

The auto industry was expanding and prospering during these decades, which further encouraged the rapid adoption of the automobile. By 1984, the petrochemical refinery at Yarraville was expanded to cover 48 acres, employing 250 people and processing two billion litres of refined product per annum: "one of the largest throughputs of any oil terminal in the Southern Hemisphere" (City of Footscray 1984, p. 40). That same year, the 'Button Plan' was introduced, which reduced tariffs to improve the economies of scale in the Australian market and increase sales of motor vehicles (Conlon and Perkins 1999). By the time the Button Plan wound up in the early 1990s, the auto sector was the biggest manufacturing industry in

Australia—accounting for 25% of GDP, and employing 162,000 people directly or indirectly, as well as being a significant end-user of other Australian production (MacKenzie 1990).

When Jeff Kennett's Victorian state government was elected in 1992, it inherited its predecessor's plans for the construction of new freeways and city bypasses. A $A1 billion construction project (which ended up costing $A2 billion) was outsourced to a private company and became "the world's largest privately constructed, privately owned and privately operated toll road" (Davison 2004, p. 246).

Notably, these road plans did not provoke as much resistance as the freeway proposals in the road building heyday of the 1960s and 1970s. Davison (1996) suggests this is because there would be relatively minor disruption to inner city homes, where other environmental and political issues were felt to be more pressing: "now the gentry drive their Range Rovers to Gippsland to save trees, rather than walking to Clifton Hill to save inner-city terraces" (Davison 1996, p. 23). Moreover, the tolls for the new freeways were mostly incurred by Labor electorates. Consequently, the new freeways "pitted car-driving working-class battlers from the outer suburbs against cycling yuppies from the inner city" (Davison 2004, p. 254).

While road construction and car sales were flourishing, public transport systems continued to languish under poor planning and management and inadequate investment (Mees 2000). The 1996 'Transporting Melbourne' strategy recommended the separation and privatisation of train, tram and bus services (Mees 2000). The government predicted that privatisation would improve service levels, patronage and profitability, but this was not achieved (Mees 2005).

7.4 Life Without the Car Becomes Unimaginable

At the end of the twentieth century, Australia's Bureau of Transport Economics (Bureau of Transport Economics 1998) projected that Australian car ownership rates would plateau at an assumed 'saturation' rate of 520 per thousand people by 2014. This supposed 'saturation' was exceeded almost straight away. By 2005, there were over 680 vehicles per thousand people in Australia and, in 2010, that number was over 720 (Australian Bureau of Statistics 2010).

These trends in growing car sales have not been limited to Australia. In the United States, car ownership rates have begun to exceed the number of licensed drivers. Market research suggests that families are accruing multiple cars to fulfil different social purposes: the 'date' car for special occasions; utility vehicles to collect items from the hardware shop; four-wheel drives for holidays; minivans for chauffeuring children; and a fuel-efficient vehicle for commuting (Naughton 2003).

Despite their many car-free childhood experiences, at the time of interview the great majority of our Baby Boomer respondents said that they could not imagine life without a car and that life would be *much, much harder* and *so unworkable*. The car is essential for these Baby Boomer parents to ferry children to school and other activities, shopping, and above all to get between home and the paid workplace.

The car offered not only a means to travel to important destinations, but—perhaps more crucially—it is considered the optimal mode of transport for the efficient scheduling of multiple activities into the day. As Karen explained:

> *Things are not direct and you would have no flexibility. Like tonight, when I finish work, I want to drive to another campus and go to a Pilates class. I wouldn't be able to do that! I wouldn't be able to pick up shopping. I don't think I could imagine it. It wouldn't be efficient.*

Another interviewee, Michelle, expressed a similar view about the necessity of the car for orchestrating multiple activities:

> *I wouldn't be able to fit nearly as much into a day as I do now because every single moment of my day is pretty much taken up these days. So I have to kind of finish here [at the interview], race home and then see private clients, and my daughter doesn't have a car, so I have sometimes to go and pick her up from work if she's working. Shopping—the car gets pretty constant use. So I wouldn't be able to fit all of that stuff in.*

The car was described as a time-saving device; indeed it was nominated by a few respondents as their favourite labour-saving device. As Catherine explained, *if you didn't have the car you wouldn't be able to do half the things you do. So the car is the best time saving device*. Respondents said that the car saves them time and effort because driving allows for more activities in a given period of time. Such car reliance is partly due to the relative paucity of fast public transport options. John explained:

> *There's public transport not too far from us. We could get by but we'd have to rearrange enormously and set a lot more time aside for that travel you know, an extra hour here and an extra hour there.*

When prompted to consider exactly how life might change if the car was no longer an option for them, some conceded that it might be possible with greater organisation, although many felt the journey to work would be particularly difficult without a motor vehicle. Julie described the logistical implications of what it would mean to be car-free:

> *If I didn't have my car ... I can organise to have my [golf] clubs kept at one of my golf clubs and I could get a lift, like public transport. Again, I would have to organise myself and certainly allow more time, but I could still maintain golf, I could still maintain badminton. I could probably maintain yoga, but I couldn't get to work. There's no way I could get to work.*

For Belinda, not having a car would mean being less *spontaneous about getting things done,* explaining:

> *I would probably leave the [list of things to get done] until the weekend when I could get hold of the car, if we were sharing one. I'm sure I would get used to it after a while but after having a car for so long, or having two cars in one family, so as far as getting things done—it would take a lot longer.*

Belinda felt that without the car and having a young child *I wouldn't leave the house pretty much*. She thought that this situation would be like her Lucky Generation mother's situation, which she described:

> *I can remember my mum saying she didn't go out very much at all. And she didn't really socialise much at all. But that was more to do with having six children. They didn't have a*

car so for shopping and things like that they just had to wait until one partner came home and looked after the children and then you could do it on your own. But I wouldn't be getting on public transport with one baby in like a knapsack and trying to negotiate… [scream from child in background]. I think it sounds like hard work.

Other respondents, such as Nicole who lives in a semi-rural area, are very dependent on their motor vehicle because there are no other options available. Nicole recently experienced life without her car when it broke down. She also reflects on the increasing financial pressure she incurs to maintain her car, because it is so essential:

I have to use a car. My car broke down a few weeks ago, the head gasket went on it, and I was stranded. I couldn't go shopping, there is no public transport. You are totally stranded. So you have to have a car. And if you want to go and do shopping you have a 45 minute drive that way or 20-30 minute drive that way to go do shopping… [Without a car] I'd be stranded. There would be no groceries, no bills would get paid, there would be nothing. You have to have one. That makes it really hard, if you have to have it. The fuel keeps going up, you have to put it in there, you can't say 'that doesn't matter I'll catch the train for the week'. You have to have it. So when things go up, you have to cut back elsewhere.

For Peter, the consequences of not having a car would be emotional as well as practical. Racing and fixing up cars and motorbikes with his friends is a hobby and he said that relinquishing the automobile from his life:

would be like cutting off my arm… [My friends and I] just go out together and go cruising, and have a coffee together as well, because that is what we like to do. My life would be turned upside down if I didn't have a car.

Several spoke about the car's importance in terms of taking holidays, which was also a theme for the Lucky Generation. Denise noted, *when we go away on holiday, we've done a lot of trips where we've driven, and we've gone places like Central Australia.* Patricia explained: *we have our holiday property… which we drive to. I mean you can get a train and a bus, but I wouldn't do it, you'd just have to sell it. [Life] would change dramatically*, and Stephen said *we need [the car] for every second weekend, at least, to get up to the caravan… got to be able to get away.*

Although the automobile has become an essential part of the lives of most Australians, many respondents discussed their preference for minimising their car use and using alternative modes of transport. Some discussed using other forms of transport to increase their physical activity. Nicole and Belinda, who both have young children, told us how they try to walk rather than drive to achieve daily tasks, such as going to the shops, because they found it hard to dedicate specific times in the week to exercise. Nicole said *we try and walk everywhere, because I figure it's good for us.* Similarly, Gregory cycles to work:

I ride a bike to work. So that is kind of my main physical activity actually. It doesn't sound much, it is only five [kilometres] to work from here. But you know that is forty minutes a day of strenuous exercise, so I think it is quite important.

The participants who felt the least car reliant lived in the inner city of Melbourne. They had access to public transport and could walk or cycle to places they visit regularly, such as work or the shops. For example, Stephen, who cycled to work, structured his life to minimise the travel he had to undertake during the week. Living in the inner city meant Stephen was able to cycle to work. He said *I think driving's the slowest [option], it takes me about 20 min to run, about 12 min to cycle and 35 min to walk.*

7.5 Contending with Car Dominance—Generation Y

Australian transport systems are now dominated by the automobile (Hinde and Dixon 2005; Laird and Newman 2001; Mees 2000). In 2003, there was one registered vehicle per licensed driver in Australia: 13 million cars on the road and 13 million drivers (Austroads 2005).

Adults are not the only heavy users of car transport: increasingly, children are chauffeured to school instead of walking, cycling or taking public transport. A survey of over 1,000 families from 19 Melbourne primary schools revealed that less than half of 5 and 6-year olds, and less than two thirds of 10–12 year-olds, walk or cycle to school once a week or more (Timperio et al. 2004).

Most of our Generation Y respondents embodied this trend; by 18 years of age, most of them already had a car of their own. This was often encouraged by their Baby Boomer parents, including with financial support, because it helped to diminish the amount of chauffeuring required of the Baby Boomers. For example, as each of Peter's children got old enough to drive, he and his wife lent them money to buy a car:

> *We felt if we could lend [our kids] the difference, to make up the money for a car, then they can pay us back rather than paying the bank interest. Because with their sporting interests there was an incentive to help them get cars because then we didn't have to be the taxis all the time.*

Australian cities rank among the most 'car dependent' in the world (Laird and Newman 2001). Compared to other developed countries, Australia is highly car reliant as indicated by high rates of car ownership and use, an extensive network of roads, abundant space for car parking in urban areas and very cheap fuel (Austroads 2005; Laird and Newman 2001). Unlike many European cities where public transport is the quickest way to get around, the average travel speed of Australia's urban public transport is significantly slower that motor vehicle (Laird and Newman 2001) and 80% of Australians never use public transport (Australian Bureau of Statistics 2005).

In 2005, Australia boasted over 800,000 km of road, a system that costs $A7.5 billion per year (Austroads 2005). Vehicles are becoming more fuel efficient, while low fuel taxes contribute to the provision of some of the cheapest petrol in the developed world. Unsurprisingly, the total volume of automotive fuel consumed continues to increase each year (Austroads 2005).

The Australian Government has continued to play an active role in promoting the automobile sector. Although Australia's Industry Commission in 1997 recommended gradually eliminating protectionist car manufacturing industry tariffs in line with the rest of the nation's manufacturing, the Federal government opted to continue them until 2005 (Conlon and Perkins 1999).

When the tariff debate emerged again in 2002, the Federal Government was pressured to act in favour of the auto manufacturing industry. As articulated by Victorian Member of Parliament, The Hon Mark Birrell (2002):

> *Australia's automotive industry, which is principally headquartered and based in Victoria, is a major contributor to our national economy and Australia's skills base. I wish to use this budget debate to urge clear-cut government facilitation of car companies and automotive companies in this state... I emphasise the need for high-level advocacy of the long-term case for our efficient automotive sector.*

The Federal Liberal Government of the time, led by Prime Minister John Howard, decided the general automotive tariff would be reduced from 15 to 10% at the start of 2005, and then to 5% by 2010, with a view to rendering the sector more globally competitive. The announcement came alongside an extension of an automotive industry assistance scheme: an outlay of $A4.2 billion between 2006 and 2015. This news was received with pleasure by business leaders (Donald 2002).

The Australian Government's enthusiasm for this sector is also apparent in the numerous other interventions which facilitate ongoing car reliance. A 2003 review of financial subsidies to fossil fuel consumption and production in Australia estimated the government incurred $A6.54 billion annually through road and car parking subsidies, and lost revenue from taxes, import duties and excises (Riedy and Diesendorf 2003).

Taking into account the gradual adoption of the car in Australia, and the depth of support car transport has received, it is unsurprising that most people travel to work by motor car. More than four out of every five people who employ one mode of transport to get to work use a car. The motor vehicle share vastly outweighs the total contribution made by the other modes including public transport, walking and cycling. Only a small proportion of these car users share a vehicle: 75% of Australian workers drive; 8% are vehicle passengers (Australia Bureau of Statistics 2002).

Most Generation Y participants in our study had owned an automobile at some point in their lives, which reflects the dominance of the automobile revealed in national transport statistics. However, when talking about the reliance on the motor vehicle, the Generation Y respondents conveyed less of a sense of dependence on the car. There are at least two possible reasons why this would be so. First, they were younger and had fewer years to become habituated to being a 'driver' rather than a passenger. Second, only one Generation Y participant had a child—and parenthood was a key moment when the parents and grandparents of Gen Y had come to appreciate the car.

The Generation Ys could imagine life without a car, but agreed with the Baby Boomer participants that it would be very difficult to continue scheduling multiple tasks within constrained periods of time. As Daniel explained:

> *I don't think I'd have as much time to do as many things, 'cos if I was having to catch public transport or wait for someone to give me a lift or something like that it obviously takes up a lot more time than just being able to drive where ever you want, so yeah that would be the biggest thing.*

Sarah works at night and also feels the car is essential for her to accomplish all of her current activities:

> *I am so reliant on my car. I would have to catch the bus to work and wait for my mum to come and pick me up. And I wouldn't be able to go to my boyfriend's house. It would be terrible... I wouldn't be able to work as late as I do. It would take me longer to get to uni so I probably would go less, which is probably not a good thing. I would be very reliant on friends still. I was really relying on friends when I was 17.*

Compared to their parents, the Generation Ys appeared to feel a greater need to have a car to see their friends and family members. As Christopher explained:

> *I don't have anyone within walking distance or...I suppose if I thought about it maybe I could get public transport to a few people's houses but it would be almost impossible to time frame it, catching public transport around.*

Similarly, Andrew explained how the people in his life were geographically distributed, which meant he needed a car to maintain relationships with them.

> *I mean public transport is alright if everyone I knew, and needed to and wanted to see, kind of lived in the kind of inner suburbs, I wouldn't need a car...But once you move out of the inner suburbs it just sucks, it really does, the trains are hopeless and there's no trams and buses and some days just don't fully don't run it, it sucks... getting out to see my family that would be harder but it wouldn't be impossible.*

The extent to which public transport was used varied. Like the Baby Boomers, the Gen Y participants mainly described using active transport going to the city, because of traffic and the high cost of parking. Those who used public transport generally lived in the inner suburbs of Melbourne or worked in the city, places which tend to be better served by public transport and where car use can be difficult.

The majority of Gen Ys did not feel that using public transport was an option, as it was not available where they lived, or did not go to the places where they were employed. Emma summed it up: *where I am, we're not linked in to the train line, so it means catching the bus, catch a train to get to wherever.... so I kind of do rely on the car.*

Emma felt she relied on her car as there were no direct public transport routes to her workplace, so she would have to catch a bus, and then a train, to get to work.

> *I could [imagine not having a car], but I just imagine it being so much harder. More time consuming more than anything... It's just the fact that it would mean getting up even earlier than I get up and just that inconvenience. And also the safety issue, even though I'm not terribly scared, it is dark when you get out in the morning... I'd have to be more disciplined in my hours at work, like the temptations to stay a bit longer... and you'd really have to plan your time better and probably cut down on the activities that you fit into your life.*

It also was not considered suitable for those who worked shift work or late hours. Rebecca explained that after she acquired her driver's licence:

> *I drove everywhere... Very rarely I'll catch a train to the city if there's not going to be any parking... or going out for the night or something. But usually, I drive.*

So it is perhaps no wonder that the collective distance travelled by Australians each year has inter-planetary dimensions! The Australian Bureau of Statistics reported that in a 12-month period, Australia's vehicles had together travelled "the equivalent of going to Pluto and back 23 times" (Australian Bureau of Statistics 2003 media release). Australians are spending growing quantities of time accelerating across ever-increasing distances. The total kilometres travelled in Australia grew 80% in the 20 years to 1998; this rate of growth was more than double the population growth for the period (Austroads 2000).

The significant pitfalls have become abundantly clear to the Australian public, especially over the last decade. Car reliance is implicated in a range of ill-health outcomes (Kjellstrom et al. 2003; McMichael 2001). Injuries due to motor vehicle accidents remain a prominent cause of disability and death. Pollution from cars is associated with respiratory illness such as asthma. Other negative consequences include noise disturbance and community disruption. In the longer term, the contribution of the motorcar to greenhouse emissions may have far-reaching negative health impacts. A reduction in car reliance, in favour of active forms of transport such as walking, cycling and mass transport, is therefore a worthwhile objective for public health (Mason 2000a, b).

The displacement of physical activity associated with car use is considered to be a significant contributor to rising rates of obesity and many argue that transport is essential to 'activating' the population (Sallis et al. 2004). Physical activity is displaced when people use a motor vehicle instead of an active transport mode such as walking, cycling or using public transport (Mason 2000b). Even in a car-dominated transport environment, it is estimated that the physical activity gains from regular cycling would provide a net benefit to personal health that outweighs its risk of injury by a factor of 20 to 1 (Hillman 1993). Even public transport is considered more active than car commuting, with some evidence that people who travel by train take 30% more steps than automobile users (Wener and Evans 2007).

While there has been some discussion of the role of transport in physical activity levels, there has been relatively limited research to confirm and quantify this relationship. One important UK study showed that walking for transport offers the greatest quantity of high-intensity activity for children (Mackett et al. 2005). Although physical education classes at school offered slightly more intense exercise, these contributed fewer hours of activity across the week, rendering walking for transport the overall greatest source of exercise for children.

Apart from offering direct activity benefits, walking for transport also has an indirect relationship with other kinds of physical activity. In a study of physical activity in 10–13 year-old children, Mackett et al. (2005) found an interesting relationship between walking for transport and levels of physical activity:

> Children who walked to sport, rather than travelling by car, experienced greater levels of exercise intensity at those events.

Car use tends to be the most frequent mode of transport for attending structured events outside the home (e.g. organised sport), whereas children more often walked to unstructured events (e.g. playing). Unstructured events—i.e. those usually attended by walking—generally resulted in greater intensity of activity.

In our interviews with Gen Y and their parents, we found that Gen Y used a variety of transport modes during their childhood to get to and from school. Active modes of transport were more common among our respondents than the literature might suggest. During primary school the majority either walked or rode a bike and then, on entering high school which was usually farther from home, public transport was common. The mother of Gen Y children, Lisa, recalled:

As soon as [my kids] went to secondary school they had to travel for an hour on public transport to go to school. Prior to that, they were at the local primary school, so they walked.

When it came to getting to and from sports, or other out-of-school activities, the parents of Gen Y drove them—and often long distances. Although Lisa did not drive her children to school, she and her husband spent a lot of time driving their children to social events:

But [my kids are] incredibly committed to the cross-suburbs [friendships]... partly because of what schools they went to. They travelled quite far to school... You could send your kid an hour-and-a-half away for school and people are sending their kids an hour-and-a-half away from other directions. I think the last party we drove [my son] to was an hour-and-a-half drive, dropped him and his mates off, came home and then sat for an hour and then drove out to pick them up again, so it's the nature of where we send them to school.

Baby Boomer Peter also talked about how his children's sporting commitments required a lot of driving, and that these demands increased as the children grew older:

They were being taken around by us, until they were old enough to have cars, then they took themselves. They had bikes for going to school; they went to school on bikes. But that was about it, the novelty wore off for going any further afield [laughter]. And with their athletics they couldn't, it was too far and wrong times of the day. It was 8.30 on a Saturday morning and it was way over in bloody Burwood. And parents had to be helping out anyway... And the time pressures got tighter too. It was: leap up in the morning, belt them over to little athletics, get home by such and such a time because you were playing soccer in the afternoon. There probably wouldn't have been time for them to ride home and get changed any way. So it became a convenience thing as well. And a safety thing as well. Society changed a bit as well... you know where they are, you're having time with them, and helping them out, and they are not coming to any harm.

Sandra's car reliance decreased as her Gen Y children grew up and her time was no longer as committed to driving them around.

I guess I do more walking now, I mean during the day I do more walking, because I don't have to look after the children and do things, you know. ... I had to save time and drive to wherever you picked them up ... It is easier not having the children... I guess the time constraints are not so rigorous. I mean, when the children were at home, you sort of meant to have dinner at a fairly reasonable hour and be a bit more organised ... running around, things to do for them.

In a survey of over 10,000 people, Frank (2004) demonstrated that daily time spent in the motor vehicle is correlated with risk of being overweight or obese. For every hour spent in the motor vehicle, the risk of obesity increased by 6%.

Disturbingly, time spent in the car ranged up to more than 5 h per day for a small number of participants, translating to a 30% increase in risk of obesity for those people. Another survey revealed that active transport is less common amongst people who are overweight, than those who are not (Gordon-Larsen et al. 2005).

While the acquisition of a car might reduce the time that Baby Boomer parents spend driving, a number of Gen Y respondents told us that buying a car has led to a rapid decline in their use of active transport. For example, Christopher told us that he got his car the day he turned 18 and that his bicycle *hasn't been touched since*.

The Lucky Generation reflected rather negatively on today's car dependence; one participant saying *it's sad really*. In contrast to the two younger generations, the Lucky Generation were not as car reliant over their lifecourse. Although most of them still owned a car when we interviewed them, they described the amount of driving they did as having decreased to the point that they rarely needed to drive. Irene said:

> *I just gave [my car] up last year. I was just using the car less and less. It got to the stage where I hadn't used it for a couple of months. I used to just use it at night for driving to church functions, then they decided they'd have the function... in the afternoon so it's easy for people to get to... and so I just found I was using it less.*

As they got older, the Lucky Generation preferred to leave the car at home when they could. They preferred walking and catching public transport, as is evident from Chap. 5 about physical activity. As Irene put it:

> *I refuse to have anyone pick me up when I'm walking to church or up the street shopping or whatever, that includes the night too. I like to walk to meetings at night. While I had the car I used to pick up people and drop people home and then when I gave up the car I just said, 'I don't want any lift home, I don't want anyone stopping to pick me up' and there's no variation. Anyone who offers I just say, 'no thank you'... Because the walking gives me more time away from the house, more of an outing. Like coming here today, for example—if someone could just drive me here and drop me off in 15 minutes, well it wouldn't be the same. I enjoy going on the train and looking around and seeing things.*

7.6 Conclusion

The introduction of the automobile was met with both excitement and ambivalence. As people became accustomed to driving and found the means to acquire and run a motor vehicle, cars gradually entered aspects of family life. The car was somewhat useful to the Lucky Generation as they grew up, started families, built homes, pursued careers, provided for their families and enjoyed leisure activities. The adoption of the automobile depended on its usefulness in helping people to achieve the usual priorities in life—family, work and recreation. At the same time, a building momentum of legislative, economic, cultural and geographic change was encouraging wider adoption of the automobile. So, while the Lucky Generation were putting the automobile to use pursuing a good life, their lives—and the lives of their offspring—were also being shaped by the advent of the automobile and its industries.

The Baby Boomers were born into a suburban lifestyle which increasingly depended on the car. Cars and traffic were an ever-present backdrop. Although their childhoods were largely car-free except for special occasions and holidays, by the time the Baby Boomers left home the car had become almost essential. The 1970s and 1980s consolidated the dominance of the automobile. Now, when asked to conceive of their lives without a car, the overwhelming message is that such a scenario would be extremely difficult, if not unimaginable. The car is essential to maintain the pace, scale and intensity of their lives.

Gen Y similarly have grown up with the constant backdrop of automobility, beginning with being chauffeured as kids, but also with the flow-on consequences of that automobility, including: the fast pace of life, traffic, and emerging concerns about peak oil, petrol prices, climate change and, more recently, economic strife. Perhaps this is why the Gen Ys have returned to the more ambivalent attitude of their grandparent's generation: accepting the positive benefits the car offers, a view which is leavened by awareness of the pitfalls of the car's dominance over ways of living.

Over the course of the entrenchment of the motor vehicle in Australian society, the people we interviewed from the Lucky Generation appear to have remained relatively unmoved by the enthusiasm that industry and government might have wished them to feel. They retained a relatively sceptical attitude towards the car, and while they are not necessarily as frightened or intimidated as their parents had been at the car's first introduction, many have gladly relinquished driving from their daily lives. For the Lucky Generation, as Chap. 5 attests, walking and not car use is associated with freedom and the good life.

Image 7.2 Cars near major shopping street, Melbourne, 2012 (Source: J. Dixon)

References

Australia Bureau of Statistics. (2002). *Census basic community profile*. Canberra: ABS.

Australian Bureau of Statistics (2003, April 8). Driving to Pluto and back: Australians drive 190 billion kilometres (Media Release Cat. No. 9208.0). Retrieved October 15, 2003.

Australian Bureau of Statistics (2005). *Sales of new motor vehicles, Australia. Table 1: New motor vehicle sales by type, All series*. Catalogue No. 9314.0.55.001 (electronic file). Canberra: Australian Bureau of Statistics.

Australian Bureau of Statistics (2010). *Motor vehicle census Australia* (Cat 9309.0). Canberra: Australian Bureau of Statistics.

Austroads. (2000). *Road facts 2000*. Sydney: Austroads Incorporated.

Austroads. (2005). *Road facts 2005*. Sydney: Austroads Incorporated.

Banwell, C., Hinde, S., Dixon, J., & Sibthorpe, B. (2005). Reflections on expert consensus: A case study of the social trends contributing to obesity. *European Journal of Public Health, 15*(6), 564–568.

Birch, T. (2003). The best TV reception in Melbourne: Fitzroy 'lowlife' and the invasion of the renovator. *Traffic, 3*, 9–29.

Birrell, M. (2002). The Australian Automotive Industry (A speech on the strength and future potential of the nation's car and automotive component industry). *Budget Papers 2002–03*. Canberra.

Bureau of Transport Economics (1998, October). *Forecasting light vehicle traffic* (Working Paper 38).

City of Footscray. (1984). *City of Footscray 125th anniversary celebrations*. Melbourne: City of Footscray.

Conlon, R., & Perkins, J. (1999). Australian governments and automotive manufacturing, 1919–1939. *Australian Journal of Politics and History, 45*(3), 376–391.

Conlon, R., & Perkins, J. (2001). *Wheels and deals: The automotive industry in twentieth-century Australia*. Aldershot: Ashgate Publishing Ltd.

Davis, P. (1980). Motoring. In *Australia in the 1960s*. New York: Rigby.

Davison, G. (1978). *The rise and fall of Marvellous Melbourne*. Melbourne: Melbourne University Press.

Davison, G. (1996). Melbourne's triple by-pass. *Arena Magazine, 22*(April–May), 19–25.

Davison, G. (2004). *Car wars: How the car won our hearts and conquered our cities*. Crows Nest: Allen and Unwin.

Donald, P. (Writer). (2002). *Tariff cuts, assistance in new car package*. Australia: ABC Radio National.

Forster, C. (1999). *Australian cities: Continuity and change*. Melbourne: Oxford University Press.

Frank, L. D. (2004). Economic determinants of urban form: Resulting trade-offs between active and sedentary forms of travel. *American Journal of Preventive Medicine, 27*(31001), 146–153.

Fredman, M. (1975). The horseless doctor—transition from horse to motor transport. *Victorian Historical Journal, 46*(1), 283–302.

Gordon-Larsen, P., Nelson, M. C., & Beam, K. (2005). Associations among active transportation, physical activity, and weight status in young adults. *Obesity Research, 13*(5), 868–875.

Hillman, M. (1993). Cycling and the promotion of health. *Policy Studies, 14*(2), 49–58.

Hinde, S., & Dixon, J. (2005). Changing the obesogenic environment: Insights from a cultural economy of car reliance. *Transportation Research Part D, 10*(1), 31–53.

Kjellstrom, T., van Kerkhoff, L., Bammer, G., & McMichael, T. (2003). Comparative assessment of transport risks—how it can contribute to health impact assessment of transport policies. *Bulletin of the World Health Organization, 81*(6), 451–457.

Knott, J. (1994). Speed, modernity and the motor car: The making of the 1909 motor traffic act in New South Wales'. *Australian Historical Studies, 26*(103), 221–241.

Lack, J., & Ford, O. (1986). *Melbourne's Western region: An introductory history*. Melbourne: Melbourne's Living Museum of the West and Melbourne Western Region Cultural Heritage Study.

Laird, P., & Newman, P. (2001). How we got here: The role of transport in the development of Australia and New Zealand. In P. Laird, P. Newman, M. Bachels, & J. Kenworthy (Eds.), *Back on track: Rethinking transport policy in Australia and New Zealand*. Sydney: UNSW Press.

Lees, S., & Senyard, J. (1987). *The 1950s: How Australia became a modern society, and everyone got a house and car*. Melbourne: Hyland House.

Logan, W. S. (1985). *The gentrification of inner Melbourne: A political geography of inner city housing*. St. Lucia: University of Queensland Press.

MacKenzie, A. (1990, July 11). Industry report: Cars. *Australian Business*, pp. 37–48.

Mackett, R. L., Lucas, L., Paskins, J., & Turbin, J. (2005). The therapeutic value of children's everyday travel. *Transportation Research Part A: Policy and Practice, 39*(2–3), 205–219.

Mason, C. (2000a). Healthy people, places and transport. *Health Promotion Journal of Australia, 10*(3), 190–196.

Mason, C. (2000b). Transport and health: En route to a healthier Australia? *Medical Journal of Australia, 172*(5), 230–232.

McMichael, T. (2001). *Human frontiers, environments and disease*. Cambridge: Cambridge University Press.

Mees, P. (2000). *A very public solution: Transport in the dispersed city*. Carlton South: Melbourne University Press.

Mees, P. (2005). Privatisation of rail and tram services in Melbourne: What went wrong? *Transport Reviews, 25*(4), 433–449.

Naughton, K. (2003). Three for the road. *Newsweek*, p. 34.

Riedy, C., & Diesendorf, M. (2003). Financial subsidies to the Australian fossil fuel industry. *Energy Policy, 31*, 125–137.

Sallis, J., Frank, L., Saelens, B., & Kraft, M. K. (2004). Active transportation and physical activity: Opportunities for collaboration on transportation and public health research. *Transportation Research Part A, 38*, 249–268.

Sandercock, L. (1990). *Property, politics, and urban planning: A history of Australian city planning, 1890–1990*. New Brunswick: Transaction Publishers.

Sperritt, P. (1987). Cars and the people. In A. Curthorys, A. W. Martin, & T. Rowse (Eds.), *Australians from 1939*. Sydney: Fairfax, Syme & Weldon Associates.

Timperio, A., Crawford, D., Telford, A., & Salmon, J. (2004). *Perceptions about the local neighborhood and walking and cycling among children preventive medicine, 38*, 39–47.

Tranter, P. (2003). Motor racing in Australia: Health damaging or health promoting? *Australian Journal of Primary Health, 9*(1), 50–58.

Tranter, K. M. (2005). The history of the Haste-Wagons': *The motor car act (1909) (Vic.), emergent technology and the call for law. *Melbourne University Law Review Association, 29*(3), 843–879.

Wener, R., & Evans, G. (2007). A morning stroll: Levels of physical activity in car and mass transit commuting. *Environment and Behavior, 39*(1), 62–74.

Chapter 8
The Weight of Time: From Full to Fragmented in 50 Years

Image 8.1 Labour and time saving devices, 1946 (Source: State Library of Victoria)

Reports of increasing time pressure are ubiquitous and widely debated. A key point of contest is whether these are 'mere perceptions' in the minds of people who feel rushed, or whether they are real and understandable responses to socio-economic and technical change (Szollos 2009). Overall, excessive time pressure is felt to be undesirable; yet perhaps paradoxically, busyness is also culturally valued, signalling productivity and personal importance (Gershuny 2005; Greenfeld 2005; Yakura 2001). The experts in our Delphi study told us that 'time pressure' was one of the top two major social trends underlying the rise in contemporary population

C. Banwell et al., *Weight of Modernity: An Intergenerational Study of the Rise of Obesity*, DOI 10.1007/978-90-481-8957-1_8, © Springer Science+Business Media Dordrecht 2012

obesity (Banwell et al. 2005). Indeed, other research shows that a sense of time pressure—feeling stressed by having too much to do in the time available—is becoming widespread (Hochschild 1997; Strazdins and Loughrey 2007), so it is important to understand what might underlie these experiences of time.

Conceptually and analytically, however, time and time pressure present significant challenges. Time is a multilayered, ambiguous term whose referent can shift rapidly (Wilk 2009). In the sentence 'What time is it?', the speaker implies a very different implicit understanding of the term than if they were to say 'I don't have time for that.' These ambiguities complicate the study of temporal experience, and the interpretation of both textual and statistical data about time. Thus, instead of constituting a clearly defined social trend, experiences of time are embedded in all aspects of daily life, including paid employment, domestic work, childcare and social relations. They are also implicated in social practices (Egger and Swinburn 1997), including the practices that ultimately constitute patterns of physical activity and food consumption. The structures organising and shaping patterns of time use simultaneously *arise from* and in turn *contribute to* major social institutions, especially the family and household and the economy. In this chapter, we offer a detailed exploration of the experiences of time and time pressure from the perspectives of three generations of Australians whose lives span the unfolding of contemporary culture, and hence the emergence and proliferation of the modern culture of hurry.

The chapter begins by sketching briefly the historical context before reporting in more detail what the interviewees said, and how we have interpreted the development of temporal profiles from decade to decade, and from generation to generation.

8.1 Times Past

Philosophical and social science discussions of time observe that for most of human history, time has been understood as fundamentally cyclical, with human life governed by the movements of the sun and the seasons (Tainter 1995). Such a view of time is still held in the majority of societies globally. However, understandings of time are being altered by several large-scale changes, notably the economic and technical transformations of urbanisation and industrialisation. More recently those two broad developments have combined with globalisation and innovations in communication technology to generate a revolution in people's ways of viewing and managing time. While the onset of a new temporal/spatial perspective is neither abrupt nor decisive, retrospectively a 'sea change' may be evident (Dixon et al. 2006). New approaches to time have reinforced the contemporary linear understanding of the passage of time which assumes moving from a specific origin toward a conclusion or goal. This linear perspective has become dominant and is now largely taken for granted in urban life and business, even as it co-exists with other understandings (Stein 2001). For example, Baumann proposes that contemporary society is 'pointillist', suggesting that everyday life has come to be characterised by ever shorter events, punctuated by constant interruptions (Bauman 2008). As Southerton and colleagues put it, "activities appear to be divided into ever-shorter episodes... which [contributes to] a sense of being 'harried'" (Southerton et al. 2001, p. 9).

Davison has described these temporal transformations in Australia since European settlement in 1788. Despite agrarian societies being tethered to the dictates of daylight, weather and season, the Protestant virtue of punctuality formed part of the colonial Australian agenda for the moral improvement of children, convicts and Indigenous people. Prisons and factories operated according to strict institutional timetables in the effort to cultivate self-discipline among inmates, while people who worked the land still lived according to the ancient rhythms. For the first century of European settlement, any reference to clock time was local, marked by church or municipal bell-towers (Davison 1993).

During the nineteenth century, the construction of the rail and telegraph systems necessitated a gradual regulation and synchronisation of society, and an Australian national standard time was established in 1895. Pocket watches were initially markers of occupation (railway employees, tram driver) or status (businessmen) and gender (pocket watches were men's possessions) (Davison, pp. 68–70). New technologies (including domestic) began to regulate time not only on the job but in the home. For example, the availability of gas stoves enabled much more precise management of cooking temperatures than was possible with solid fuel, leading to recipes that were "expressed in precise hours and minutes rather than in the old fashioned formulae of risings and thickenings" (Davison, p. 95). As more men's work lives came under precise time discipline, home life necessarily followed. While a farm wife might have scheduled the evening meal by anticipating the fading of daylight, the urban wife ordered her domestic duties by the clock which governed the beginning and end of her husband's workday and children's school hours. Servants typically had longer work hours than their employers, with daily rhythms dictated by the families for whom they worked, and conventions of class and gender.

Scientific management, time-and-motion studies, and a range of new technologies such as conveyor belts and the punch clock expanded the relations of production that were regulated by the clock. World War I produced new forms of temporal order, requiring the recognition of standardised time across geographic distance to make strategic coordination possible. As men were mobilised for the military and women replaced them in the factories and fields, a new need for efficiency emerged. The interwar years are described as "the heyday of domestic punctuality," as "the punctual household seems to have been a source of both pride and security" to a generation unsettled by "...the uncertainties of war and depression" (Davison, p. 138). World War II made efficiency a priority again, and the introduction of the 40-h workweek (in 1948) prompted managers to focus on minimising 'wasted' time on the job in order to get maximum value from the hours employees were at work. This has been described as the 'Taylorisation' of time as "increasingly more spheres of daily life are regulated by principles of the efficient sequencing of tasks" (Southerton 2006, p. 438).

Thus, people's experiences of time—apparently so intimate and personal—reflect and embody a wide range of cultural, economic, political and social dimensions

(Wajcman 2008). In light of those multiple contributions, perhaps it should not be surprising that discursive and personal representations of time are so diverse.

The cultural time norms and values prevalent in Australia at the beginning of the twenty-first century form the symbolic location from which the people we interviewed talked to us about time in their lives. When the oldest generation were growing up, the foundations of a modern time-scape were being laid in urban Australia. We wondered whether they noticed temporal changes that were occurring. Similar issues—at a different stage in their development—could be relevant to the middle generation. For all three generations, we wanted to know how they managed their own time at different phases in their lives. What did they notice about the temporal lives of friends and family members? How did they experience and explain current patterns?

8.1.1 Talking About Time

People spoke of being busy in a variety of ways and for a range of reasons. Their accounts contain rich descriptions of their time-biographies and time-styles, showing both continuity and change over the decades and from generation to generation. Generally, they were quite nuanced in the ways they described being busy, often explicitly distinguishing it from time pressure, or what we would describe as time scarcity or not having enough time to do all that they want to do or all that they feel obligated to do. Occasionally, the subject of time came up spontaneously in an interview, but we usually had to ask about it specifically.

The accounts from the people we interviewed suggest that at particular stages in the lifecourse, people will notice qualitative differences in their experiences of time, and that additional cultural and economic changes in time-stories may have occurred as well. That is, we identified both age or lifecourse patterns in people's apparent 'time-styles', as well as period and generational (cohort) patterns (Mackay 1997), themes elaborated in Chap. 9.

8.1.2 Not Busy, Just Life: Busiest Times for the Lucky Generation

In response to our asking when they had been the busiest, the overwhelming majority of both the Lucky Generation and the Baby Boomers said it was while they were having and raising their children. For the oldest respondents, this period in their personal lives corresponded to the era of post-war reconstruction (1945–1970) which has been described as a 'golden age' in modern Australian history (Hancock 2002): an era of nearly full (male) employment, rising real wages, and an industrial relations regime that protected the interests of many vulnerable workers. Nearly two thirds of participants mentioned the child-rearing stage as the busiest. This was intensified for employed mothers who had 'the second shift'[1] of responsibility for household work and childcare as well as a paying job (Bittman and Wajcman 2000; Pocock 2003). For example, Shirley jealously guarded a little time each weekend to do her 'own thing' while her husband and children went go-karting, but Sunday night would come the reckoning.

> *... getting organised for Monday morning, that was always hanging over my head. Have to do that so that I'm ready for the week. That's the time that used to stress me out. I needed to be organised so that when Monday came I was finished and everybody had their clothes for the week and I had everything ready for the week to go, so yes, Sunday nights that was always on my mind that hey, I've got still a lot of things to do.*

Other research (such as studies using time diaries) confirms this lifecourse pattern in time pressure (Apps and Rees 2005; Goodin et al. 2002; Rice et al. 2006).

One woman said the time pressure she experienced during her child-rearing resulted from the number of children she had: she felt that four had been manageable, but five was *too many*. Several mentioned the number of children, with children's ages defining the time demands for some. For example, having babies who needed hands-on care, or teenage children involved in many activities outside the home generated busyness for their parents. Women's responses placed caring for others in the foreground of their accounts of being busy. Edith's circumstances were particularly taxing because of the number of dependants for whom she was caring.

> *I had four children under three and a half. I can't remember what happened, it was so busy. That was the time I had my mother and she was incontinent and I would be up during the night to her and then the children, and it was just a very, very hectic time for me.*

She gave up netball, socialising and other relaxation, concluding *I was never able to do anything.* As Peggy summed it up, *I'd say you can't dispute that when you've got small children, you're at your busiest.*

In addition to both male and female respondents who identified the child-rearing life stage as the busiest, a number of men described a specific employment situation (being in management, starting a small business, working two jobs, having their wife go back to work) as the source of their busiest phase. William said *any management type of position there is always pressures, always.* Richard, who ran his own retail business which involved long hours, 6 days a week recalled, *I don't think I ever had time to stop for lunch.* Even men who also mentioned having children at home when they were busiest tended to represent their family situation as part of the context, but their account of being busy emphasised what was happening at (and because of) work, or very occasionally, the conjunction of family and work. Charles observed that *having a family and that and when you're working, you don't seem to have any time. I couldn't take up golf until I retired.* John said he had *always been described as a 'workaholic,'* and indicated that he had only recently begun *to slow down a bit.*

---

[1] While the percentage of married women in paid employment in Australia stagnated below 20% at the end of World War II, and remained low until the 1970s, more than 60% of our female participants had worked for pay at some stage, many part-time and usually after children were all in school.

Although most had been very busy during the active parenting years, and in retrospect remarked on all they accomplished, very few described this life phase as unpleasantly pressured. In drawing the distinction between being busy on the one hand, and being time-pressured on the other, they were likely to observe that 'having a lot on' was preferable to being bored, as long as there wasn't too much or too many competing demands. Having some household support may have affected the view of Frank, a father of six.

> *We were both working, used to get someone to come in to be there when they came home in the afternoon. And we knew we were busy but we fitted things in, did things together... We didn't feel we were missing out.*

A common theme in the interviews with this generation is summarised in the statement reiterated by a number of the Lucky Generation: *We didn't think of it as being busy. It was just life. You just got on with it.*

Being busy had multiple sources and meanings. Some respondents said that urgent deadlines, numerous or competing claims on their time, and the need to juggle demands all contributed the feeling of being busy—perhaps too busy. They also mentioned periods when life seemed particularly fast-paced which might be related to (but was still distinct from) having many things to get done. William recalled:

> *At one stage, my doctor, I developed a rash on the body which I couldn't overcome, shall we say. He said, "You will have that till the time you finish work". Since I retired, it has disappeared.*

In fact, the pressure of a promotion to a more senior management position with more responsibility prompted him to take early retirement when the opportunity arose. Time pressure (distinguished from being busy) was mentioned particularly when people described life with long hours, shift work, financial and material hardship, heavy responsibility, anxiety and fatigue. Experiencing material hardship might amplify a sense of time pressure, such as for those whose fathers lost their jobs during the Depression, and individuals who worked two jobs in order to pay the bills. But sometimes money problems eclipsed time pressure. As Lindsey put it: *There were more worrying things. Like financial matters.*

Those who were caught by severe time pressure recalled the circumstances as distressing and costly to personal health and wellbeing, and to family relationships. For example, Margaret described circumstances similar to Edith's: caring for young children and an incontinent mother-in-law which she said was *Terrible. Very debilitating. Very exhausting.* Several mentioned missing out on time with their children, and two men volunteered (sadly or with some bitterness) that long work hours and career ambition had cost them their marriages. Robert was another self-described *workaholic* who held down two jobs. His wife also worked, and they enjoyed a level of material comfort that was unusual among our Lucky Generation respondents (two cars, frequent entertaining, restaurant food), but the marriage ended when their children were still in their teens. Broken sleep (from either paid or caring work) was a form of time stress. Caring for a frail elder at the same time as a growing family (or in one case, a disabled grandchild) generated extreme time pressure, bordering on what has been labelled a "chaos narrative" (Frank 1995).

These experiences of time pressure share a common feature: lack of time sovereignty. That is, people do not believe that they have the capacity to decide how they allocate their time, and to what. The importance of time sovereignty was revealed in some positive accounts of busyness. Several older people said *right now* was the busiest time in their lives, as being retired allowed them to travel or become more involved in volunteer activities, hobbies and social commitments than they could when they were employed or had children at home, but none complained of this kind of busyness. *Going out* (of the home) was frequently virtually synonymous with 'being busy' for these people. Most enjoyed their current level of busyness because they had control over how they spent their time and the activities they chose to engage in.

Their preference for being busy (rather than being *bored* or not having enough to do) is not surprising, given that our oldest respondents were born during the interwar years when punctuality and efficiency were prominent national values, synonymous with patriotism and civic virtue. That is, respondents appeared to subscribe to prevalent social norms and values. They seemed to agree with the saying that 'idle hands are the devil's workshop,' to share in the broad cultural value that has become attached to busyness and the implicit attribution of laziness to anyone who is not busy. *I guess I've always been a busy person* and *I've got to be doing something* were typical self-descriptions. People who represented themselves this way seemed to embody being productively occupied, rather than harried, pressured or rushed. They have made being busy part of their personal identity.

Several also mentioned rushing (generally described as unpleasant) in contrast to being leisurely (preferred), taking one's time or having enough time to do things. The relevant aphorism here was that 'something worth doing is worth doing well'. A number mentioned that age and illness *slow you down*, so however people might have felt about hurrying, it became more difficult to do with the passing of years or onset of disability.

The theme of choice or having control appeared in people's accounts repeatedly. When they were doing what they wanted, or when they intentionally chose to take on numerous activities, they didn't feel oppressed by being busy. These periods in their lives and circumstances exemplified the image of the benefits of the positive form of busyness: being fruitfully engaged with rewarding activities. On the other hand, negative experiences of busyness were characterised by having responsibilities imposed upon them or feeling helpless, a victim of circumstance. During such periods, people had—by definition—little or no time sovereignty; instead they had a feeling of frantic rushing which made it difficult to enjoy much of anything. Edith's situation (described above) exemplifies such pressures, however willingly she may have assumed the responsibilities.

8.2 Managing Time Pressure

When people described the period in their life they were most pressed for time, we asked them about how they managed in those circumstances, and whether they took shortcuts or made sacrifices to cope. Most said they did not, although a bit of probing uncovered some practical compromises. For example, a few women said they cut down on housework, and when they spoke in more detail, it was evident that some adjustments had to be made. Instead of *sacrifices*, they tended to talk about meticulous planning and about being highly organised. Indeed, devising detailed schedules (with little margin for error) became a new chore as the increasing demands on their time required almost military coordination of people and tasks. Women mentioned preparing meals in batch lots and freezing them, paying for a particular task to be done (for example, ironing) or getting extended family or friends to supervise children after school, but none reported having had household servants.

A few (all employed women) mentioned leaving their children unsupervised before or after school, perhaps with responsibility for meal preparation, a chore that several recalled performing when they themselves were children to help their (employed or perhaps ailing) mothers. Judith (who worked afternoons and evenings) described her routine in some detail.

> *They would be leaving school as I was getting the train, and I would leave ... it sounds shameful now—it seems horrifying, but everyone did it, but I would leave the young girl to having her afternoon sleep because I knew that the older ones would be home from school. ...Then, their father would come home, because he started work early. He would get home about 4:30–5:00 and ... I'd have got the meal to a reasonable stage, and he would go ahead with it and see that they were bathed and got to bed, and so on.*

She and others commented without prompting that nowadays, children are virtually never left to fend for themselves unsupervised. *My children wouldn't dream of doing such things, and they're horrified to think ... I just ... it was a calculated risk, and I felt that it was OK.* Such observations noted that this shift had occurred even though many more mothers are now employed (another change on which they commented) and might need their children to be responsible for themselves occasionally. These contradictions are elaborated in Chap. 9.

Apparently issues of safety and security had not worried our participants much when they were parenting. Another Lucky Generation participant who had been employed during her active mothering years mentioned sending her children to school even when she knew they might be sick, hoping that they wouldn't become really ill or get a fever and be sent home. She had worried both about their health, and also about the possibility of having to leave work to care for them. This is a dilemma mentioned often by contemporary employed mothers (Vuckovic 1999).

Respondents who said they made sacrifices to cope with time pressure were likely to mention missing out on social life, not going out (or going out less), or giving up hobbies, relaxation or sports. As Lindsey put it: *We didn't go out, we didn't socialise, didn't have time, didn't have ready transport ... we didn't have babysitters, so we stayed home and looked after the family.* There was less *enjoyment time* (perhaps free time) during the child-rearing years, while they managed numerous overlapping tasks (Floro and Miles 2003). That is, generally people sacrificed what they defined as leisure activities so that they could fulfil obligations to family care and paid work.

Sleep might be another casualty of time pressure, so fatigue was both an indicator and a concomitant of being exceptionally busy. Virtually no one described taking shortcuts with the family's food to save time, with the exception of resorting to a very occasional take-away meal (fish and chips or Chinese were the only options), or giving up preparing home-made deserts, relying instead on ice cream and fruit (see Chap. 4) (Banwell et al. 2010). Apparently preparing cakes and steamed puddings was construed as a leisure activity, one that women relinquished with reluctance and perhaps guilt since they were—in that respect—not feeding their children quite the same way they had been fed when they were children themselves (Warde 1999).

8.2.1 Busy Boomers

In many ways, the accounts of the Boomer generation closely resembled those of the Lucky Generation. Like their parents, most of the Boomers identified their early parenting years as the busiest (except, of course, for the five who had not had children). Several still had dependent children at home when they were interviewed, so child-rearing and *right now* were the same for them. A mother with two adolescents at home remarked, *I don't find there's a lot of periods where I'll sit down and say "What'll I do next". It doesn't seem to happen.* The role of child-rearing in legitimising a claim to be time-pressured is evident from an interview with a single woman working full-time with no children, whose account was faintly defensive: *Even though I haven't got children and I'm not studying, I still feel quite time poor because I'm still out 10 h a day.* By contrast, another woman with no children (divorced, employed full-time) was remarkable in describing her weekends as relaxing, saying she *might get seven videos out…Just generally veg out for the day*. The only other participant (a man) from the Boomer generation who had no children used similarly exceptional language: *I think I have enough time to do whatever I wish to do.* No interviewee with children spoke in these terms.

Leanne (age 47) described the things she relinquished when she was busy.

> *It's my sport. Whether it be my exercise, swimming, my social tennis days, they are the things that have gone. And the garden, that gets put on the backburner until I have a day off. So probably the things I like most are the things you miss out on. But I guess I do see them as a luxury, as a hobby, whereas other things are seen as more of a necessity.*

Stephen left a job because he found *there wasn't time to do any of my sports or do the things that I like*, but not everyone could adopt that strategy. The addition of full-time work to family responsibilities prompted Lynette (age 51) to reorganise her life in order to be able to continue exercising.

> *I used to get up early every morning because I was paranoid about getting no exercise. So I would get up early every morning and go for a run or walk or swim before work. So that was being organised basically.*

Although we didn't ask about stress specifically, some respondents used the term, and made a distinction between being stressed and being busy. For example, Peter had held several volunteer positions (with APEX, Scouts, State Emergency

Services and Army Reserves) while he and his wife were rearing their children, as well as doing part-time jobs (for extra income) in addition to his regular occupation. Despite these multiple commitments, he said he did not find the demands stressful until restructuring within the large organisation where he worked led to *massive retrenching... and the bar was raised higher, and everyone had to keep jumping higher*, including working longer hours. His own job changed considerably and became *a very responsible position* which he described as *more stressed rather than busy*. These changes were compounded by an injury, *so it was becoming an existence, not a life*. Consequently, when he was offered a voluntary redundancy with a substantial payout, he accepted the option of early retirement.

His experience points to the role of choice and control that was also highlighted by the Lucky Generation. When the time demands had been of his own making, he enjoyed what he was doing. But when external forces came to determine more of the allocation of his time and energy, it ceased to feel like *a life*. Also similar to their Lucky generation parents, those Boomers who have retired remarked that they are now busy with things they have chosen to do, and hence enjoyed it, reinforcing the theme of the centrality of choice and control.

Despite the similarities in their ways of speaking about time, there was evidence of the beginnings of significant change in the parenting years of the Boomers, particularly when their children reached adolescence. Multiple structured extracurricular activities appeared much more frequently in their narratives—activities that relied on parental involvement for transport, at least. Peter remarked that they became so time-pressured by their Gen Y teenage children's numerous extracurricular activities that they bought them cars as soon as they were old enough to drive to be relieved of having drive them all over town. This was a marked contrast to what the Boomers described about their own teenage years when they walked, cycled or used public transport. If they got a car before leaving home, they had to save a long time to buy it. It also contrasts with the largely unstructured non-school time of most Lucky and Boomer childhood and adolescent life. The effort needed to organise and coordinate many extracurricular activities appears for the first time when the Boomers described the lives of their teenagers, and of course the Boomers' teenagers are our Gen Y interviewees.

8.2.2 Gen Y: Already Hectic

Because they do not (with one exception) yet have children (and indeed some never will), the Gen Y participants in this study have no child-rearing phase on which to reflect, but a few were aware of the generational differences in the age sequencing of life transitions. The contrast with her own relatively unencumbered life as a teacher prompted Julie to observe, *when my parents were my age, they had three kids... they were married... living off my dad's PhD scholarship or whatever.* Those who do go on to have children may eventually concur with their parents and grandparents about when they were busiest. But for now, they say that it has generally been study (particularly when combined with paid work) that generated time pressure for them. Several described their final year of high school as particularly busy and requiring them to relinquish some activities such as sport and socialising with friends. Some commentators suggest intensifying stress surrounding the standard of academic (and perhaps other) accomplishment for the Gen Y respondents, perhaps compounded by time pressures. For example, a divorced Boomer mother with two grown children thought there were *more demands on them from an educational point of view. There is more pressure to do really well, so they studied harder. And there is more choice of things to do after school. And they are more social.* Another Boomer Lisa said the *expectations on teenagers are really climbing*. At age 20, Daniel seemed to confirm the impression. He really enjoyed playing football, but he found he had to give it up when he was doing his final year of high school. University studies, typically in tandem with part-time jobs, also generated considerable time-related stress for those from any generation who embarked upon such combinations. Those who participated in competitive sport faced what were typically very heavy time demands for training, and several had a range of commitments to music, competitive dance or drama, all of which could be time-consuming. Chap. 5 documents those demands, highlighting that while time scarcity is a culprit in adding to life pressures, it acts alongside performance anxiety, lack of money and frustration at not being able to be more flexible with scheduling, especially in relation to seeing friends.

Several from Gen Y were concerned about finding time to spend socialising with friends, and were aware of making what might be difficult trade-offs in order to do so. David (aged 27) usually preferred to protect *my social time* rather than *spend time by myself at the gym,* echoing the experiences discussed in Chap. 6 about dancing and aerobics as increasingly individualistic pursuits, chosen because they are time-efficient ways of keeping fit.

Even though (with one exception) they are not yet parenting, some of them have adopted time management strategies reported by the two older generations, such as developing detailed schedules, and pre-preparing food for several meals at once. Melissa tried not to give up other activities while she had a lot of academic demands and a paid job, and as long as she continued to live at home, that was feasible because her mother managed meals and domestic tasks, and her parents helped her with homework and drove her places. When she moved into her own accommodation, she found she needed to plan her time more carefully. *I use my diary a lot more.* She felt that it *puts pressure on whether you eat healthy, and whether you stay fit.* She now works full-time as a teacher and lives with her partner who is also a teacher. Reflecting on balancing the need for food that is both healthy and quick to prepare when they get home, she commented on the ease of eating out as a solution, *I'm sure we'd love to be cooked for every night, but it just doesn't happen.*

The experience of a hectic, pressured life is evident in the description of Melissa, who began dancing in high school.

> *From 18–20, I was dancing a lot and working a lot, and it was really, like, Saturdays used to be my main day for training....I used to dance from like at least 9.30 in the morning until about 3.30, and then drive straight to my job and work until 12.30, 1 o'clock in the morning...I don't know. I just used to go flat out all the time for those couple of years.*

Only an injury prompted her to stop dancing, acknowledging in retrospect that *it was just…too much pressure actually.*

8.2.3 Generations of Time

In addition to their personal experiences of time, we asked our respondents how they saw busyness for their parents, and (where relevant) their adult children and their grandchildren. Exploring these comparisons supplied perspectives covering the whole of the twentieth century.

The relevance of the qualitative aspects of time was prominent in these discussions, as it had been in describing particular phases of their own time biographies. Virtually all of the oldest generation said their parents had a lot to do, and many people commented on the physicality of housework, transport and chores when they were young. *To me that was normal* said Valerie (Lucky Generation) who had helped her father with heavy farm work while she was growing up.

Cooking, cleaning and laundry were arduous and time-consuming when they entailed the literal hewing of wood and (less often) drawing of water as part of the task. Laundry was a demanding process for the mothers of the Lucky Generation, and might occupy an entire day (usually Monday). This continued for many of the Lucky Generation themselves into their young adult years: stoking the wood-fired copper in which to boil clothes and linen, manual scrubbing on a washboard, feeding wet items through a mangle, and hanging on a clothesline or perhaps inside in front of the fireplace or stove in inclement weather. When we asked what labour-saving devices they remembered their mother particularly appreciated, the most popular answers (requiring little reflection) were: a washing machine, a gas stove or a hot water system (closely followed by a refrigerator). For the first few years of their married lives (during the period of post-war material scarcity), many of our older respondents lived in circumstances very similar to their parents (perhaps initially with their parents). Consequently, when we asked them about their own favourite labour-saving device, they often also listed the washing machine or refrigerator as what they had welcomed most. Like the Luckies, many Baby Boomers and even a few Gen Y participants could recall their parents' appreciation at getting a washing machine. When she was asked about the most useful labour-saving device she ever had, Shirley replied immediately

> *Good old washing machine. My mother had a copper, boiled up every Sunday night, was all set in the ready waiting for Monday morning, that was the ritual. Monday morning washing, Tuesday morning ironing, so I have to say a washing machine.*

Similarly, walking, cycling and using public transport—now called active transport—were the norm for the first half of the twentieth century. When they were growing up, and often well into their early child-rearing years, many Lucky and Boomer respondents described cycling or walking substantial distances to school, recreation, work or shopping. The time impost of active transport was evident to them looking back on earlier years, but it was not remarkable when they were cycling many kilometres to school, the beach or a dance. *It was just what we did*, as one put it. *Everyone did the same.* Such language suggests a sense that there was no decision to be made. It was simply the way the world worked in that time and place. This was true for the two older generations, but had virtually disappeared when Gen Y reached adolescence.

Quite a few of the oldest respondents listed the car among their labour-saving devices, acknowledging that it enabled people to travel farther in the same time, to reach more destinations, and hence to become involved in a wider range of activities. How that was interpreted in terms of busyness, however, was variable. Lorraine (Lucky) saw her mother's life as much busier than her own because her mother never had a car and often had to walk long distances, yet Kevin thought his mother was less busy for the same reason. A few suggested that cars used or wasted time, even if they saved physical effort, a theme also applied to other items of technology. For example, one Lucky respondent had a dishwasher but rarely used it. *You see, I can't be bothered. If I have to wash up saucepans and that, I'd rather wash them [all]... Basically I still wash up.* This distinction between labour-saving and time-saving was a common motif, and seems to accord with analyses of automobile (Tranter 2010) and other modes of transport (Metz 2008), and with research showing the more rapid diffusion of time-using technology (radio, TV) than time-saving technology (such as the vacuum cleaner) (Bowden and Offer 1994, 1996). Thus, the effect of new technology on time or busyness is far from singular, but instead forms part of the complex relationship between time pressure and socio-technical change.

When the Boomers and Gen Y were asked whether they could imagine living without a car, the answer was often blunt 'no way!', as if shocked by the very idea. This was usually followed by a more detailed explanation that they could not do nearly as many things if they had no car. They felt they would be extremely constrained if they had to rely entirely on walking, cycling and public transport, as discussed in Chap. 7 on the rise of automobility.

Very few of our respondents mentioned having any regular paid help with domestic work, despite the fact that a 1996–97 Australian survey of over 1,000 couple families found that almost 20% used paid household help (housework or garden) (Baxter et al. 2009). Indeed, domestic service was a major occupation for many women in Australia until World War II (which recruited women to work in factories) and the era of post-war prosperity and industrialisation generated other alternatives. Indeed, the difficulties bourgeois families experienced recruiting and retaining household servants is in some ways a good indicator of the toil involved in domestic work until the advent of a few genuinely labour-saving technologies (Broom 1986). Women who could find alternative employment did so, and use of paid domestic help almost disappeared during the 1960s, beginning to rise again only in the 1990s (Baxter 2009).

New domestic technologies and their associated household routines are more evident to conscious observation than the less visible but potentially no less significant cultural change over the decades. Several people commented on shifting housework standards, or rising women's employment as relevant to time use. But no one said anything about new personal practices such as 'daily bathing…, once a dangerous folly, then a luxury, and finally a necessity.' (Wilk 2009, p. 149). Yet such a dramatically revised personal practice may have major implications for time and time pressure.

Looking both up and down the generations, many from the two older generations were convinced that the pace of life has sped up during their lifetimes. Baby Boomer Stephen with a primary-school age daughter described a strategy that might be called tag-team parenting with his wife so that they could each have time to exercise. Comparing his own life to his parents' at the same age, he said

> *Probably a lot more hectic now. Probably [we] try to cram a lot more into our lives than they did. And then they tended to have more fixed hours. Pretty much routine…there's a lot more these days.*

The car was particularly implicated in the ever-quicker pace of life. But they drew a distinction between work or transport involving time and effort (being physically hard), and the speed with which tasks (including transport) must be performed. The physical demands had been considerably reduced during the lifetimes of the oldest interviewees, while the speed of performing tasks had increased. *The pace of life has increased. Everybody's in a hurry these days*, was Lucky Generation Kenneth's succinct (and widely shared) opinion. They often contrasted their own experiences with those of their adult children and grandchildren. *The demands on your life are greater now…[There is] pressure to do things quickly* as another Lucky Generation member said. According to Brian, *My kids, they're moving around faster now than I was at their age*. Kenneth observed how much more quickly international news reaches people today, compared to their experience during World War II when *the news we got was often out of date*. This was in vivid contrast to contemporary instant and constant online access.

Like the contrasting assessments regarding cars and time, older respondents had various evaluations of other aspects of life. A particular commitment (such as ferrying children to activities and engagements) was an indicator of busyness in some people's views, and a signal that the person was *not that busy* for others. That is, despite the many similarities in their early lives, and their concurrence regarding when was their busiest life phase, people's reflections on specific elements of time pressure were far from uniform.

Whatever people said about time pressure, they tended to volunteer observations about these distinctions as refinements, clarifications of their descriptions of time. When we asked them to describe how busy their own lives were compared to their parents and their children, quite a number of felt that it was *impossible to compare*, saying that each generation is *different busy*. That is, they wanted us to note the qualitative (not quantitative) differences. Several of the Boomers had spent some early adult/child-rearing years in Papua-New Guinea or elsewhere in the Pacific, affording them a very culturally different perspective on time and time use than was developing in urban Australia in those years, and they referred to those experiences in commenting on what is happening now.

8.2.4 Choice: Part of the Problem or Part of the Solution?

Several of our oldest respondents proposed, either directly or indirectly, an hypothesis to account for the contemporary experience of time pressure. Nearly all suggested in one way or another that the plethora of choices now available to their children and especially grandchildren is central to the growing prevalence of time pressure. Joy said that when her mum was getting older, *there was the church and Senior Cits [Citizens]. That was it. There was nothing else. There is so much available now.* The dramatic increase in options from which to select is one of the main markers of difference between the generations, a change that has been documented in some detail (Schwartz 2004a, b). In one woman's view, *The variety of life ... avenues presented to you are greater, so there's a demand to try to do them all.* Combined with the escalating pace (*Everybody is in a hurry*), perhaps paradoxically, the perception of choice—the very element that can protect people from experiencing busyness as time pressure—has multiplied to the point that it is now coming to feed the sense of time pressure. In a dynamic that recalls *The Omnivore's Dilemma* (for food), our older respondents see the proliferation of sites, activities, commodities, and possibilities as fuel for the fire of time pressure to which the rising generations are subject (Katz-Gerro and Sullivan 2010). The Lucky Generation appears to have experienced little of the 'confusion and anxiety' (Pollan 2006) surrounding schedules and time commitments that are so characteristic of the kinds of time pressure reported by Baby Boomers and Gen Y. The "fragmenting of time slots" generates a need for family members and friends to arrange to see each other, since a common schedule can no longer be relied upon to bring people together. "The imperative to organise time… has invaded everyday life, eroding routines and compelling …. People…to embark on scheduling strategies." (Warde 1999)

In a description that combines the themes of speed and the number of activities, James told us that his son worked weekends and often travelled overseas for work, saying *I think I can describe it as maniacal*. Several respondents distinguished among their children, noting that one individual might be extremely busy while another was not. That is, not everyone offered the simple generational-difference perspective to which others subscribed. Sometimes, it was not clear whether they were drawing distinctions or were simply supplying specific details. *I know my boy that's married, he's got great demands on his kids to get them [around]… They're into all sorts of things. There's so much more activity now.* (Lindsey)

Superficially, the possibility that choice may drive time pressure seems to contradict the notion (mentioned above) that having choice or control over the allocation of one's time often made the difference between being busy versus being weighed down or trapped. People told us that time demands assumed voluntarily were welcome; those beyond the person's control could escalate to leave them overwhelmed and debilitated in the effort to do everything that needed to be done.

On closer inspection, however, the contradiction may be more apparent than real. Time sovereignty—the resource that distinguishes productive engagement from strain—is partly a result of objective circumstances (such as the number of co-residents who are physically dependent) and partly a function of what has been called 'perception'; that is, the sense that one is subject to excessive or conflicting demands. Critics of contemporary time–pressure discourse have insisted that such perceptions are generally mistaken; cases of people ignoring significant 'degrees of freedom' that are 'objectively' available, and failing to allocate time to what they say are important priorities. Some commentators have suggested that if people would reflect more thoughtfully on their circumstances, they would discover that their feeling of time pressure is self-inflicted, a consequence of their own decisions that could be modified. Occasionally, such criticism implies or explicitly names various individual shortcomings (laziness, greed) as the root causes of time pressure: wanting 'everything', being unwilling to wait and save for things, or being neurotically overprotective of children.

At least two important elements are missing from these judgmental analyses of the contemporary time crisis: a detailed consideration of people's diverse socio-economic circumstances, and the operation of a competitive culture in structuring people's understandings, experiences and management of time. While it may seem simple and obvious (if counter-cultural) to recommend 'downshifting' (working fewer hours for a lower income), setting more modest goals for the family's level of consumption, or ignoring media headlines about child injuries and abductions (to free parents from the need to supervise children or enroll them in numerous expensive and time-consuming activities), those are not options for families who already spend long hours in low-paying jobs, commute long distances from suburbs where housing is more affordable, or who live in unsafe neighbourhoods.[2] Part-time jobs—when available—might reduce work hours, but typically entails minimal control over when hours are worked, diminishing an important aspect of time sovereignty that is particularly crucial during the parenting years. Lone parents, who are reckoned as the most time-pressured by virtually all research, are unlikely to be able to consider a more 'modest' lifestyle as a way to relieve their time pressure. Many dual-earner households achieve improved incomes at the expense of time (Strazdins et al. 2011), sacrificing personal recreation and sleep in order to meet the demands of the workplace and to preserve time with children (Craig 2007). Even families on more substantial incomes living in comparatively safe areas will require an unusually high level of cultural critique or self-awareness to refuse contemporary incitements to hyper-consumption, to decline electronic interaction and entertainment, or to cease raising their children according to newly demanding norms of parenting (Banwell et al. 2007). Only two Boomers talked about consciously restricting their children's choices, thus resisting the trend. For example, Carol (aged 60) had six children, four boys followed some years later by a girl and a boy. She made a distinction between being active and being busy, and noticed the change between the two groups of children. Of the older four, she observed: *They weren't as busy in those days, they were more settled, somehow,*

[2] Those who may wish to downshift must now consider that option in the context of persistent global financial turbulence that is provoking new anxieties about future job and income security.

than the younger two. She had rationed the range of activities, even for the four boys, requiring them to agree on one sport they would all play in order to limit the driving she had to do:

> *I said to them 'Look, I'd love you to have sport, play sport'—that's the four boys—'and I'm not going to be running from one thing to another'. You know, because it's too fragmented. So they decided—they chose to play baseball, which was really good. And so my husband would help on weekends. ... they'd have to travel to different games and they had one night a week of practice. But that was really all. ... So baseball was the thing and so that kept them busy, but not too busy. Because they had their homework, their schoolwork and stuff like that and, because we value education highly and we were very strong on that.*

She went on to reflect, *I don't know whether it's just the expectations of our culture, but with the younger two, they're just so much busier... the meals, therefore became more disjointed.* Dealing with the plethora of choices itself becomes a time-consuming task. When the Lucky Generation were young, there were comparatively few consumer products, and very few brands or models of any particular product: effectively there were two brands of cars for sale, two washing machines, two banks. Having few decisions to make as a consumer may have contributed to the kind of time sovereignty that characterised most of the Lucky generation's lives. The regularity, predictability and relative simplicity of their childhood and parenting years generated little need for the elaborate temporal-spatial coordination that they see in the lives of the next generations, and that appeared in the accounts of the Boomers' parenting adolescents and in the stories from Gen Y of their own teenage years. The details of these developments are woven through the chapters on food and physical activity. In the middle of the three generations, Karen, a Baby Boomer and lone mother, expressed the emerging change.

> *I like to walk, but time is of the essence.*
> So is walking more of a leisure thing?
> *Yes, totally a leisure thing. Everything else is in the car, out of necessity.*

The sacrifice of whatever is defined as 'leisure' was evident for all three generations. The contrast between the grandparents and grandchildren, however, is that the Luckies had a habitus of habit: a life of comparatively regular routines and rhythms that required occasional adaptation but rarely necessitated new decisions. Most of the schedules, strategies and technologies of modern time management were absent because there was relatively little flexibility about what to do or when; those decisions were culturally, institutionally and technologically fixed, thus sparing people the temporal anxiety they see in their grandchildren.

Due in part to an increasingly commodified culture of time-saving, efficiency and vigilant attention to scheduling, the seeds of that particular form of time pressure were sown in the childbearing years of the Boomers, expanded markedly when their children reached adolescence, and have fully developed in the young adult lives of Generation Y. Their lives and experiences confirm the argument of Schwartz that having 'a surfeit of alternatives' is as harmful to wellbeing as having no opportunity to choose how one will invest one's energies (Schwartz 2004a, b). The 'sweet spot' between no choice and too many options seems to elude many from Gen Y, and perhaps future generations as well.

8.3 Conclusion

In a sense, these three generations may represent a particular form of temporal reversal. What was special and unusual in mid-twentieth century Australia (frequent use of pre-prepared and catered food, involvement in multiple activities outside the home, school and workplace, reliance on the private motor car) had become the norm by the 1990s and early 2000s. On the other hand, fixed routines for work (both paid and unpaid) and highly predictable menus for home-cooked family meals that were typical for much of the twentieth century were gradually replaced by constant variety and change in what happens and where on any given day at any given time, generating a kind of temporal turbulence requiring real-time communication, constant vigilance and rapid adaptation on the part of individuals and households. The lone mother (Boomer) quoted above said evening meals now are *anarchy*. When asked to describe a typical evening, she said:

> *Well, there isn't one...Three adults living in a house, with three lives. No two evenings are the same. And my eldest son has a partner and she has a 6-year old. So it can go from a night in...If I know I'm the only one home, which is rare...the first thing I will get out is a Lean Cuisine. My idea is that I can get that over and done with and do something entertaining. Use that time by yourself...It can go from that to ringing up [son] and saying "What's happening tonight?" "Oh, [son's partner] is coming over with [partner's child]" and we could have the whole catastrophe. My two sons, me, a 6 year-old, and a girlfriend. So some nights it's all of us sitting around. And then [other son] saunters out and cooks his own meal because he is a vegetarian. But if we are all there I say "Let's try and pull it together" so we all sit down.... Sometimes I get home and [son and his partner] are already there and they have started. He finished early, he's a tradesman. So I might get home at 5.30 and it's already started. Or if I've rung him from work and he's said they are all coming, I'll say "I'll get a cooked chook and we'll do veggies when I get home." So its very ad hoc.*

That is, what used to be exceptional (unpredictability, constant negotiation) has become the norm, while the previous norm (predictable routine) has become the exception. In Chap. 9, these themes are examined in detail in light of all the findings in this book and in the context of social science theory.

We did not set out to conduct a time use study, nor do we aim to resolve the debates about time pressure or to intervene in the development of various competing social theories of time/space (May and Thrift 2001). Research that focuses on such matters often identifies paradoxical temporal effects, such as the persistence of time spent on some housework tasks (such as laundry) despite reductions in the physical effort required (Vanek 1974). Changing norms and standards, and the fragmentation of tasks may contribute to some of these unexpected changes (Shove 2003). They also help make sense of the seemingly irresolvable debate about whether people today actually have more free time than previous generations. Few people feel they have much time they describe as free, spare or leisure, no matter how surveys and statistics may measure the average objective expenditure and disposition of time.

Image 8.2 Multi-technology for managing time, 2012 (Source: J. Dixon)

References

Apps, P., & Rees, R. (2005). Gender, time use, and public policy over the life cycle. *Oxford Review of Economic Policy, 21*(3), 439–461. doi:10.1093/oxrep/gri025.

Banwell, C., Hinde, S., Dixon, J., & Sibthorpe, B. (2005). Reflections on expert consensus: A case study of the social trends contributing to obesity. *European Journal of Public Health, 15*(6), 564–568.

Banwell, C., Shipley, M., & Strazdins, L. (2007). The pressured parenting environment: Parents as piggy in the middle. In J. Dixon & D. H. Broom (Eds.), *The seven deadly sins of obesity: How the modern world is making us fat* (pp. 46–63). Sydney: University of New South Wales Press.

Banwell, C., Dixon, J., Broom, D., & Davies, A. (2010). Habits of a lifetime: Family dining patterns over the lifecourse of older Australians. *Health Sociology Review, 19*(3), 343–355.

Bauman, Z. (2008). *Does ethics have a chance in a world of consumers?* Cambridge: Harvard University Press.

Baxter, J. (2009). The sources of time pressure: Work, family and more. *Family Relationships Quarterly, 13*, 21–23.

Baxter, J., Hewitt, B., & Western, M. (2009). Domestic outsourcing: Choice and constraint in hiring household help. *Feminist Economics, 15*(1), 1–26.

Bittman, M., & Wajcman, J. (2000). Rush hour: The character of leisure time and gender equity. *Social Forces, 79*(1), 165–189.

Bowden, S., & Offer, A. (1994). Household appliances and the use of time: The united states and Britain since the 1920s. *Economic History Review, 47*(4), 725–748.

Bowden, S., & Offer, A. (1996). The technological revolution that never was: Gender, class, and the diffusion of household appliances in interwar England. In V. de Grazia (Ed.), *The sex of things: Gender and consumption in historical perspective*. Berkeley: University of California Press.
Broom, D. H. (1986). The occupational health of houseworkers. *Australian Feminist Studies, 1*(2), 15–34.
Craig, L. (2007). How employed mothers in Australia find time for both market work and childcare. *Journal of Family Economic Issues, 28*, 69–87.
Davison, G. (1993). *The unforgiving minute: How Australians learned to tell the time*. Melbourne: Oxford University Press.
Dixon, J., Hinde, S., & Banwell, C. (2006). Obesity, convenience and 'phood'. *British Food Journal, 108*(8), 634–645.
Egger, G., & Swinburn, B. (1997). An "ecological" approach to the obesity pandemic. *British Medical Journal, 315*, 477–480.
Floro, M. S., & Miles, M. (2003). Time use, work and overlapping activities: Evidence from Australia. *Cambridge Journal of Economics, 27*(6), 881–904. doi:10.1093/cje/27.6.881.
Frank, A. W. (1995). *The wounded storyteller: Body, illness, and ethics*. Chicago: University of Chicago Press.
Gershuny, J. (2005). Busyness as the badge of honor for the new superordinate working class. *Social Research, 72*(2), 287–314.
Goodin, R. E., Rice, J. M., Bittman, M., & Saunders, P. (2002). *The time–pressure illusion: Discretionary time versus free time* (SPRC Discussion Paper No. 115). University of New South Wales.
Greenfeld, L. (2005). When the sky is the limit: Busyness in contemporary American society. *Social Research, 72*(2), 315–338.
Hancock, K. (2002). Work in an ungolden age. In R. Callus & R. D. Lansbury (Eds.), *Working futures: The changing nature of work and employment relations in Australia* (pp. 6–26). Sydney: The Federation Press.
Hochschild, A. R. (1997). *The time bind: When work becomes home and home becomes work*. New York: Henry Holt and Company.
Katz-Gerro, T., & Sullivan, O. (2010). Voracious cultural consumption: The intertwining of gender and social status. *Time & Society, 19*(2), 193–219.
Mackay, H. (1997). *Generations*. Sydney: Pan Macmillan.
May, J., & Thrift, N. (2001). Introduction. In J. May & N. Thrift (Eds.), *Timespace: Geographies of temporality* (pp. 1–46). London: Routledge.
Metz, D. (2008). The myth of travel time saving. *Transport Reviews, 28*(3), 321–336.
Pocock, B. (2003). *The work/life collision*. Sydney: Federation Press.
Pollan, M. (2006). *The Omnivore's dilemma: A natural history of four meals*. New York: Penguin.
Rice, J. M., Goodin, R. E., & Parpo, A. (2006). The temporal welfare state: A crossnational comparison. *Journal of Public Policy, 26*(3), 195–228.
Schwartz, B. (2004a). *The paradox of choice*. New York: Harper.
Schwartz, B. (2004b). The tyranny of choice. *Scientific American, 290*, 70–75.
Shove, E. (2003). Converging conventions of comfort, cleanliness and convenience. *Journal of Consumer Policy, 26*(4), 395–418. doi:10.1023/a:1026362829781.
Southerton, D. (2006). Analysing the temporal organization of daily life: Social constraints, practices and fair allocation. *Sociology, 40*(3), 435–454. doi:10.1177/0038038506063668.
Southerton, D., Shove, E., & Warde, A. (2001). *'Harried and Hurried': Time shortage and the co-ordination of everyday life* (CRIC Discussion Paper, p. 21). Manchester: Centre for Research on Innovation & Competition.
Stein, J. (2001). Reflections on time, timespace compression and technology in the 19th century. In J. May & N. Thrift (Eds.), *Timespace: Geographies of temporality* (pp. 106–119). London: Routledge.
Strazdins, L., & Loughrey, B. (2007). Too busy: Why time is a health and environmental problem. *NSW Public Health Bulletin, 18*(11–12), 219–221.

Strazdins, L., Griffin, A. L., Broom, D. H., Banwell, C., Korda, R., Dixon, J., et al. (2011). Time scarcity: Another health inequity? Time-Space and Life-Course. *Environment and Planning A*, 43(3) 545–559.

Szollos, A. (2009). Toward a psychology of chronic time pressure: Conceptual and methodological review. *Time & Society, 18*(2–3), 332–350. doi:10.1177/0961463x09337847.

Tainter, J. A. (1995). Sustainability of complex societies. *Futures, 27*(4), 397–407.

Tranter, P. (2010). Speed Kills: The complex links between transport, lack of time and urban health. *Journal of Urban Health: Bulletin of the New York Academy of Medicine, 87*(2), 155–166.

Vanek, J. (1974). Time spent in housework. *Scientific American, 231*(November), 116–120.

Vuckovic, N. (1999). Fast relief: Buying time with medications. *Medical Anthropology Quarterly, 13*(1), 51–68.

Wajcman, J. (2008). Life in the fast lane? Towards a sociology of technology and time. *British Journal of Sociology of Education, 59*(1), 59–77.

Warde, A. (1999). Convenience food: Space and timing. *British Food Journal, 101*(7), 518–527.

Wilk, R. (2009). The age of agency: Routines, habits and volition. In E. Shove, F. Trentmann, & R. Wilk (Eds.), *Time, consumption and everyday life: Practice, materiality and culture* (pp. 143–154). Oxford: Berg.

Yakura, E. K. (2001). Billables: The valorization of time in consulting. *American Behavioral Scientist, 44*(7), 1076–1095.

Chapter 9
Social Forces Shaping Life Chances and Life Choices

Image 9.1 Intergenerational family and friend celebration for Baby Boomer bithday, Adelaide, 2012 (Source: J. Dixon)

One of the hallmarks of modern societies is their capacity to provide their citizens with an overwhelming sense of choice, agency, or freedom to select from many alternatives: how to use their individual talents, how they identify in terms of religion, politics and other social status attributes, or what goods and services they can buy. The narrative that brings these alternatives together promotes the idea that anyone can be whatever they want. A favoured mass media trope which celebrates this cultural characteristic is the millionaire who comes from a 'humble background',

C. Banwell et al., *Weight of Modernity: An Intergenerational Study of the Rise of Obesity*, DOI 10.1007/978-90-481-8957-1_9, © Springer Science+Business Media Dordrecht 2012

the paraplegic who excels at physical feats, the cancer victim who 'beats' the disease, the high school drop-out who becomes a High Court judge. According to these narratives, life choices trump life chances.

Thus, success is especially admired when the individual is considered to have overcome their destiny. These days, people of normal weight are viewed as successful: they have made healthy choices in the face of the overwhelming odds of succumbing to the many temptations that comprise the obesogenic environment. Descriptive epidemiology supports this view: in a near majority of OECD countries and an increasing number of Asian and Middle Eastern countries, the person who is normal weight is exceptional (Finucane et al. 2011; Sassi 2010).

However, our concern is to explain the unequal, and often unwelcome, choices and chances that are buried in obesity trend averages. More than six decades ago, Mills (1959/2000) called attention to problems in which public issues and personal troubles are intimately connected. Mills could have been discussing obesity when he said, "Nowadays men [and women] often feel that their private lives are a series of traps. They sense that within their everyday worlds, they cannot overcome their troubles, and in this feeling, they are often quite correct" (Mills 1959/2000, p. 3). One way of releasing the trap, according to Mills, is to "grasp history and biography and the relations between the two in society" (p. 4). Our research design is informed by an approach in sociology that operates at the intersection of the impersonal, remote transformations at the societal level and the intimate features of the self.

Here, we adopt Mills' argument to reconsider some of our data. 'The personal troubles of the milieu' are an individual's experience of his or her social setting, "and to some extent his [or her] willful activity" (p. 8); they are akin to the notion of life choices available to each cohort. This is the realm of biographical agency, of personal actions and rationales. Chapters 3 through 8 provide the accounts of 160 socially situated individuals, with each chapter focusing on the way particular socio-cultural dynamics influence life chances and life choices. These chapters bring together social environmental history and biography.

In them, readers can glimpse the extent to which individuals act in concert with the ebb and flow of the four obesogenic socio-cultural trends that were the focus of this book, and whether they feel they can resist the trend's undertow. They capture the 'personal troubles' or struggles to do what feels both personally correct and socially appropriate, which may be contradictory. Here is a brief overview of our major findings from those chapters.

9.1 How Socio-Cultural Trends Have Affected Diet and Physical Activity Over Three Generations

Chapter 3 shows that a shift has occurred from a rather restricted menu of foods and meals eaten at regular times and in a weekly pattern (during the Luckies' childhood) to today's easy access to a wide variety of foods and eating habits. The importance of eating with the family is diminishing, not because this is considered unenjoyable, but because solitary eating is an imperfect solution to the need to be flexible to accommodate the scheduling of other activities including: socialising with friends, paid work, study, house work, shopping, caring, physical activity. An important facilitator of flexible eating is the marketplace of convenience foods and the growing legitimacy of consuming them.

Convenience foods are often criticised for their calorie-rich nature, but it must be remembered that our Lucky Generation regularly ate high-calorie desserts. Whether recipes have changed so that marketplace offerings are more calorific, whether the portion sizes were more modest (in keeping with household budgets or social norms) is not known. Chapter 4 indicates that a home-made sweet daily in the context of a 'meat and three veg' meal and simple lunch does not appear to have been harmful. The question that is raised is whether health harms are the result of this routinised, home-based approach to meals and snacks being bypassed in favour of the extensive range of commercially prepared deserts, cakes, biscuits, ice cream and other sweets that are now widely available.

Chapter 5 offers two starkly different scenarios between the physical activity routines and experiences of the Lucky and Y generations. It documents how the incidental exercise of daily life coupled with social sports enjoyed by the Lucky Generation have given way to programmed physical exertion which competes with other activities like jobs and study. Like their Lucky Generation parents, adult Baby Boomers recognise the pleasures afforded by unstructured leisure social activity and hobbies but along with their Gen Y children, they struggle to juggle being physical in a context of work, family and community commitments. Further, as a national ethos of excellence in sport has been consolidated, people of all ages and capacities (witness the Masters Games, Paralympics) are encouraged to identify as 'sporty' or 'not sporty'. Those who are sporty spend considerable time and money in keeping fit, sports training, performing and attending to injuries. The social aspects of their endeavours become less important than personal and team achievements; and for Gen Y, parental support can add a layer of expectation.

Chapter 6 elaborates on the escalating expectations regarding being accomplished in physical activity. It describes how the physical activity dispositions of Gen Y are in stark contrast to their grandparents, who also valued staying fit but in a way that met other objectives, namely enjoyment and companionship. This chapter illustrates how fitness commodity cultures—in this case, the gym and aerobics culture—re-educate or reorient individual behaviours. They structure the chances of becoming physically active when other choices are denied because of higher-order structuring trends, especially labour force participation and transport systems that privilege the private automobile.

The material in Chaps. 3, 4, 5, and 6 leads us to the conclusion that food consumption and leisure-related physical activity practices have both become underpinned by processes of individualisation and commodification over the last 50 years. Furthermore, they are enmeshed and should no longer be considered discrete practices, as we have argued elsewhere. Food and car use have become increasingly intertwined (Hinde and Dixon 2005). For example, in the last few years, large supermarket chains have begun to collaborate with petrol retailers in co-promotion of their products (Evans 2003). Practices such as 'eating on the run' are facilitated by petrol stations that sell food, drive-thru fast food and gadgets that facilitate eating while travelling. A US study of driver practices revealed that 70% of drivers eat or drink while using their motor vehicles (Stutts et al. 2005). To complicate matters, in a car-reliant society, access to healthy food depends on access to an automobile. Our ethnographic research describes the intersection between the automobile and the food system and in particular the different roles of transport in procuring fast food and slow food. Fast food is accessible to people who travel by all modes of transport, but the purchase of slow food tends to rely more heavily on the consumer having access to automobile transport (Banwell et al. 2006).

The potent influence of commodity cultures on population behaviours reappears in Chap. 7. From being virtually non-existent when our Lucky Generation were children, car reliance is a ubiquitous feature of living 80 years later. It facilitates the relatively speedy movement across considerable distances which are a feature of Australian suburbs. Life without a car is deemed unimaginable, because the car allows the complex scheduling of daily life. Considered by some to be a labour-saving device, especially when they reflected on how earlier generations shopped, it can also be thought of as a 'time machine': a socio-technical system for organising society's movement and routines. The importance of the auto manufacturing sector to the Australian economy has made car ownership something akin to a civic duty until recently.

Chapter 8 approaches time from a sociological perspective, specifically examining how people had experienced the way time is socially organised and constructed. It is a matter of academic debate whether people are now busier because of increases in "obligated" time to work and caring demands, or whether they are attempting to fit more activities into their day. All three generations thought that the Baby Boomers and Gen Y were likely to be more time-pressured than the Lucky Generation had been at the same ages. Certainly, the need to manage and schedule multiple, diverse and time incompatible commitments, and to coordinate the travel and timetables of several family members, are key dynamics fostering acceptance of the social changes documented in the five previous chapters.

9.2 Emergent Socio-Cultural Trends

Re-reading the data that underpins Chaps. 3 through 8, we have identified three additional socio-cultural trends: the rise of health consciousness; the changing nature of family dynamics from a more hierarchical, patriarchal structure to a more child-centred structure; and the attenuation of habits and the embrace of cultural change. We explain what we found in general terms about these trends, before illustrating them through vignettes from one particular three-generation family.

9.2.1 The Rise in Health Consciousness

Over the three generations, health concerns ceased to be products of advancing age and ill health, and became a pervasive aspect of culture, regardless of age or health status. For the Lucky Generation, a focus on health arose most prominently in their 60s onwards, as specific problems (such as heart disease or arthritis) prevented them from undertaking their preferred activities. The Baby Boomers became aware of health linked to wellbeing in their young adult years. The younger generation, however, has always been aware of the health implications of physical activity and diet. Indeed, the duty to exercise and eat 'healthy food' seems to appear at younger ages with each successive generation. Perhaps because of this state of heightened reflexivity, being physical in particular has lost its positive connotations with freedom and enjoyment. This increasing awareness and concern for health maintenance is part of what has been described as the development of normative healthy citizenship (Cockerham 2007). It has arisen over the course of the twentieth century as chronic diseases associated with individual lifestyle health risks have replaced infectious diseases as the main causes of morbidity and mortality.

Perhaps surprisingly, one aspect of the growing health *zeitgeist* derives from an understanding of a genetic predisposition to health risks. Biomedical research shows the relevance of a genetic component to some chronic diseases, including those that are associated with obesity such as heart disease, high cholesterol and Type 2 diabetes. These are interrelated diseases in which family history is considered to play an important role. While individuals cannot change their genes or family history, many health promotion campaigns attempt to persuade people to modify their lifestyle to reduce their inherited risk. Such ideas have been widely promoted in Australia and have been adopted by study participants. Through this understanding of risk, a common familial approach to diet and physical activity over several generations of family members is promoted. One Baby Boomer said *I live in a family of cancer people.* In another family, the father had major heart problems at an early age and his children are aware that heart problems have a genetic component so they monitor their health and health-related activities. Karen, a Baby Boomer, explained that the effect of her father's diabetes diagnosis (considered genetic) had "trickled down" so that she and her sister were careful about their diets. Her statement below illustrates the difficulties individuals and families have in absorbing and acting upon health messages from a range of sources.

> *He was diagnosed in 1995 and he was so wounded by that because he had been so disciplined. He had this idea that people who have diabetes are obese. You watch..... The media would have you believe and I know most people are, they have eaten themselves into diabetes. But dad's is just genetic, his mother was diabetic. So he was perfectly well and he went to the doctors one day and he said "I'll just give you a little check up"—diabetic. And that has changed their [parents'] lives and it's trickled down. If you go to your parents for dinner and the whole conversation is "have you read the back of this product?" And if you go shopping with mum and she says "You know it all ideally has to be under 10, the sugars and fats have to be under 10". And they are so savvy about all of that it has trickled into [us]... it has to really. And my sister is fanatic, she is a vegetarian. She is obsessed and fanatical and it has permeated my mind set a little bit I think.*

Nicolette, a Gen Y member, explained about her partner: *His dad's got some heart problems, and I think he's getting a bit of a sort of shock that he needs to actually do something about his own health, so he doesn't end up like his father.*

The rise in health consciousness is part of a broader transition in values (at the societal culture level) between generations (Inglehart and Baker 2000). As societies become wealthier and institute social protection policies, concerns for economic and physical security are displaced by valuing wellbeing and quality of life. Being 'freed' from constant vigilance over personal income permits people to focus on the other aspects of their daily lives. This cultural transition has become dominant in advanced industrial societies over the last 35 years; and at the same time, life expectancy has risen substantially.

9.2.2 A Shift to Child-Centred Parenting

Chapters 3 and 5 show how parental involvement with children has swung from comparatively low to high levels of engagement. They also reveal a simultaneous growth in children and young people dictating new food consumption patterns and leisure routines for the whole family. These dynamics become particularly marked in the high degree of parental involvement of the Baby Boomers in the lives of their children. There are numerous reasons for this shift (Banwell et al. 2007, 2010), but in part it coincides with a general tendency for the post-Lucky generations to value winning, excelling, triumphing and general reflexivity regarding personal performance.

Rather than children's activities having to fit in with household needs and routines, Chaps. 3 and 5 also indicate that Gen Y children are having an impact on Baby Boomer activities, with some parents adopting particular physical activities so that they can do them with their children and altering meal times to fit around their children's activities. One family vividly illustrates the rise in adult involvement in children's activities over the generations. When she was young, Lucky Generation Alice was a good enough runner to be asked by a trainer to participate in serious training. Her father gave permission but would not transport her to training sessions so she could not accept the offer, something she has since regretted. By contrast, as her Baby Boomer daughter, Catherine, explains, their family holidays are now organised around Alice's grandchild's sporting activities.

> *My daughter plays hockey for Victoria and every year they are in a different state [hockey championships]. So we used to go to a different state to follow her. So we went to Perth about five years ago. And we went to Canberra as well, Darwin, Sydney, Adelaide. We have been every year following her around. That's our family holiday, we all go off and watch her play hockey.*

In this family, it isn't just family schedules that are adapted to accommodate the child's interest; even family holidays are planned around attending Gen Y elite sporting events.

9.2.3 The Attenuation of Habits and Embrace of Cultural Change

Participants attributed family patterns that persisted across several generations to force of habit from childhood, to a family characteristic such as being a sporty family, or to a genetic predisposition that led family members to attempt to modify their health risks through lifestyle changes. What we observe is that the 'habitus of habits' which characterised the Lucky Generation way of life (see Chap. 8) is less entrenched among the Baby Boomers and is certainly absent for their children.

The notion of family habits was relatively strong between the two earlier generations especially in relation to diets, and was offered by a few as a primary explanation for why people ate in the way they did even down to the third and fourth generations. Nicolette (Gen Y) illustrates the way in which family food preferences are replicated across generations, including with her own daughter. Nicolette's grandmother grew up on an orchard and members of all three generations talked about the importance of fruit in their diets.

> *So just yeah, mostly my mum and what she fed us, we eat fairly similar things, I think really, to what mum fed us. And I guess what [partner] does have a say, and it's a bit about what his mum fed him and that sort of thing, and he... he doesn't eat any fruit...And I think that's... he doesn't like it, but his mum doesn't like fruit, and so she probably didn't give it to him nearly as much as... as she would've if she'd liked it. And maybe that's been an influence. I love fruit, and I give it to my daughter, so hopefully she won't inherit his dislike of fruit.*

Nicolette's aunt has expert dietary knowledge and she referred to her aunt's active influence over their attitudes to food.

> *I think diet's important... very important, I think mum, and the food she fed us is the major influence, and I've got an auntie who's a dietician, and she's always talking about good things to eat.*

Nicolette's mother suggested that the influence went back another generation to her own mother.

> *...oh my mother, my mother is an influence, she probably influenced me during my training as well. She always told us you've got to eat this because it's got vitamin A and things like that, and this is good for your brain and is full of B vitamins and calcium....*

Familial attitudes to diet extended to, and were interwoven with, their attitudes to body size. As Baby Boomer Karen said:

> *It's that really subtle influence of your family. You just couldn't end up the size of a house and be part of my family [laughter].*

She went on to explain that her mother has always promoted the idea of moderation and restraint in food consumption:

> *We wouldn't be the sort of family at Christmas lunch where there were prawns piled [high]. We would think that was very tasteless.*

Here we see confirmation of the proposition that the unconscious or semi-conscious daily practices of individuals—including diet and physical activity—are socialised during childhood and are maintained to a greater or lesser degree in adult life. Many families were physically active and often the parents introduced their children to their own preferred activities, a point reinforced in Chap. 5. For example, Baby Boomer sisters Lynette and Margaret joined Girl Guides because their mother was a Girl Guide leader. When talking about her grandchildren, Joyce (Lucky Generation) said:

Their father played hockey and their mother played hockey and their father rode for Victoria, played hockey for Victoria and was captain of the lacrosse team, so it's no wonder they're sporty.

However we also found the instigation of new habits. Karen, a Baby Boomer, describes the force of childhood socialisation that occurred during family meals in terms that evoke the Bourdieuian notion of habitus, but she no longer replicates it with her own children.

I think I tried, either consciously or unconsciously, to replicate the same thing [as the family meal she had when young]. When they [the children] were young we sat down to a set table and sat around and chatted. Because that is just my expectation. We don't do it now.

The Baby Boomer Generation is renowned for its embrace of change. The term the 'Generation Gap' came into use in the 1960s to refer to a pronounced shift in values and behaviours from the Lucky to Baby Boomer generations. The Baby Boomers, who were reaching young adulthood in the 1970s, led the country in adopting political, social and economic change introduced by the Australian Labor Party under leader Gough Whitlam. These perspectives are still evident among them. Recent American research shows that among internet users the adoption of social media is dramatic among the 50–65 year olds (http://www.pewinternet.org/Reports/2010/Older-Adults-and-Social-Media.aspx). Because there are so many of them, the Baby Boomers can influence trends because marketers cannot afford to ignore their demographic weight. Another characteristic of the Baby Boomers has been their resistance to ageing in its many forms. As they have grown older, sayings like "50 is the new 40" have multiplied. Baby Boomers have tended to downplay the influence of their life stage in their adoption of new social trends, sometimes leading to paradoxical pressures in their lives. Thus Baby Boomer women have borne the brunt of time pressures as they have attempted to apply intensive, child-centred mothering practices while also participating in the workforce. Another example is their ready adoption of culinary novelty, diversity and abundance as well as labour- and time-saving devices, such as cars. Despite their resistance to the physical signs of ageing they have become fatter at an earlier age than the Lucky Generation (Allman-Farinelli et al. 2008). Their interviews are full of examples of rejection of the frugality and predictability of their parents' food habits. The Generation Gap of the 1960s still exists for the Baby Boomers who are more likely to identify with the lifestyles of their own children rather than those of their parents. If they return to the mores and practices of the Lucky Generation, it is often couched in new language or revolutionary phrases. So, riding a bike or catching public transport are not seen as a continuation of a Lucky Generation habit but rather as a revolutionary act against climate change or an attempt to resist the ageing process.

With successive generations, participants increasingly became subject to influences beyond their immediate family: from families they married into, work mates, friendship groups and others with whom they identified. Chapter 5 notes the rising importance of social networks as conduits for new behaviours. More broadly, the proliferation of internet activities alongside older forms of media like newspapers, magazines and television multiplies the array of possible choices for any individual.

As teenagers and young adults, Gen Y has grown up with the fast-moving social and technological change encouraged by the Baby Boomers. They are exposed to almost 52 h of media per week (Shoebridge 2011). High levels of media engagement are all they know; and because of their youth, they cannot judge it in the context of a long lifecourse. And yet in terms of obesity, the multiple and complex effects of social trends and generational shifts in values that we have identified have come to rest in their bodies. While individual Gen Y participants in this study may or may not be heavier than their parents, research shows that as a generation they are indeed heavier than earlier generations at the same age and they are more likely to become overweight at an earlier age (Allman-Farinelli et al. 2008).

9.3 Do Cultural Change and Attenuation of Habits Mean Life Choices Are Trumping Life Chances?

The study contains seven three-generation families. By reading down the generations (in contrast to reading across them), we find individuals within families who follow the family trajectory while others choose to depart from 'the family culture'. Some Baby Boomer and Gen Y participants had deliberately endeavoured to break away from family patterns of eating or exercising, sometimes because they either wanted to be different in terms of their behaviours or their identity or both. Thus within the family setting, there are instances where individual behaviours illustrate choice trumping the life chance that is associated with the family into which an individual is born. That is, individuals follow a way of life that may be different in terms of their education or career, for example, that is very different to the rest of their family, or perhaps choose to eat or exercise in a different way.

In Chap. 3 we observed that culinary habits have become attenuated as recent generations have embraced choice. In recent times the notion that we all have choices is a powerful mantra. Our findings do not readily support this line of reasoning. Even when families attempted to maintain habits such as a shared family meal or healthy eating, they were often unable to. As Gen Y children got older, the evening family meal became increasingly difficult in the face of multiple schedules built around different employment, study and other activities. Not only do these schedules make it difficult for the families to eat together, people must mobilise complex planning and organisation to maintain a healthy diet and adequate physical activity, and they experience all sorts of psycho-social pressures when they cannot bring their numerous life domains together in a desired way.

Here we report on the food practices of the Williams family, a family which is unique in our sample, in the extent to which all members apparently regularly eat healthily and exercise in line with health expert advice. However, it is not unique in exemplifying what we heard throughout the research: there are tensions in managing life choices, or the extent of being able to both capitalise on and modulate the socio-cultural trends, given other life chances including employment policies, the structure of transport systems and educational opportunities (Fig. 9.1).

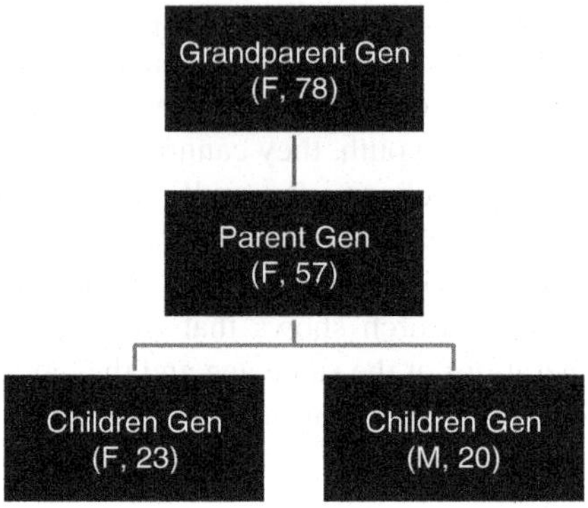

Fig. 9.1 The Williams family

The Williams family is close-knit. Members of the three generations regularly visit each other and dine together. As a family they are all passionate about their chosen sport and have a long-term commitment to it. They appear to fit their physical activity into their lives easily, and continue to do so across their lifecourse. They all identified themselves as 'middle class' even though some men in the family are blue collar workers. Two women members work in the service sector. All three generations attended Catholic secondary schools.

Alice's account of childhood meals was typical of her era. Her family was poor, but her grandfather had a market garden so they had fresh veggies in season. She can't remember going hungry. A typical evening meal was when the family sat down together to eat corned beef with cabbage, carrots and spuds and sometimes a rhubarb pie or something similar. Now in old age, she now eats many meals without meat. She is health conscious or *very good* about her diet. She cuts the fat off meat and does not use commercially prepared foods. She sometimes uses the microwave to cook, and often makes stir fry and pasta. She no longer eats sweets or desserts.

Her daughter Catherine remembers her childhood evening meals as *old traditional meat and two or three veggies*. The family ate around 6 pm. *We always used to sit with the family around the table*. Alice cooked the meals and Catherine and her sister helped dry the dishes. However, *Friday night was fish and chip night… I think we occasionally had Chinese. If we went out for a meal we used to go to the local Chinese place… maybe once a month, not very often*. For snacks she had fruit, and remembers eating Twisties, and bread and vegemite.

Catherine observed that food seemed to change around the time that she married and she became *a bit more adventurous*. She and her husband went out quite a bit to cheap restaurants. They ate with their extended family once a week. Home-cooked meals were more varied than in the past and the family ate less red meat. She observed that there had been a rise in health consciousness and *people [had] became more aware about diet*. Personally, she was health conscious and made an effort to make sure that the family ate well by cooking and freezing food so that she did not resort to *short cuts* when *stressed*.

Rebecca, Catherine's daughter, remembers that when she was young the family would often have pasta once a week, veggies and sometimes chips. *We'd had either like a steak and veggies or chops and veggies, it was pretty healthy...probably had takeaway once a week.* Evening meals were usually at a set time but as the children got older the family sometimes ate sitting around the television. Once she reached her mid-teens she started cooking for herself because her sporting activities conflicted with the usual family meal times.

Now that she is an adult, Rebecca dines with her family quite often even though she has left home. She often goes to her grandmother's place on Sunday for a roast dinner with the family. Sometimes she eats out with friends. She tries not to have take away too often but she does when she's tired and she doesn't have time to cook. She often shops for food late at night or after sporting practice. She takes her own lunch to work; this often includes fruit, a sandwich, or leftovers. Like her mother she cooks and freezes food in preparation for busy times. Lack of time influences her diet. *If you want something more healthy then it's you know, it takes more time, you have to cook it yourself.*

Daniel, Catherine's son, reported eating the same sort of food when he was young. As a young adult (still living at home), he eats with his family unless he is working late. He also has meals at local cafés with his girlfriend and gets takeaway at least weekly. He has started cooking regularly with his girlfriend. *I cook every Monday night. My girlfriend comes over and we both cook together. So that's our night to cook. We're building our own recipe book. We've got a couple of pasta dishes and some chicken dishes that we do.* Like his sister, he sees take-away food as a solution to a busy life.

The three generations of the Williams family show an increasing rise in health consciousness concerning their diets, a desire to eat healthily and to resist the pressures coming from work and sporting demands to take what they see as unhealthy short cuts, such as packet foods or takeaway foods. They are fortunate because they reinforce one another's healthy food dispositions. Nevertheless, the two Gen Y children demonstrate the difficulty of maintaining these standards in the face of competing time pressures and demands. Family culture and the personal choice to preserve it must buck the headwinds of socio-cultural change.

9.4 Social Forces Across the Twentieth Century

The bulk of our material lends support to the sociological canon: that life chances constrain life choices, sometimes radically. The generation into which one is born and the social position and geographical space that one inhabits can act to anchor or liberate life chances. These factors structure opportunity and constraint, aided and abetted by the socio-cultural trends prevailing at the time.

All seven of our three-generation family narratives elicit similar tensions, begging the question as to the sources of the predictability in life chances and the way chances circumscribe choices. Instead of common expressions of individual choice-making, we regularly heard about choices foregone. People would express a

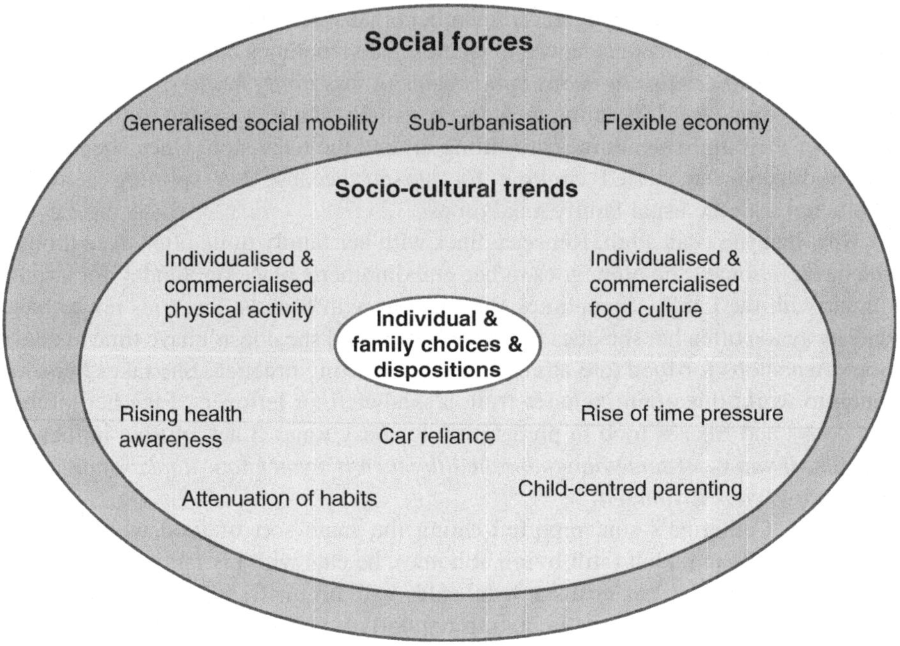

Fig. 9.2 Social forces, life chances and life choices

desire to make changes to their behaviours and quickly follow with a list of reasons why change would be too difficult given the financial, temporal and social demands of work, study and travel. It is these people who are quickly labelled by some media commentators and politicians as passive, indolent or irresponsible.

Thus, the remainder of this chapter is concerned with addressing our second research question: What are the social forces that infuse the socio-cultural trends with their potency? A combination of re-analysing the interviews plus examinations of social and economic histories of Australia over the last eight decades elicited three social forces which have given rise to one of Mills' public issues of twentieth century social structure, namely, obesity as the new statistical norm in body weight. The social forces are: generalised social mobility, flexible economy and suburbanisation.

Figure 9.2 illustrates the relationship of the social forces to the seven socio-cultural trends described in this book.

The first social force concerns a generalised social mobility due to an overall rise in income and educational and employment status. This is best illustrated by looking at social mobility within the seven families. As Baby Boomer Nicole observed, reflecting on differences between her own and her parents' financial position:

> *I think we probably have more money than either of them did, either side did when we were growing… I think we're pretty lucky, but I'm working, so that's one of the reasons we have more money.*

When we considered the data collected from the seven three-generation families, a clear trend towards increasing levels of education is evident. Most of the Lucky Generation women had limited secondary education, and one had attended primary school only. That this group of women had lower education levels than their children and grandchildren conforms to the social expectations of the time that militated against women gaining a tertiary education. When they were in their teens and twenties, the social norm was that they would become wives and mothers and therefore did not require further education. Furthermore, during the Depression and World War II when many families were struggling financially, the young women of the family often left school to get a job so that they could contribute to the family income until they got married. A further disincentive to higher education and career was that reliable contraception was not available at this time (before the 1960s), and whatever their preference, women lived with the possibility of a pregnancy for most of their adult lives. Most of the Lucky Generation began their childbearing in their early 20s while their Baby Boomer daughters often had their first children in their mid- to late 20s. During the infrequent times when they were employed (usually during or after the hours when their children attended school), Lucky Generation women worked mainly in clerical or sales jobs.

Within the three generation families, eight of the ten Baby Boomer children (nine of them women) had either undergraduate or post-graduate education and were employed as professionals. Their careers as teachers and nurses were quite typical for the time. This rise in women's educational and employment status illustrates the social changes that occurred in the 1950s and 1960s, including the so-called sexual revolution, enabled by the invention of the contraceptive pill and the rise of feminism, that saw women further their education and enter the workforce in increasing numbers. Furthermore, a democratisation of education occurred as tertiary education in Australia became free in the 1970s to those who gained a scholarship to university. At the time of our research, nine of the 12 Gen Y participants were either secondary school graduates or university undergraduates. One was employed in a professional category, while two were undertaking PhDs.

As the Lucky Generation grandparents were all retired when they were interviewed, it is difficult to gauge their income during their working years. Three Baby Boomers had household incomes below $50,000 and two had incomes above $100,000. Nine of the Gen Y grandchildren lived at home although four had independent incomes as well. One lived away from the family with a household income over $70,000.

Participants were not recruited on the basis of their class identification, although all participants were asked to identify where they sat on a five-point scale of class ranging from working class to upper class. The Lucky Generation family members declared themselves to be in the working to middle-class categories, with several displaying some signs of discomfort with this question. All their Baby Boomer children declared themselves to be lower-middle to middle class; while with the exception of one family the Gen Ys stated that they were middle to upper-middle class. Thus, the families' understanding of their social position points to a gradual upward mobility over the three generations while there is little class or other socio-demographic variation between the families.

Occasionally a participant hinted at class-associated behaviours. For example, a Baby Boomer on a limited income who described herself as coming from lower-middle class background emphasised that when she was young her family meals were plain and repetitious. In her adult life she had deviated from this approach slightly by expanding her menus.

> *The repertoire is a bit more colourful than my upbringing, it's a wider selection but it's not very wide. I keep nutrition in mind and I have a repertoire of about six things.*

She also described how when she was struggling financially (because she was a single mother) and her children were young she filled them up on bread, a strategy akin to her parents' generation in straitened circumstances. According to Coveney (2004), a limited dietary repertoire accords with a working-class emphasis on the functional aspects of food rather than a middle class use of food to display knowledge, taste or distinction. Coveney argues that the use of technical language emphasising the importance of nutrition indicates a middle-class attitude to and knowledge about food. In contrast, working-class parents were more likely to judge their children's diet on the basis of children's appearance and healthiness. The statement (above) about meals thus illustrates a transition from the generally working-class Lucky Generation to the Baby Boomers' more middle-class attitude to food.

Yet, another family displayed some signs of middle to upper-class upbringing. The Lucky Generation grandmother went to boarding school. She adopted the upper-class English habit of feeding young children before the adults, serving food cooked specifically for them and then dining with her husband later in the evening. Whether she was aware that these are class-based practices from the UK is not clear, as she explained that she adopted this practice because her husband came home late. However, it is likely that the time at which the evening meal was held followed class-based distinctions since men employed in blue collar jobs often finished work before five, making it easier for the whole family to eat together. She gave up university to marry, and her children and one of two grandchildren are professionals. Across the three generations this family shows a great concern about managing weight through careful eating and physical activity. As one of her Gen Y grandchildren explained: *we've always grown up that we should be fit, and we should be healthy, kind of what we are, I guess.*

In our fairly homogeneous sample, behavioural differences based on social class have probably been swamped by the successive waves of socio-cultural and economic change in which each generation grew up. Because of incremental upward social mobility, all classes became subject to the same socio-cultural trends permeating modern life, including those that pose health risks.

The material in Chaps. 3 through 8 provides ample evidence for distinctive generational behavioural patterns which followed from the diffusion of new commodities and conditions of paid employment. The generational dietary trends included a shift from a basic, repetitive, and inexpensive diet for the Lucky Generation to one for the Baby Boomers and Gen Y that is increasingly diversified and individualised in terms of food styles and ingredients, more industrialised, and partially or fully prepared outside the home. Similarly in terms of physical activities, there was a move from activity performed for sociability, pleasure or the requirement to move from one place to another, to an emphasis on activity for health and for competition with an increasing role for the market in the provision of activity opportunities. Even the experience of time pressure is widespread across and increasing among the younger age groups. This is despite, or perhaps in part because of, time-saving and energy-saving devices—cars, electronic home entertainments, washing machines, freezers—rapidly becoming part of the Australian domestic scene from the 1950s onwards. The car which was used for an occasional outing by the most privileged in the 1930s is now a daily essential of household life for close to 100% of the adult population. Much of the dominance of these socio-cultural trends arises from their increasing affordability and accessibility (assisted by an aggressive marketing to make them acceptable) of the commodities which underpin them over the second half of the twentieth century; so that by the 1980s only the very disadvantaged and marginalised had not been able to adopt convenience foods, car reliance and or purchased home entertainments. Rarely, did we hear, for instance, Baby Boomers and Gen Y members bemoan the economic costs of gyms or DVDs.

In this regard Australia has been a forerunner among both developed and middle-income countries. It has been comparatively affluent with low levels of inequality for decades, although inequality has begun to grow in the last 20 years. Based on a survey of over 400 Australians conducted in 1996–1997, sociologist Michael Pusey explained that "the new capitalism's insistence on 'flexibility'" had led middle Australia to view economic reform with a mix of moral anxiety and anger. He argued that "citizens are being asked to deliver themselves, their savings and their future, into a so-called global economy....that coordinates markets for goods and services over our heads and without reference to social meanings, intentions, and consequences" (Pusey 2003, p. 174). It is this disconnect between daily life and social meaning that the Baby Boomers expressed as they described the frustrations in their daily lives.

The second and related social force can be encapsulated in terms of a flexible economy, built on twin bases in the last 50 years: government policies regarding flexible labour markets and widened opportunities for all but the most marginal groups to embrace commodity consumption.

In the past 30 years, when the rise in obesity has been most pronounced, Australians have become familiar with the notion of a deregulated economic system. Most Baby Boomers and their offspring have experienced this system as employees and household members who have a variety of working conditions and household routines. Indeed, domestic arrangements are often instigated to accommodate the spread of hours and tasks demanded by the flexibilised economy. A deregulated economy, promoted by governments and corporations as unleashing resources and talents previously locked away by bureaucratic regulations and customs, has delivered significant innovation in firms, products and services. The entrepreneurial spirit has created myriad consumption possibilities and liberation from what some might consider stultifying guiding authorities, including ruling class mores. Australian producers and consumers are repeatedly told that 'anything is possible'.

While there is no denying that the flexibilised economy and culture open up choices and opportunities, the evidence in this book indicates that Gen Y's shift work and casual employment along with 24/7 access to goods and services means that the scheduling of basic household activities (what used to be called social reproduction) has become destabilised, undermined or eroded. They find that choice is a promise that is often not fully realised. Spasmodic around-the-clock engagements, or the practices of pointillism, make it very hard to be as self-reliant in terms of food preparation and active transport as in the past. Thus, family meals or 'sitting down to eat' according to Christopher (Gen Y) must sometimes be sacrificed.

> *Yeah. If I'm at work or if I'm organising stuff like the car or anything I usually just grab whatever I can eat while I'm driving or whatever yeah.*

Alternatively, the family struggles to co-ordinate multiple members' various schedules and people. According to a Baby Boomer Peter,

> *Well we still try to achieve (sitting together). We try to know who's coming and whether partners are coming. And we try to time the meals so we can sit down together. But we don't get bent out of shape over that if that doesn't happen... But it doesn't matter if you are wanting to eat around 6.30 and one isn't here. We will keep some aside for him. That's the thing there can be anything from three of us to six or seven of us. And thank god for SMS. About 5 pm [we'll ask] are you home for tea. Yes I'm bringing [friend] Ok we need enough for five.*

Variegated lifestyles are the new norm, but they all lack "traditional signposts" (Giddens 1991, p. 82), with few or no limitations on possibilities. As Polanyi (1944) and Mingione (1991) noted some time ago, "a market regulated economy means the subordination of society to market laws" (p. 22). With each generation there has been an earlier reliance on the market for goods and services, setting up the conditions for the development and sedimentation of a more commodifed way of life. This is the world in which the Baby Boomers and especially Gen Y have grown up, with ramifications for future social changes. As Inglehart and Welzel (2005 p. 99) have argued, "if younger generations are socialized under significantly different conditions from those that shaped earlier generations, the values of the entire society will gradually change through intergenerational replacement".

However, resentment appears to be growing, according to a highly regarded survey of Australian values. In the most recent report Being Australian, focus group participants were quoted as saying: "Big business undermines our way of life"; "Your weekend isn't your weekend any more"; "They get to decide when your weekend is and your time with your family". Reflecting on Australia's social policy history, one person told the researchers, "Big business has made shops open longer and, even though we might be part-time, our week is stretched out a lot more because they can make the hours any time they like and we have to fit our lifestyle around it. So your whole weekend is wrecked" (West 2011, p. 17). A few respondents were similarly jaundiced in their view of business. As one member of the Lucky Generation commented:

> *Of course, big business ... they are out to make money. They are not interested in the health or lifestyle of the people, as long as they can sell their product and make a profit for their investors.*

Despite the veneer that people have greater opportunities to express their individuality through how and what they consume, we find extraordinary uniformity in the choices that individuals are making. This extends to widespread acceptance of a pervasive, but not necessarily welcome, culture of choice. As Giddens has noted, late modernity has ushered in lifestyles based on the assumption that "we have no choice but to choose" (1991, p. 81). This social practice of constrained choice-making has become a social structure in its own right, a life chance of limited choice.

Suburbanisation or the spread of low to medium density suburbs is the third social force relevant to Australia, one that is shared with other 'young' and large countries where the car became entrenched early (Canada, US, New Zealand). We heard about the importance of this form of spatial organisation through the intergenerational accounts of changing physical activity patterns, car reliance and the time it takes to cross the city attending appointments and ferrying children to their many activities. Harvey (1990) has described the necessary relations between the emergence of more flexible modes of capital accumulation, the rise of postmodernist cultural forms, and a new round of space-time compression in the organisation of capitalism. In other words, where dynamic capitalism and a culture of choice operate, there are requirements to make the temporal and spatial demands of daily living accord with their processes. However, contradictory forces also operate. In Australia it is common for people living in the suburbs to manage their lives over considerable geographic distances and to travel at all times of the day and night. At least one car per family is the solution that most Australian families turn to, even though commuting times for car drivers living in the outer suburbs of major cities can take up to several hours (Flood and Barbarto 2005).

Suburbanisation receives less attention than the process of urbanisation, which is mostly portrayed in positive tones because it describes an increase in population density and diversity and the incubation and diffusion of new opportunities and ways of life. Australia is now identified as the most urban nation on earth, with 85% of the population living in cities and towns (Capon 2007). In reality though, Australian cities are not nearly as densely populated as most, and Melbourne, where we conducted the research, is no exception. It has few geographic or topographical impediments to curb residential settlement expansion, and possibly for this reason is growing faster than Sydney or Brisbane. The combination of new housing estates and infill in older inner suburbs taking over pockets of scrub and parklands was noted by the Lucky Generation and Baby Boomers when they reflected on their physical activities as children, reported in Chap. 5.

In a chapter entitled 'Australia as suburb', social historian Hugh Stretton noted that as the Baby Boomers were being born, "Most Australians choose to live in suburbs, in reach of city centres and also of beaches or countryside" (Stretton 1975, p. 7). At the same time as this choice was being made, he describes the books, plays, poems and intellectual critiques of the 1960s which questioned the value of the Australian way of life lived in the suburbs. The suburbs were seen by many to be dull and conformist, robbing their residents of money through high mortgages and of time due to commuting, denying people freedom to be different. In short, the suburbs were portrayed in some quarters as the antithesis of what city living was all about.

Yet this was a decision that our Lucky Generation and their Baby Boomer offspring were making, with the encouragement of the government of the day. We heard very little criticism of the way of life afforded by suburbanisation from

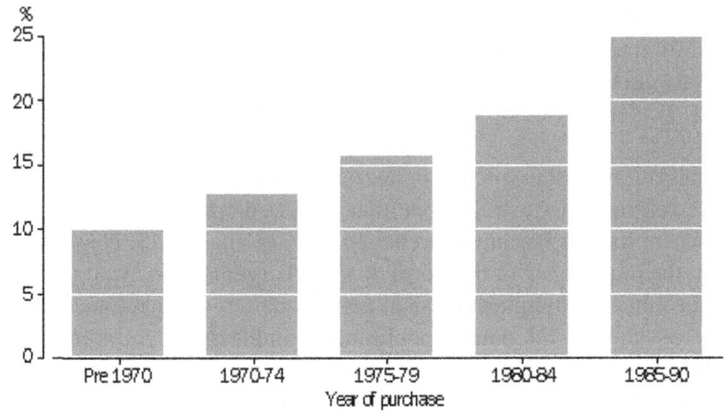

Fig. 9.3 Proportion of income spent on housing by home purchasers, 1970–1990 (Source: ABS 1994)

the Lucky Generation, although some women did reflect on the fact that high mortgages required two incomes. This sometimes forced them into paid employment, which robbed them of time with their children. Still, during the 1950s, house prices were comparatively low when Lucky Generation participants were buying or building their houses in the suburbs. Moreover, for many decades houses were being erected on quarter-acre blocks, and there was still enough space within the suburbs in backyards and public places for children to play freely. *You play a bit of cricket with the boys down the paddock—you know?* The relatively car-free nature of suburban roads was a common refrain prior to the 1950s. Members of the Lucky Generation told how they would play in the middle of the bitumen road.

Housing became less affordable for the Baby Boomers. Between 1975 and 1990, when the Baby Boomers were becoming house purchasers, the proportion of income spent on housing by couples with dependent children rose from 15 to 21%. Low-income families, however, were spending 50% of their incomes on home purchases while high-income families were spending half of that (Australian Bureau of Statistics 1994). The rise in the proportion of incomes spent by all home purchasers prior to the 1970s, when the Lucky Generation was buying, was around 10%, as Fig. 9.3 shows.

Baby Boomer women's participation in the labour force from the 1970s on is often attributed to the liberating effects of the second wave of the Women's Movement. These figures suggest that economic forces were pivotal if the Great Australian Dream of home ownership was to be kept alive. Since 1990, housing affordability has fluctuated in line with interest rates. By 2006, when Gen Y could have been considering buying a home, affordability was worse than in the 1980s when interest rates were higher and mainly due to rapid rises in house prices in the cities (Australian Bureau of Statistics 2010). It is not surprising that nine of the 12 Gen Ys were living with parents, as they struggled with the costs of higher education and finding consistent, well-paid employment.

With the increasing density of housing in suburban areas, the loss of paddocks and unclaimed land, and the heightened role of the car, physical activity options had changed by the time of the Gen Y childhood. Baby Boomer mothers told us that because they were working, their children's after-school activities were dictated by their availability to chauffer them around. There was little reference to them 'running wild' or neighbourhood play. It is hard to know whether the home-based leisure was a response to homework demands or parental guidelines to stay close to home due to 'stranger danger' and car traffic danger (Timperio et al. 2004).

Joyce from the Lucky Generation described playing *ball games and racing up and down the street, because we could play on the road. It wasn't a big deal. You'd just stop while a car went by and then... I don't know, we just went out and did things.* In contrast, when asked about what she did when she wasn't at school, her granddaughter talked about organised physical activities several afternoons after school as well as school-based sports.

Some Gen Y men described childhoods that included outside play and a fair amount of freedom, whereas others did not proffer such descriptions, leaving us wondering if they did not think such things worth mentioning. We surmise however, that the combination of suburbanisation, supported by the socio-cultural trends of car-reliance, commercialised (including the plethora of screen based alternatives) and competitive physical activities, and child-centred parenting, precluded children from this kind of play.

Due to low population density and "newness" in urban form in comparison with relatively prosperous European nations, spatial constraints on the spread of the socio-cultural trends have been minimal. In particular, Australian houses have been built to accommodate labour saving devices, while urban landscapes have been constructed around cars. Stretton points out that during the 1960s, very few of the many government plans for vibrant city centres in Victoria were being realised in the new suburbs and even when they were, their access and amenity were radically compromised by roads and car parks. While Melbourne is the only city to have maintained an extensive network of tramlines, and has well-established train and bus networks, it has become a highly car-centric city as Chap. 7 showed. To get access to employment and entertainment opportunities and to reduce their car reliance, Chap. 7 also reported that a few Gen Y were hoping to be able to move close into the city where there is good mass transport.

A century ago, the public health and town planning fields were championing suburban living: wide open spaces, clean air, better housing stock and waste disposal possibilities. Now both fields are advocating high-density urban living on grounds of environmental sustainability and promoting physical activity (Capon et al. 2011). Planners now have evidence that suburban sprawl is related to high levels of commuting and mortgage stress, which in turn exacerbate parental absence and family breakdown (Head 2011). There is belated acknowledgement that maintaining and building active and mass transit systems is too expensive outside cities, and yet unless people have alternative transport systems, life without a car will continue to seem unimaginable.

9.5 Conclusion

Which generation an individual is born into constitutes a life chance, and this chapter consolidates our view about the importance of one form of 'life chance'—historical time features—to particular socio-cultural exposures and subsequent behaviours. Indeed, this chapter indicates that broad social forces operating across the twentieth century hold greater potency in relation to dietary and activity practices than do cohort specific and family habits. Although the occasional hint of class-based influences appears in within-family patterns related to food and physical activity, these are far outweighed by upward class mobility for the three generations across the time period under discussion and by the lack of strong class differences between the families within each generation. Furthermore, the socio-cultural trends under discussion in the book, and which we argue have contributed to increasing obesity over time, have become affordable, accessible and acceptable for all but the most disadvantaged.

In regard to the choice-chance conundrum, we typically observed situations where the older Lucky Generation cohort who had lived through some marked cultural shifts continued to practice habituated behaviours, largely ignoring the new approaches. Whether this can be called 'exercising choice' is debateable. As Bourdieu (1984) has pointed out, habitus mainly operates at a sub-conscious level, so making major alterations to daily practices would be too hard to contemplate and maybe impractical. We also had a few instances, like Alice Williams, who had intentionally modified her diet in line with contemporary health advice.

For all of the participants who displayed independent or idiosyncratic behaviours, more of them told us that their behavioural 'choices'—the ability to 'freely' or independently decide when and what to eat and exercise—are heavily circumscribed by their life chances as they operate at the societal and family levels. Thus it is not surprising that we observed marked within-generation similarities and across-generation differences in approaches to 'being physical' and diet.

References

Allman-Farinelli, M. A., Chey, T., Bauman, A. E., Gill, T., & James, W. P. (2008). Age, period and birth cohort effects on prevalence of overweight and obesity in Australian adults from 1990 to 2000. *European Journal of Clinical Nutrition, 62*(7), 898–907.

Australian Bureau of Statistics. (1994). *Australian social trends, 1994*. (4102.0). Canberra: ABS.

Australian Bureau of Statistics. (2010). *Measure of Australia's progress 2010*. (1370.0). Canberra: ABS.

Banwell, C., Dixon, J., Hinde, S., & McIntyre, H. (2006). Fast and slow food in the fast lane: Automobility and the Australian diet. In R. Wilk (Ed.), *Fast food/slow food. The economic anthropology of the global food system* (pp. 219–240). Lanham: AltaMira Press.

Banwell, C., Shipley, M., & Strazdins, L. (2007). The pressured parenting environment: Parents as piggy in the middle. In J. Dixon & D. H. Broom (Eds.), *The seven deadly sins of obesity: How the modern world is making us fat* (pp. 46–63). Sydney: University of New South Wales Press.

Banwell, C., Dixon, J., Broom, D., & Davies, A. (2010). Habits of a lifetime: Family dining patterns over the lifecourse of older Australians. *Health Sociology Review, 19*(3), 343–355.

Bourdieu, P. (1984). *Distinction: A social critique of the judgement of taste*. London: Routledge and Kegan Paul.

Capon, A. (2007). The way we live in our cities. *Medical Journal of Australia, 187*(11/12), 658–661.

Capon, A., Johnson, M., Head, P., Agarwal, S., & Lawrence, R. (2011, July). The view from the city. *Design and Health*, pp. 6–9.

Cockerham, W. C. (2007). Health lifestyles and the absence of the Russian middle class. *Sociology of Health & Illness, 29*(3), 457–473.

Coveney, J. (2004). The government of the table: Nutrition expertise and the social organisation of family food habits. In J. Germov & L. Williams (Eds.), *Sociology of food and nutrition: The social appetite* (2nd ed., pp. 259–275). South Melbourne: Oxford University Press.

Evans, S. (2003, August 23–24). Supermarkets try to make petrol a happy purchase, *The Weekend Australian Financial Review*, p. 5.

Finucane, M. M., Stevens, G. A., Cowan, M. J., Danaei, G., Lin, J. K., Paciorek, C. J., et al. (2011). National, regional and global trends in body-mass index since 1980: Systematic analysis of health examination surveys and epidemiological studies with 960 country-years and 9.1 million participants. *The Lancet, 377*, 557–567.

Flood, M., & Barbarto, C. (2005). *Off to work: Commuting in Australia* (Discussion paper number 78). Canberra: The Australia Institute.

Giddens, A. (1991). *Modernity and self-identity: Self and society in the late modern age*. Stanford: Stanford University Press.

Harvey, D. (1990). *The condition of postmodernity: An enquiry into the origins of cultural change*. Cambridge MA: Blackwell.

Head, P. (2011). Healthy cities in an ecological age. *Healthy City Design*, pp. 10–14.

Hinde, S., & Dixon, J. (2005). Changing the obesogenic environment: Insights from a cultural economy of car reliance. *Transportation Research Part D, 10*(1), 31–53.

Inglehart, R., & Baker, W. (2000). Modernization, cultural change, and the persistence of traditional values. *American Sociological Review, 2000*(65), 19–51.

Inglehart, R., & Welzel, C. (2005). *Modernization, cultural change, and democracy: The human development sequence*. New York: Cambridge University Press.

Mills, C. W. (1959/2000). *The sociological imagination*. New York: Oxford University Press.

Mingione, E. (1991). *Fragmented societies: A sociology of economic life beyond the market paradigm*. Cambridge: Basil Blackwell.

Polanyi, K. (1944). *The great transformation*. New York: Holt, Rinehart and Winston.

Pusey, M. (2003). *The experience of middle Australia*. Cambridge: Cambridge University Press.

Sassi, F. (2010). *Obesity and the economics of prevention: Fit not fat*. Paris: OECD.

Shoebridge, N. (2011, June 18–19). TV stays switched on. *The Weekend Australian Financial Review*, p. 1.

Stretton, H. (1975). *Ideas for Australian cities*. Melbourne: Georgian House.

Stutts, J., Feaganes, J., Reinfurt, D., Rodgmana, E., Hamlett, C., Gish, K., et al. (2005). Driver's exposure to distractions in their natural driving environment. *Accident Analysis and Prevention, 37*(6), 1093–1101.

Timperio, A., Crawford, D., Telford, A., & Salmon, J. (2004). Perceptions about the local neighborhood and walking and cycling among children. *Preventive Medicine, 38*, 39–47.

West, A. (2011). What's on our minds. *The Saturday Age*, p. 1.

Chapter 10
Restoring Coherence to a Stressed Social System

> [In the last twenty years], we epidemiologists have suffered a whole series of embarrassing failures. …Our model is to identify the risk factors and share that information with a waiting public so that they will then rush home and, in the interests of good health, change their behaviours to lower their risk. It is a reasonable model, but it hasn't worked. In intervention study after intervention study, people have been informed about the things they need to do, and they have failed to follow our advice (Syme 2005, p. xi).
>
> …unless we can identify the pressure points in our culture, we will never be able to draft policy that aims at [obesity] prevention (Cottam 2004, p. 1203).

10.1 Obesity as Cultural Disturbance

One hundred and fifty years ago, Rudolph Virchow—doctor, statesman and anthropologist—proclaimed disease to be a disturbance of culture (Virchow 1848/2006). He asserted that epidemics are warning signs against which the progress of states can be judged. We are not alone in arguing that the time has come to heed the warning signs of what has been called the epidemic of obesity. We began the book by noting that the Cochrane Systematic Review on Obesity (Baker and Young 2006) made depressing reading for policy makers, offering little guidance for effective obesity prevention programs. Indeed, the report lends support for the quotation above from Leonard Syme, a leading social epidemiologist, who went on to argue that the failure to follow health advice comes about because "people have lives to lead". We too have found that the food and physical activity choices of the three generations are rational choices in a context of priorities in life other than health: people have jobs to hold down, children to educate, parents to care for, hobbies to pursue, housing to maintain.

In our investigation, the objective was not to document whether children now spend less time in physical activity than they did on average when the Lucky Generation were young, or whether middle-aged women are now consuming more or fewer calories than similar women would have done in the 1960s. Instead, our

C. Banwell et al., *Weight of Modernity: An Intergenerational Study of the Rise of Obesity*, DOI 10.1007/978-90-481-8957-1_10, © Springer Science+Business Media Dordrecht 2012

focus is on the lives that people lead, and how the experiences and meanings of the "proximal" causes (McMichael 1999) of obesity have been transformed over the decades and generations we study. The chapters on food and physical activity show that during the childhood years of the Luckies and the Boomers, family meals and incidental exercise were unremarkable components of daily routines. Whether they were bored by or liked the weekly rota of menus, 'meat and 3 veg' at a set time was how (and when) they ate. They walked and cycled not to 'get exercise' but as means of transport. It was how they got around.

Our interest is in how the decades have altered the meanings and practices (important aspects of culture) that comprise the 'risk factors' for obesity. First, food has ceased to be organised and delivered according to habitual cycles of season and day-of-the-week, served to a predictable cast of family members at the same time, day in and day out. Provisioning, preparing and eating have become for many of our respondents sites of anxious and incessant decisions about the components of a meal, mode of preparation and portion size, as well as when, where and with whom it will be eaten. From a blandly conventional source of fuel, food has become a significant health issue requiring expertise and minute-by-minute vigilance, often complicated by new (perhaps competitive) norms of culinary performance and consumption. Eating meals as a family has not lost its normative value, but scheduling the acquisition and preparation of food and coordinating with the availability of hyper-mobile individuals makes it much more challenging to achieve. It is, as Warde (1999) puts it succinctly, "about timing rather than about time".

Similarly, current descriptions of physical activity are markedly different from the picture of routine incidental physical activity, perhaps supplemented by enjoyably sociable pursuits such as tennis or dancing that prevailed for the Lucky Generation until very recently. Like food, 'physical activity' once happened in the process of getting places and being social. By the end of the twentieth century, that pattern had been transformed into one where people are constantly reminded by health professionals and other experts that they must exercise regularly in order to maintain a healthy weight, reduce excess kilos, and prevent or manage chronic conditions such as diabetes and heart disease. Moving enough has become a civic duty rather than an unconscious, inevitable and unremarkable consequence of living day-to-day.

Our material highlights that obesity is the result of the behavioural consequences of the interaction between social forces and cultural trends. Figure 10.1 summarises our overall argument about the complex interactions operating at multiple levels that have given rise to the spike in obesity over the last 50 years. The three social forces described in Chap. 9 operate to structure social relationships, leading to unequal life chances most commonly measured in terms of socio-economic status, neighbourhood deprivation, ethnicity and gender. The social forces also lend potency to the socio-cultural trends. For example, the trend toward car reliance is the result of a cascade of legislative decisions, wartime imperatives, taxation arrangements benefitting auto manufacturers, and urban planning decisions that advance the agendas of those interests with a stake in the flexible economy, social mobility and suburbanisation.

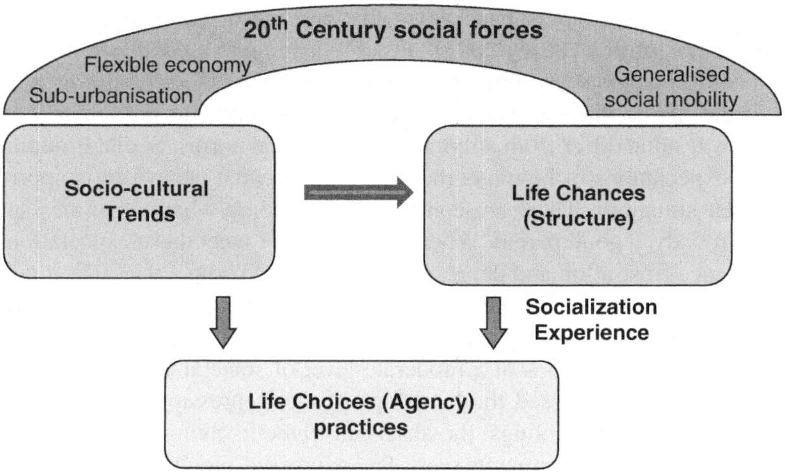

Fig. 10.1 Social forces, socio-cultural trends and social practices

Together the life chances and socio-cultural trends influence what is imaginable and doable in terms of social practices. Importantly, what is imaginable and doable varies across the population, giving rise to the inequalities in obesity described in Chap. 1.

10.2 Culturogenic Stress and the Fiction of Choice

Some years ago, Antonovsky (1985) reported on associations between stress, health and a psycho-social sense of coherence. He described this sense as "a global orientation that expresses the extent to which one has a pervasive, enduring though dynamic feeling of confidence that one's internal and external environments are predictable and that there is a high probability that things will work out as well as can reasonably be expected". He continued that a sense of coherence is a "crucial element in the basic personality structure of an individual and in the ambiance of a subculture, culture or historical period" (pp. 123–124). He proposed that there are health benefits to engaging in pursuits that feel right, where there is a perception of a natural fit between what one thinks and does and what the surrounding society thinks and does.

The Lucky Generation is fortunate to have been engaging in activities that continue to feel right. As we have already noted, they have tended to be cautious in their adoption of new behaviours, preferring to maintain the habits of their childhood. Some of the changes they have made have been responses to their own unavoidable ageing, ill-health, or death of a partner, rather than an enthusiastic embrace of change. It is likely that this 'habitus of habits' has protected them against some of the health effects of late modernity.

Since Antonovsky, others have noted that a sense of coherence is difficult to maintain in eras of flux (Pusey 2003), possibly leading to a condition identified by medical anthropologists as culturogenic stress (Helman 2007). Culturogenic stress refers to the harms that can arise when people subscribe to particular values or behave in ways that differ from cultural or sub-cultural norms. Social groupings are bound by expectations of how members should act, what behaviour is appropriate in particular situations. There are conventions regarding what constitutes success, beauty, a fit body, a good parent. When people cannot meet these expectations they can experience frustration and depression (Helman 2007, pp. 294–295).

The generally good spirits of our older group, combined with their pride in what they had achieved and how well-equipped for life they had felt, prompts our research team to argue for the virtues of a moderate level of societal coherence. While the participants readily discussed the hardships of the Depression and World War II, the childhood deaths of siblings, the absence of labour-saving devices and limited range of organised entertainments, very few expressed regret about growing up in what was considered an era of material hardship. They talked animatedly about the freedoms of walking, bike and horse riding, mucking about, games of imagination, the opportunities that a big strong tree presented for play. Their reflections highlight how an enduring passion for one or more social activities and a routine approach to eating has contributed to their sense of wellbeing. These older Australians shed valuable light on the benefits of adherence to a few cultural pursuits as well as the converse: how ignoring or rejecting more faddish cultural activities and commodities need not compromise contentment.

At a psycho-social level, participating in social institutions—whether they are devoted to religion, culinary culture, sport or leisure—can promote a sense of wellbeing due to their incorporation of learning through social mimicry, familiar rules and rituals, a common language and the culturally regulated behaviours that follow. In contrast with the weekly footy match as a major form of family entertainment in the 1930s to 1970s, Baby Boomers revealed a growing struggle to do the right things by themselves and their children. In order to widen their children's learning and leisure opportunities, many described ferrying several children to numerous different activities a week, often outside the local area and at some distance from each other. Ironically, this schedule of running around to different activities has robbed the Baby Boomers and Gen Y of whole-of-family times.

The Lucky Generation's observations about the resource-intensive nature of their grandchildren's more variegated lifestyles raise questions about their capacity to maintain these ways of life over the long term. The Baby Boomer emphasis on Gen Y's success at school, sport and leisure activities seems to have some unwanted side effects, including performance-related stress. Whether the elite sportspeople among them can maintain their levels of activity is debateable, given the frequent injuries and the demands of family formation and responsibilities. While their Baby Boomer parents appeared to maintain team-based sports into their mid-age, some sociable dimensions to their participation have moderated the impulse to winning above all.

An important theme emerging from our research concerns people's incapacity to adopt or maintain behaviours that 'feel right' in a context of pronounced cultural flux. This conundrum is the most pronounced for the Baby Boomers, who are in the position to look back and forward over several decades.

One indication of cultural flux is the notion of choice, which may be unravelling, with commodity choice becoming devalued and lifestyle choice being revalued—as happened in the 1960s suite of cultural revolutions. This shift in the desired nature of choice is evident in the domain of food. Despite being an omnivorous species, food commodity choice now overwhelms people. Fischler (1980) points to a "breakdown of the 'fit' between human biology and the environment, the latter having been radically modified by social evolution". One marked environmental alteration concerns the rapid introduction of new foods and tastes. While humans crave novelty they fear it at the same time, leading to what has been identified as the 'omnivore's dilemma': a situation in which familiarity breeds both contempt and content. Fischler argues that instead of governments acting to modulate the consequent anxiety, they intensified the dilemma by accepting changes to food systems; here he nominates the explosion in processed 'snacks' as a prime example. While not acting to curb the processed food market, governments are issuing dietary advice telling people to avoid, or at the very least to minimise, foods high in salt, sugar and fat. Such contradictions are a recipe for public cynicism and confusion.

Baby Boomers were both embracing of change and yet reflective of what they felt was missing in their lives and the lives of their children. A capacity to welcome change is an essential feature of a resilient society and a resilient person. Our primary concern is that some sub-populations can succeed even as they resist or moderate changes that do not 'feel right', while other people cannot. Current investigations of cultural transitions indicate that more advantaged groups are not only able to fashion and be early adopters of cultural shifts (Katz-Gerro and Sullivan 2010), they can do 'what feels right' more easily than other groups. Despite Australia's more egalitarian approach to certain cultural pursuits (Turner and Edmunds 2002), it helps to have money, education and confidence to take cultural risks and push the boundaries (Emmison 2003), and this extends to saying "no" to health risk-taking (Dixon and Banwell 2009). It is important to note that socially advantaged groups do not necessarily repudiate the old, more traditional pursuits and approaches (Bourdieu 1984; Elchardus 1994). People with high incomes and good educations can elect to limit their range of choices, thus preserving their sense of coherence, while those with fewer resources in human or financial capital are left with the fiction of choice: a dominant discourse asserting everyone's wealth of options which is at odds with their experience of constraints imposed by their circumstances.

We do not want our attention to the cultural ways of the advantaged to be read as saying all people should or could adopt similar dispositions. At the heart of pluralist societies lie demands for a respect and tolerance of cultural difference. The call for social inclusion became impossible to ignore with the events of the 1960s and 1970s when the new cultural movements of the Women's Movement, Civil Rights and Equal Opportunity Movements emerged, along with the counter-culture movements of the peace, self-reliance and environment movements. These movements gave voice to the aspirations of vast numbers of people who had previously been marginalised by their structural position or by their beliefs, and they contributed to the social mobility we described in Chap. 9. Their emphasis on lifestyle and political choices was coopted by the flexible economy which we also described in Chap. 9, with one profound effect: commodity choice became central to lifestyle choice. This metamorphosis of one trend into another is well described by Belasco (1993), when he attributes the spread of ethnic cuisines in the United States to the corporate response to the calls for multiracial equality. He then charts the community backlash to the corporatisation of ethnic diversity.

Rather than celebrating how people's chance to be different arises from the exercise of individual choices, we emphasise how life chances and hence choices are unevenly distributed. Due to their particular location within the employment system, for example, it is entirely rational and unsurprising for people living in outer suburbs to be more car reliant. Similarly, those who are paying high housing costs may need to economise on food (Kearns 2010), which often means buying more energy-dense and fattening foods.

In attempting to distil the features of modern life that are stressful, we are proposing that the culturogenic stress evident in our interviews reflects the truncated choices that many people are experiencing. The OECD, a body not known for radical economic diagnoses, released a Briefing Paper *Health Choices* for the 2010 Health Ministers' Meeting describing the relationship between lifestyles and lack of choice in the following terms:

> Lifestyles should not be viewed merely as the result of individual choices. Choices are often influenced, and even constrained in some cases, by environmental conditions, including social structures, cultural and political conditions, physical and economic environments (OECD 2010, p. 4).

Given this understanding of the constraints on lifestyle decisions, health education campaigns urging people to change behaviours which ignore the exigencies of daily life are unlikely to reduce obesity. Indeed, because health promotion campaigns and individual behaviour change programs "do not work directly on population exposure to risk factors, they do not address inequalities in risk factor profiles in subsequent cohorts" (Capewell and Graham 2010, p. 3). Thus, for governments with a focus on disease prevention, supporting whole-of-environment changes are more likely to interrupt the trajectory of risk exposure for future generations.

10.3 Foregrounding Culture as a Determinant of Obesity

Cottam proposed that it is *within* culture that the pressure points of obesity would be found. The preceding chapters contain a wealth of evidence indicating a cascade of environmental conditions, of interactions between disparate trends and personal circumstances. Those who frame obesity as a systemic problem are vindicated by our findings (Newell et al. 2007). The simple insight that "people have lives to lead" is far from simple in its implications when it comes to weight control. Fortunately, public health researchers are now directing attention towards understanding how culture operates in a causal, contributory or protective fashion in relation to ill-health

(Banwell et al. in prep; Hahn 1995; Helman 2007; Hruschka and Hadley 2008; Lang and Rayner 2007; Thomas et al. 2004; Trostle 2005). Belatedly, culture is coming to be recognised as part of the multi-factorial aetiology of illness operating in concert with social and psychological factors. Like socio-economic status, culture "helps to produce asymmetries in the abilities of individuals and social groups to define and realise their needs" (Johnson 1986/87, p. 39). Cultural processes are important because they facilitate and constrain decisions about how, when, where and what everyday actions to take. Culture operates at multiple levels.

Returning to the topic of social dancing provides another view of the polysemic nature of culture. The Lucky Generation grew up in an era when mass forms of popular culture were exerting great influence: the reading of newspapers with their coverage and debate of what different segments of society were doing; the early films with evocative dance scenes; the travel by entrepreneurial Australian and English citizens who subsequently set up dance halls; and the early importation of US cultural artefacts including dance studios, big bands and jazz music. From the outset, dancing was a valued means of social participation, albeit one that required the acquisition of modest skills through repeated copying. It had the advantage of being comparatively inexpensive. For those who grew up in straitened circumstances, dancing was an enjoyable form of enjoyable leisure for three reasons: there were few alternatives, so the risk of failure in electing the 'right' activity was negligible; dance hall proprietors provided dance lessons and multiple and novel entertainments at little extra cost, making any night out a worthy escape from the hard labour of household duties and paid work; and the standards for performance were largely set by peers with dollops of fantasy from Hollywood movies, rather than by Olympics committees, TV judges and professional stars.

Baby Boomers continued to appreciate dancing for its social benefits, and they too saw fitness and health as by-products of dancing rather than as reasons to do it. However as they entered the workforce, Baby Boomer women began to eschew dancing in favour of gym services which could be more flexible. For some, the priority to remain or acquire fitness at the gym displaced opportunities to dance: there was neither enough time nor money to do more than one activity. Compared to their parents, Baby Boomers were also more subject to a growing sense of pressure to perform well on multiple fronts, including being fit and healthy, and this pressure encouraged an intense focus on apportioning time in the most efficient ways, which in turn consolidated the appeal of the most efficient forms of fitness. That is, the Baby Boomers inherited a commercialising and broadcast dance environment as they grew up, but one that was increasingly suffused by the imprint of the second wave of the Women's Movement, the counter-culture and the self-help movement. Together these disparate developments amplified ideas of individual empowerment through self-improvement, including disease prevention and occupational success, and enticed this generation into patterns of physical activity which can be too onerous to maintain.

What the cultural economy histories of social dancing, lost family meal times, the rise of convenience foods, car use, and time management all indicate is how a few disparate socio-cultural trends have crept up and interacted to have far from

Table 10.1 Submission to the House of Representatives Standing Committee on health and ageing executive summary

1. A powerful cultural transition, or cultural disturbance, is contributing to the recent and rapid rise in obesity in Australia.
2. Cultural transitions encourage changes to ways of thinking about, and 'practising', daily living: including physical activity and diets.
3. The contemporary transition involves the convergence of four factors: time pressure; the valuing of convenient solutions to eating; the valuing of convenient solutions to being mobile; and for parents, pressure to practice child-centred rearing. The four are closely interlinked and are mutually reinforcing.
4. Household valuing of convenient solutions—particularly car reliance and eating foods prepared outside the home—escalated from the early 1980s and coincided with policies to deregulate the economy. They were viewed as 'solutions' because they facilitated flexible working lives by allowing more flexible routines.
5. The new forms of daily life are best understood as an adaptation to economic deregulation. They help to resolve tensions in managing working-family life dynamics and being a modern parent and consumer.
6. We argue that the rise in obesity across society is a warning sign against which the progress of the Australian government should be judged; and we call on the government to take cultural forces as seriously as it does structural economic forces.

benign effects on the enjoyment of everyday life and on population health risks. The implications of these transformations for a consideration of obesity prevention could not be more profound. Certainly the multi-factorial nature of our findings accords with the meta-reviews of obesity prevention (Sassi 2010) and other analyses in the field of behavioural economics (Fuller 2010): that one-off environmental changes like accessible park networks or affordable fresh food outlets will make very little difference to obesity levels.

In 2008, we provided a submission to an Inquiry into Obesity in Australia sponsored by the House of Representatives Standing Committee on Health and Ageing (House of Representatives Standing Committee on Health and Ageing 2009). Our submission presented a systems view of the obesity problem based on preliminary analysis of the data reported in this book. At the heart of our submission lies the proposition that Australians (and the citizens of many industrialised nations) are subjects in a great, uncontrolled natural experiment: namely, the subordination of cultural and social relations to the meta-narrative that presents economic progress as automatically enriching those very relations. This is not turning out to be the case. In the last quarter century, economic developments in advanced economies have failed to deliver greatly enhanced social and health status progress for the majority of populations (Pusey 2003) (Commission on Social Determinants of Health 2008). Rising rates of morbid obesity are but one manifestation of this failure.

We reproduce an excerpt of the Executive Summary of the submission in Table 10.1.

Unlike many of the submissions tendered to the Inquiry, we opted to address complexity and the interconnected nature of disparate social problems. We stressed that no one sector or set of policy decisions was to blame. However, we also noted that the government's economic de-regulation policies of the 1970s appeared to act as a tipping point in the adoption of cultural flexibility as a behavioural disposition. Australia replicated economic policies in the United States under Ronald Reagan, Britain under Margaret Thatcher and New Zealand under Roger Douglas; and it is noteworthy that all these nations are among the fattest on earth.

Fuller argues that governments can reduce the fiction of choice, which is encouraged by economic de-regulation, through: "(1) policies tailored to specific choices and habits, and (2) policies to support 'domain general' habits, which underpin patterns of good choice" (Fuller 2010, p. 3). Within the context of the obesogenic system, we now turn to consider in more detail Fuller's second realm of essential policy action, 'domain general' habits.

10.4 Dismantling the Obesogenic System

To this point, our book has chronicled the evolution of economic and cultural systems through the last 70 years. It has been one of growth followed by consolidation and the marked health consequences of those phases. More recently we entered a phase considered by resilience scientists to be one of release/collapse, in which locked-up resources are suddenly freed (Cork et al. 2008); an apt description of the influx of married women into the paid workforce that accompanied economic de-regulation. In Australia and elsewhere there have also been numerous signs of collapse, including high levels of poor mental health and life dissatisfaction (Helman 2007; Pusey 2003).

The fourth phase of a resilient system is one of re-organisation: a situation where previously dominant system elements can be reconfigured (Cork et al. 2008). In Australia which is entering this phase, there is an opportunity to eliminate the drivers of the obesogenic system. This, in turn would mitigate the need for large numbers of people to practice crude survival responses (Boyden et al. 1981) like gastric banding.

Luhmann (1995) argues that social systems change requires a change to the prevailing expectations that structure the system, and influence actions. Redefined expectations lead to new actions, which in turn will modify the system. At the heart of this social change dynamic is the public taking control of the cultural realm of values, and demanding practical support for the pursuit of their values. There is evidence that this dynamic is underway as large numbers of people are urging a revision of societal expectations about what is possible in an era when vital resources are reaching their 'peak'. The public is becoming exposed to scientific assessments that the earth has reached peak, or maximum, resource capacity in terms of fossil fuels, soil nutrients, clean water supplies and bio-diversity. Some are suggesting peak population has been reached or exceeded. To re-establish the conditions for system sustainability in these circumstances requires questioning existing resource distribution mechanisms, which in turn elicits alternative scenarios to mainstream and orthodox approaches. We draw hope from economic and cultural actions in three domains general (following Fuller's terminology).

The first is the very gradual acceptance of the need to transition to a low-carbon and low-consumption economy. The second (which will aid the first) is a view that many major first world cities may have already exceeded peak automobility. The third area of action (which could also aid the first and second) involves the growing diversity in alternative food systems and a diminishing reliance, by the upper middle classes in the first instance, on the industrial food supply of energy-dense foods. Action in each of these domains has the potential to alter the unequal and unhealthy life chances which result from the current operations of the obesogenic social forces identified in Chap. 9: social mobility, flexible economy and suburbanisation.

The first domain: As we finish writing this book, the Australian Parliament has been in acrimonious debate over the policy settings that could help the country move from being one of the world's highest per capita carbon dioxide polluters to becoming a low-carbon economy. A price on carbon can also serve a cultural change function because it highlights the environmental consequences of a modern way of life. For some, carbon pricing raises a welcome question about what levels of consumption are required to lead the 'good life'. Of course, raising the spectre of lower levels of household consumption sends shivers down the spines of economists and Treasury officials fearful of lower taxation receipts; but it also encourages a public examination of priorities and how human progress should be measured and experienced. It means stepping back from what Rostow (1960) termed "the age of high mass consumption", and questioning the merits of what we have identified as the consumptogenic environment that encourages the consumption of commodities in greater amounts, more quickly and more often (Dixon and Banwell 2011a). In this environment, consumption has an emotional intensity that can be injurious to health and wellbeing.

Recalibrating the expectations about the rewards from consumption is leading many people to revalue earlier cultural values and practices: voluntary simplicity, home production, reusing recycled goods. These actions typically involve greater personal energy expenditure than is involved in buying and consuming commercial goods and services. It returns people to an active approach to life akin to that of the Lucky Generation, but with the benefits of labour saving devices like hot water systems, washing machines and refrigerators.

Most people require assistance to downgrade their consumption. Given material in this book on the role of paid work-related time pressure in shaping behaviours, it is critical to revisit the time demands of labour market participation if broad-scale systems change is to be fostered and maintained. It is clear that when there was a 'home maker' and primary care-giver present, as pertained in the Lucky Generation, there was less need for pre-prepared meals or commodified activities (even if they had been available). Elsewhere we elaborate on how changed labour force participation has had marked impacts on Australia's culinary culture (Dixon et al. 2011). We do not argue that women should once again exit the paid workforce and be relegated to providing these unpaid and undervalued services. However, the point remains that households in which all teenage and adult members are employed, whether for a few or many hours, places enormous pressures on everyone. Our argument is that adopting a balanced life approach becomes very difficult given the influence of socio-economic forces like casualised shift work, long commutes and unaffordable housing. Without the adoption of a systems approach, such interconnections are missed.

The second domain: As the suburban way of life has become car dependent, our respondents expressed frustration at having to make time for physical activity in a modern world characterised by sedentariness. However, as a portent of wider changes that are underway, a couple of our Gen Y participants had either moved or were planning to move closer to public transport. In a sign of cultural revaluation regarding mobility, long-time leading exponents of active transport systems have recently identified the slowdown in car sales and car use in Australia as 'peak car use' (Newman and Kenworthy 2011). City residents in many of the world's large developed cities with good mass transit systems do not find a car to be essential, as Chap. 7 discussed. In car-reliant Australia and the US, the peak in car demand seems to have been reached in 2004. Several reasons are provided for a subsequent gradual decline, two of which resonate with our research: peak travel time budgets (after about 1 h in the car people begin to question the car's utility); and the ageing of populations, with older people not wanting to drive. Other factors are playing a part: rising fuel costs, and the growing availability of sufficient active transport alternatives to meet mobility requirements. In some cities, there is also a very slow reversal in urban sprawl, combined with a return to the city due to a growing appreciation among older empty nesters and young people of the easily accessible amenities and highly enjoyable cultural vibrancy.

While the alternatives to car reliance—extensive rail, bus and tram networks, bike and pedestrian pathways and bike hire schemes—have been championed in civil society, they have been provided only reluctantly by governments in the face of often fierce opposition by the automobile lobbies. The upper-middle classes are the major beneficiaries because they can afford to live in the inner cities where the best alternative mobility systems exist. However as younger generations come to expect non-auto-dependent mobility, it is possible that they will carry this habitus for ready access to a range of mobility forms with them through their lives and demand these choices at the ballot box.

The third domain: There is growing diversity in alternative food systems and a diminishing reliance, by the upper-middle classes in the first instance, on the industrial food supply of energy-dense foods. One driver is that flexibilised citizens are telling market researchers that they have exceeded their choice/opportunity comfort zone (Schwartz 2004). In one response to this situation, the original purveyors of abundant choice—the supermarkets—are now positioning themselves as 'choice editors' (Dixon and Banwell 2012). They are scaling back their 40,000 plus offerings, as middle-class customers flee to small food retailers like farmers markets and specialist retailers where the shopping experience appears more manageable and home cooking follows the purchases (Mason and Knowd 2010; Sumner et al. 2010).

These alternatives to the corporate food system are arising because of changed expectations regarding what 'good food' comprises. The increasingly popular farmers markets where consumers can meet with producers, government-sponsored school kitchen garden and cooking classes, municipal-supported community gardens and the popularity of backyard vegetable gardening all stand testimony to the possibility of new relationships between citizens and their food (Donati et al. 2009). These are local and small initiatives, which benefit relatively few people at this stage. By their very nature they cannot operate at a scale that truly challenges the fiction of choice for most people.

On a larger scale, the Australian National Heart Foundation is attempting to support a national growth in diverse food systems. It has completed a project to encourage local governments to consider urban design and planning protocols which advance access to what they call "food sensitive environments" (Donovan et al. 2011). These protocols aim to give all urban Australians food shopping and commodity choice options, while getting more physical activity and social engagement.

In Italy, a large and influential social movement is operating to protect long-standing civil society food customs against corporate-imposed ones (Petrini 2001). The Slow Food Movement was set up in 1989 to counteract what was perceived to be fast food chain provision of unhealthy and unsustainable food, which offered few connections to local cultures. The movement's emphasis is on good, clean and fair food for all, an emphasis which is supported by public health evidence about healthy food practices: eat slowly, in company, at the table. By privileging local foods, the consumption of fresh foods follows. The movement frames its operations in ecological terms, seeing links between environment sustainability, public health and conviviality.

This particular citizen-led movement (now global), alongside the many public transport users advocacy groups worldwide, shows citizens reclaiming leadership of the cultural realm. To foster the sort of system reorganisation for which many people seem to be hankering, we point to the need for more of this type of action initiated by civil society supported by governments and industry.

Governments only occasionally intervene to protect traditional food ways alongside the new. In a rare instance, the Japanese law of Shokuiku (Education Basic Law 2005) directs farmers to uphold the traditional diet through growing traditional foods and directs consumers through health education to follow what is considered Japanese culinary culture (Japanese Ministry of Agriculture, Foresty, and Fisheries 2006). While French chefs see some positive signs in McDonalds appearing in that country (as part of opening up stultifying traditions), they are also highly supportive of labour market rules which protect the option of the long lunch (Steinberger 2009). Defending traditional food practices in France, and not simply protecting the availability of favoured food products, may be related to that country's slower rise in obesity (Rozin et al. 2003).

Figure 10.2 draws together our reflections in this and the preceding chapter concerning the elements that will lead to a change in the obesogenic system. It indicates our belief that civil society is leading the way in responding to the sense of incoherence that is the current experience of the Baby Boomers and some Gen Y. It also shows the system feedbacks that are possible if government and industry truly respond to the desires of middle Australia.

Fig. 10.2 Obesity System Change

10.5 Conclusion: Advancing the Conditions of Possibility

This is the first book in the obesity field, in Australia or overseas, to draw on the experiences of three generations of people, the two most recent of which have been valiantly trying to make healthy choices. Paradoxically, ways of life promoted by governments—working long hours, living in the suburbs, attempting to excel on many fronts—can impede healthy ways of living. No one sector or set of policy decisions is to blame. Instead, a stressed social system has evolved over many decades as a result of numerous decisions, many of which were initially positive. Different trends have crept up and interacted to have far from benign effects on population health risks.

Providing evidence-based advice on interventions in the face of half a century-long evolution of a system of unhealthy dynamics seems as hopeless as stopping a bolting horse with a single thread. A review of obesity prevention policies notes that a new policy framework is required based on a whole-of-system rather than a sector-specific approach (Lang and Rayner 2007). Societies must approach the obesity problem in a manner akin to contemporary trans-disciplinary treatments of the other great global issues of the day (climate change, urban resilience), not to relegate it exclusively to the health domain, which approaches issues in terms of health system responsiveness to individual exposures.

Governments, commercial enterprises and civil society have all played roles in shaping cultures of eating and physical activity that increasingly valorise competitive performance, individual capital accumulation and the most expeditious management of time. Instead of individual and sub-population adaptation to a stressed social system, we call for economic and cultural systems change. This would include legislation and willingness by society's 'influential groupings' (peak industry bodies, governments, labour movement) to act in a comprehensive manner (Boyden et al. 1981, p. 353) alongside civil society. There are numerous instances of such responses at times of war and natural disasters. Governments should not be timid in their leadership as a result of industry-led claims of 'nanny-statism', or claims that they have no mandate to intervene in the cultural sphere beyond arts sponsorship and health education. Governments and corporations intervene in culture constantly in ways that make everyday life subservient to economic developments. If human societies are to continue to thrive, they must be treated as ecological systems in which it is possible to evolve cultural, physical and social conditions that encourage all people of all ages to engage in pursuits that bring social coherence, pleasure and health.

This leads us to conclude that there is a need for an expansion of political choices for citizens rather than more commodity choices for individual consumers. At present, the political choices in Australia and elsewhere are between two parties, both of which offer only superficially different versions of more of the same.

The latter part of this chapter has in effect outlined the 'conditions of possibility' for enhancing political choice. Based on the examples above, we propose that change of the obesogenic system will come about when:

1. citizens change their expectations about what modern social progress can achieve in an era of peak resource constraints and marked social inequalities;
2. changed expectations emerge from doing or producing alternative ways of living that are more self-reliant, and hence more socially cooperative and physically demanding;
3. labour force compacts moderate the temporal demands (including unsociable scheduling) of workforce participation;
4. governments use urban planning and design to support active transport and local food possibilities; and
5. governments learn from one another about the sensitive ways to intervene in cultural systems.

Multi-national comparisons of obesity rates (Finucane et al. 2011) demonstrate that some European and Asian nations are able to maintain and even reduce obesity rates despite being subject to the social forces described in Chap. 9. Perhaps their governments or civil society movements are operating to protect valued aspects of cultural life. More fine-grained comparisons of cultural contexts may assist Australia and other societies to understand how to align policy settings so as to foster the emerging expectations that would lead to a healthier social system than the one in which people are enmeshed at present. In turn, other countries can learn from Australia's failure to date to take a systems approach to complex social problems that have major health consequences, giving them the opportunity to avert the public health crisis of obesity.

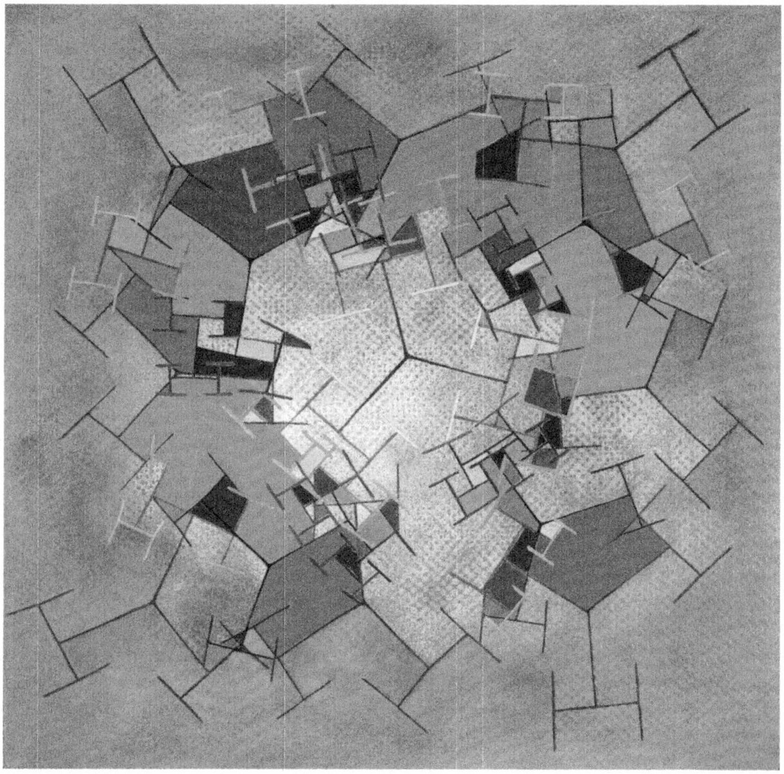

Image 10.1 Branching out Artist: Kerry Shepherdson

References

Antonovsky, A. (1985). *Health, stress, and coping*. San Francisco: Joey-Bass Publishers.

Baker, P., & Young, M. (2006). *A summary of published Cochrane and non-Cochrane Systematics reviews – Systematic reviews on obesity*. http://www.health.qld.gov.au/ph/documents/caphs/32117.pdf

Banwell, C., Ulijaszek, S., & Dixon, J. (2013). *When culture impact health: Global lessons for effective health research*. Elsevier.

Belasco, W. (1993). *Appetite for change: How the counterculture took on the food industry*. Ithaca: Cornell University Press.

Bourdieu, P. (1984). *Distinction: A social critique of the judgement of taste*. London: Routledge and Kegan Paul.

Boyden, S., Millar, S., Newcombe, K., & O'Neill, B. (1981). *The ecology of a city and its people*. Canberra: Australian National University Press.

Capewell, S., & Graham, H. (2010). Will cardiovascular disease prevention iwden health inequalities? *PLoS Medicine, 7*(8), 1–5. doi:e1000320.

Commission on Social Determinants of Health. (2008). *Closing the gap in a generation: Health equity through action on the social determinants of health*. Geneva: WHO.

Cork, S., Walker, B., & Buckley, R. (2008). *How resilient is Australia?* Canberra: Australia 21.

Cottam, R. (2004). Obesity and culture. *Lancet, 364*(9441), 1202–1203.

Dixon, J., & Banwell, C. (2009). Theory driven research designs for explaining behavioural health risk transitions: The case of smoking. *Social Science & Medicine, 68*(12), 2206–2214.

Dixon, J., & Banwell, C. (2012). Choice editing for the environment: A corporate response to the impacts of hyper-consumption on the environment. In S. Lockie & T. Meacham (Eds.), *Risk and social theory in environmental management*. Collingwood: CSIRO Publishing.

Dixon, J., Strazdins, L., Banwell, C., Broom, D., Woodman, D., & Davies, A. (2011). *Time and taste in Australian culinary culture.* Paper presented at the 18th Symposium of Australian Gastronomy, Old Parliament House, Canberra.

Donati, K., Cleary, S., & Pike, L. (2009). Bodies, bugs and dirt: Sustainability reimagined in community gardens. In G. Lawrence, K. Lyons, & T. Wallington (Eds.), *Food security, nutrition and sustainability: New challenges, future options*. London: Earthscan.

Donovan, J., Larsen, K., & McWhinnie, J.-A. (2011). *Food-sensitive planning and urban design: A conceptual framework for achieving a sustainable and healthy food system (FSPUD).* Melbourne: National Heart Foundation of Australia.

Elchardus, M. (1994). In praise of rigidity: On temporal and cultural flexibility. *Informations Sur Les Sciences Sociales, 33*(3), 211–230.

Emmison, M. (2003). Social class and cultural mobility—reconfiguring the cultural omnivore thesis. *Journal of Sociology, 39*(3), 211–230.

Finucane, M. M., Stevens, G. A., Cowan, M. J., Danaei, G., Lin, J. K., Paciorek, C. J., et al. (2011). National, regional and global trends in body-mass index since 1980: Systematic analysis of health examination surveys and epidemiological studies with 960 country-years and 9.1 million participants. *The Lancet, 377*, 557–567.

Fischler, C. (1980). Food habits, social change and the nature/culture dilemma. *Social Science Information, 19*(6), 937–953.

Fuller, J. (2010). *Promoting good choices: Patterns of habit and the role of government* (p. 26). Melbourne: Per Capita.

Hahn, R. (1995). Anthropology and epidemiology: One logic or two? In R. Hahn (Ed.), *Sickness and healing: An anthropological perspective*. New Haven: Yale University Press.

Helman, C. (2007). *Culture, health and illness* (5th ed.). New York: Oxford University Press.

House of Representatives Standing Committee on Health and Ageing. (2009). *Weighing it up: Obesity in Australia*. Canberra: Department of House of Representatives.

Hruschka, D., & Hadley, C. (2008). A glossary of culture in epidemiology. *Annula Review of Anthropology, 25*, 253–274.

Japanese Ministry of Agriculture, Food and Fisheries. (2006). What is "Shokuiko (Food Education)"? Tokyo: MAFF.

Johnson, R. (1986/87, Winter). What is cultural studies anyway? *Social Text*, pp. 38–80.

Katz-Gerro, T., & Sullivan, O. (2010). Voracious cultural consumption: The intertwining of gender and social status. *Time Society, 19*(2), 193–219.

Kearns, R. (2010). Recourse to discourse: Talk and text as avenues to understand environments of obesity. In J. Pearce & K. Witten (Eds.), *Geographies of obesity. Environmental understandings of the obesity epidemic* (pp. 297–309). Farnham: Ashgate.

Lang, T., & Rayner, G. (2007). Overcoming policy cacophony on obesity: An ecological public health framework for policymakers. *Obesity Reviews, 8*(Suppl 1), 165–181.

Luhmann, N. (1995). *Social systems*. Stanford: Stanford University Press.

Mason, D., & Knowd, I. (2010). The emergence of urban agriculture: Sydney, Australia. *International Journal of Agricultural Sustainability, 1 & 2*, 62–71.

McMichael, A. (1999). Prisoners of the proximate: Loosening the constraints on epidemiology in an age of change. *American Journal of Epidemiology, 149*(10), 887–897.

Ministry of Agriculture, Forestry and Fisheries (MAFF). (2006). What is "Shokuiko (Food Education)"? Tokyo: MAFF.

Newell, B., Proust, K., Dyball, R., & McManus, P. (2007). Seeing obesity as a systems problem. *NSW Public Health Bulletin, 18*(11–12), 214–218.

Newman, P., & Kenworthy, J. (2011). 'Peak car use': Understanding the demise of car dependence. *Journal of World Transport Policy and Practice, 17*(2), 31–42.

OECD. (2010). *Healthy choices* (p. 15). Paris: OECD.

Petrini, C. (2001). *Slow food. Collected thoughts on taste, tradition, and the honest pleasures of food.* White River Junction: Chelsea Green Publishing.

Pusey, M. (2003). *The experience of middle Australia.* Cambridge: Cambridge University Press.

Rostow, W. (1960). *The stages of economic growth: A non-communist manifesto.* Cambridge: Cambridge University Press.

Rozin, P., Kabnick, K., Pete, E., Fishcler, C., & Shields, C. (2003). The ecology of eating: Smaller portion sizes in France than in the United States help explain the French paradox. *Pyschological Science, 14*(5), 450–454.

Sassi, F. (2010). *Obesity and the economics of prevention: Fit not fat.* Paris: OECD.

Schwartz, B. (2004). *The paradox of choice. Why more is less.* New York: Harper Collins.

Steinberger, M. (2009). *Au revoir to all that.* London: Bloomsbury.

Sumner, J., Mair, J., & Nelson, E. (2010). Putting the culture back into agriculture: Civic engagement, community and the celebration of local food. *International Journal of Agricultural Sustainability, 1 & 2*, 54–61.

Syme, L. (2005). Foreword. In J. Trostle (Ed.), *Epidemiology and culture.* New York: Cambridge University Press.

Thomas, S. B., Fine, M. J., & Ibrahim, S. A. (2004). Health disparities: The importance of culture and health communication. *American Journal of Public Health, 94*(12), 2050.

Trostle, J. (2005). *Epidemiology and culture.* Cambridge: Cambridge University Press.

Turner, B., & Edmunds, J. (2002). The distaste of taste: Bourdieu, cultural capital and the Australian postwar elite. *Journal of Consumer Culture, 2*, 219–239.

Virchow, R. (1848/2006). Report on the typhus epidemic in Upper Silesia. *American Journal of Public Health, 96*(12), 2102–2105.

Warde, A. (1999). Convenience food: Space and timing. *British Food Journal, 101*(7), 518–527.

Index

C. Banwell et al., *Weight of Modernity: An Intergenerational Study of the Rise of Obesity*,
DOI 10.1007/978-90-481-8957-1, © Springer Science+Business Media Dordrecht 2012

The manufacturer's authorised representative in the EU is Springer Nature Customer Service Centre GmbH, Europaplatz 3, 69115 Heidelberg, Germany. If you have any concerns regarding our products, please contact ProductSafety@springernature.com

Printed and bound by CPI Group (UK) Ltd, Croydon, CR0 4YY
30/09/2026
02225444-0006